MW00584453

Praise for *God's Monsters: Vengeful Spirits, Deadly Angels, Hybrid Creatures, and Divine Hitmen of the Bible*

"*God's Monsters* is a hilarious treatment of a horrifying topic. With deep intelligence, literary flair, and wicked wit, Esther Hamori pulls no punches in exposing the terrors of the Bible and the multitudinous divine creatures that inhabit it—including the Almighty himself. For those of us who believe in brutal honesty and in fighting horror with humor, this book is a godsend."

—**Bart D. Ehrman,** James A. Gray Distinguished
Professor, Department of Religious Studies,
University of North Carolina at Chapel Hill

"With a perfectly pitched mix of sharp wit and deep insight, Esther Hamori creates space for us to explore the monstrous in all its biblical dimensions and the Bible in all its monstrous dimensions, raising haunting theological questions along the way."

—**Timothy Beal,** author of *Religion and Its Monsters*

"Esther Hamori's brilliant and powerful book troubles biblical waters in a profound manner! Her superb erudition and courageous vision compel us to cross the Rubicon, never again to return to a biblical literalism, ignorance, or denial of the night side of Hebrew Scripture and Christian New Testament."

—**Cornel West,** Dietrich Bonhoeffer Professor of Philosophy
and Christian Practice, Union Theological Seminary

"It's time to uncover our eyes and face the Bible's monsters! Esther Hamori is an exceptionally expert, wise, and fun guide through the Bible's most haunted realms. With a flair that dazzles and engages, *God's Monsters* turns the Bible upside down to reveal its underbelly and, by doing so, offers essential insight into the Bible's rich and relevant theology. This is a must-read for those who are willing to read

the Bible honestly and who are not afraid to discover that it expresses the fullest range of human experience."

—**Dr. Amy Kalmanofsky,** dean of List College and the
Kekst Graduate School, Blanche and Romie Shapiro
Professor of Bible, The Jewish Theological Seminary

"Esther J. Hamori's *God's Monsters* offers a Dante-esque tour of the
monstrous figures in this world, according to the Bible. Often over-
looked or played down by even the most faithful readers of the Bible,
these include the destroying angel, demons, and lying spirits, who all
work for God. This highly accessible romp across the Bible's pages
culminates in the monster of monsters, namely God. This book will
challenge many readers who believe in a just and good God, when
they confront what Hamori takes to be the Bible's evidence for God
as a monster—and the wonder of wonders. Is God a monster?"

—**Mark S. Smith,** Helena Professor of Biblical Literature
and Exegesis, Princeton Theological Seminary

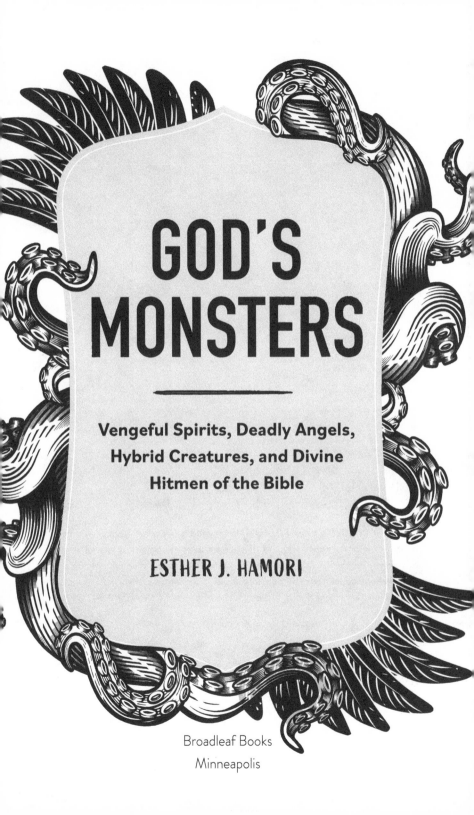

GOD'S MONSTERS

Vengeful Spirits, Deadly Angels,
Hybrid Creatures, and Divine
Hitmen of the Bible

ESTHER J. HAMORI

Broadleaf Books
Minneapolis

GOD'S MONSTERS
Vengeful Spirits, Deadly Angels, Hybrid Creatures, and Divine Hitmen of the Bible

Copyright © 2023 Esther J. Hamori. Published by Broadleaf Books, an imprint of 1517 Media. All rights reserved. Except for brief quotations in critical articles or reviews, no part of this book may be reproduced in any manner without prior written permission from the publisher. Email copyright@1517.media or write to Permissions, Broadleaf Books, PO Box 1209, Minneapolis, MN 55440-1209.

Library of Congress Control Number 2023934441 (print)

Cover design: Monica Cheng

Print ISBN: 978-1-5064-8632-1
eBook ISBN: 978-1-5064-8633-8

Printed in China

To Jack and Jonah

Contents

Part 3: The God-Monster

Author's Note

I realized at some point in the writing process that this book follows a classic monster-of-the-week format, complete with season arc leading up to confronting the Big Bad. Where I mention relevant movies or TV along the way, I occasionally resist using a recent example if it would involve too much of a spoiler, on the grounds that anybody reading this book probably appreciates the twists of a good monster show.

All translations from the Hebrew Bible and New Testament are my own (except where otherwise indicated). For readerly ease, where I include Hebrew or Greek words, I use accessible English spelling rather than a formal transliteration system.

In some parts of the Bible, like the Leviathan poem in Job, if you look at different English translations you'll see different verse numbers, because some translations follow the traditional Hebrew verse numbering and some don't. For those texts, I use the verse numbers of the New Revised Standard Version.

For the sake of readability, I sometimes refer to the writer of a biblical text using the traditional attribution (for example, "Isaiah"), even if scholars understand the writer(s) to be distinct from the character.

Monster Heaven

Every now and then, safari goers make the fatal mistake of forgetting that they're surrounded by wild animals—that no matter how well managed the environment may be, it is filled with wild things, dangerous to their core. The Bible is like that too. When we read these ancient texts—no matter how carefully managed they've been—we're visiting wild and dangerous terrain, and who knows what we'll find there.

The biblical world is full of monsters. Uncanny creatures lurk in every direction, from the hybrid monsters surrounding God in heaven to the stunning array of peculiar beings touching down on earth, and from giants in the land of milk and honey to Leviathan swimming beneath the seas. Most have been tamed by time and tradition. The cherubim—menacing, winged animal guardians—have become heavenly babies, marketed for feel-good cuteness on greeting cards and framed prints to be hung on a bathroom wall. The seraphim, multi-winged creatures with serpentine bodies and humanoid hands, have become conflated with angels. Angels, meanwhile, have acquired the soft-edged glow of a Hallmark card, even as they are some of the deadliest shapeshifters in a universe teeming with bizarre figures. Other monsters are hidden altogether, masked in translation as natural phenomena, like the demons Pestilence, Plague, and the Chill, who'd be prime comic book villains—except that they work for the Good Guy.

Who are the monsters skulking through the pages of the Bible, and what do they tell us about their God?

Strange and frightening creatures have always surrounded us. We stumble upon them—or they upon us—in legends, histories, travel reports, medical books, philosophical works, theological treatises, and epics from all places and times. Wherever there were forests, there were forest-dwelling monsters; in every wine-dark sea, giant monsters toppled ships. The ancient and medieval worlds were brimming with so many bizarre, dangerous creatures—basilisks, ogres, giants, and all manner of composite beasts—that it's a wonder humanity made it to the Renaissance.

Every culture has its monster lore, and the world behind the Bible is no exception. If anything, it seems especially overrun with monsters. The Bible is a collection of texts from ancient Southwest Asia (formerly called the ancient Near East, mapping roughly onto the region known today as the Middle East), and in literature from this region, as in Greek mythology, there are monsters spilling out the windows. From Canaan to Mesopotamia, people wrote spectacular epics and poetic masterpieces about their gods—*including* the monstrous figures who served them, fought them, and ruled among them. Being divine, you see, was not in conflict with being a monster. The best-known Babylonian creation story features the great goddess Tiamat, who's also the monstrous sea, complete with a tail. Marduk, who slays Tiamat and creates the world out of her body, is a gigantic, fire-breathing god with four eyes and four enormous ears.[1] Sometimes, the monsters are divine and the gods are monstrous.[2]

It can be more obvious who the monsters are when you're looking at someone else's mythology. When it comes to the Bible, though, even a vague sense of familiarity can fog up the picture. The Bible is made up of diverse texts that were written by people trying to make sense of the world around them, including the heavens and the earth and all they contained. It has an incredible history: texts from a world long gone, preserved and passed down for millennia, made new with each generation's reading. But this is also its great pitfall. These texts have been compiled and canonized, interpreted and misinterpreted, cherished and wielded. PG versions of stories are mistaken for what's in the texts themselves and mask what's right before our eyes.

The Bible has been domesticated, along with the eerie creatures within. Familiar images like beautiful seraphim winging and singing, and peaceful divine messengers ascending and descending, might register to the modern reader as what is in the Bible, but beware: in those pages, monsters play freely, wreaking havoc and bringing death and destruction to their divinely chosen targets.

What Makes a Monster?

I teach a course called Monster Heaven, and on the first day of the class, I ask students to name their favorite monsters. A few sea monsters are named: a sci-fi fan says Cthulhu, a rabbinical student names Leviathan, and a student from Vermont calls out, "Champ!" which I learn is the monster of Lake Champlain. But then one person mentions the Windigo, who's been devouring swaths of the general public for centuries across North America, and another adds the Islamic ifrit, a malicious djinni made of fire. A young man breaks into an exuberant rendition of "Suppertime" from *Little Shop of Horrors*, the solo of the giant singing man-eating alien plant, Audrey II.

What do these monstrous beings have in common? That part of the conversation is more complex.

Monsters have no single defining trait. Many are easily recognized by the blood dripping from their befanged jaws or the decaying flesh falling from their faces. Bodily anomalies are common, each type uniquely suited to the spread of its own brand of fear—the sharp and pointy, the huge and hairy, the grotesque and gooey. But even with the dazzling variety of anomalies in the monster compendium, they don't all advertise their monstrosity with some physical aberration. Next to your more obvious monsters, beside the gigantic thrashing sea monsters and radioactive killer robots, there stand little girls with ribbons in their hair. Sometimes the creepiest monsters are the ones we thought were innocent but turn out to be very, very bad.

Nor do monsters all share a place in the world. There are the naturalistic, like Jaws or Bigfoot; the supernatural, like succubi and incubi; and the unnatural, like the yacumama, a giant river monster at the mouth of the Amazon that devours any creature unwise enough to dip a toe anywhere within sucking distance.

Physically terrifying or perfectly innocent in appearance, naturalistic, unnatural, or supernatural, monsters share no single defining characteristic. There are nice, succinct definitions out there, but they all fall short, because it turns out you can't pin a monster down.

There is, however, a certain family resemblance, a collection of features from which monsters draw, in diverse and overlapping combinations—even across cultures, time periods, and genres. Heads up: every one of these features will come back to haunt us in the chapters ahead.

Giant size is a common family trait, from the kraken to the Mokèlé-mbèmbé, a Congolese cousin of the Loch Ness monster, and from Mesopotamian Marduk to Hellboy.

Superhuman or supernatural strength and power is another common family trait—even among the emphatically nonsupersized, like Chucky (*Child's Play*, 1988) and other killer dolls. Ruby, Meg, and *Supernatural*'s other young demon women throw the strapping heroes across the room whenever they please. Lethal superpowers, like the basilisk's literal death stare, are always a good show of monstrosity.

Perhaps the most common monstrous trait is physical hybridity, the mixing of two or more species. Bizarre composite creatures fill the pages of works both ancient and modern, spanning genres from myth (centaurs, satyrs, the Chimera) to tales of terror, from the highbrow to the low (the creations of Doctor Moreau, and *Sharktopus*, 2010).

There are other varieties of hybridity, too, like being both living and dead. These are your entry-level monsters, like vampires, zombies, and every reanimated corpse since Frankenstein's creature. Then there's the combination of animate and inanimate, like the lethal car in *Christine* (1983).[3] Yes—these, too, will resurface as we explore the biblical monster world.

Shapeshifting and realm-crossing are also common family traits. Some monsters take different forms at different times, like werewolves, and Pennywise of Stephen King's *It*. Other monsters cross between realms. A dead person who stays contentedly dead is no threat, but the moment such a soul crosses back over to walk the earth, a monster is born. Spirits might be innocuous as long as they remain on some cosmic home turf, but problems arise when they cross realms to interfere with human beings, as they all too often do.

The flip side of these traits of hybrid and multiple forms is the amorphous or formless monster, like Chaos in Ovid's *Metamorphoses*, described as a "raw unordered mass," and the invisible evil of *The Haunting* (1963).[4] Many stories of ghosts and evil spirits revolve around formless threats. Some of these are also shapeshifters: the looming threat of John Carpenter's *The Fog* (1980) would be anticlimactic if the fog didn't shift into the form of zombie pirates who slaughter townspeople (which is wicked even if the townspeople sort of deserve it).

Then there are the monsters that would seem natural . . . if only they showed up alone. One bird? Fine. A horde of birds attacking en masse? Monstrous. Like in this classic example, *The Birds* (1963), the creep factor doesn't come just from the countless creatures' activity, but from their unnatural collective will.[5]

These juicy category violations—from grotesque bodily anomalies, giant size and super(natural) strength, to forms that are composite, shifting, realm-crossing, amorphous, or countlessly multiplied—are the most common traits from which members of the monster family draw. No monster has all of these traits; all monsters have some.

As with features of monster physiology, there's a common monster geography. Monsters usually dwell outside of human society, lurking in the liminal spaces and the places *beyond*—the depths of the forest, the heart of the sea—encountering people either when they break into human territory or when people dare to enter those dangerous realms.[6] A recent *Onion* headline reads, "Report: Leading Cause of Death Still Venturing beyond the Pines."[7] Monster life flourishes in the *elsewhere* places: mountaintops and mysterious islands, cemeteries and sewers, the strange old house at the end of the road.[8] In *An American Werewolf in London* (1981), an old man in the gloomy northern pub warns Jack and David, "Stay on the road. Keep clear of the moors . . ." (They don't.)

If only the monsters would stay in the *elsewhere* and *beyond*. The problem is their propensity to break into this realm. Like the creature of *Stranger Things* who comes from the Upside Down but breaks into this dimension, monsters are forever pressing against the boundaries, threatening to breach our world.[9]

And how many *elsewhere* and *beyond* places the Bible has! All kinds of monstrous figures peer out, each kind manifesting its own combination of the classic monster family traits. In the heavens above, huge winged creatures with confusing assortments of body parts threaten interlopers. This is also the home turf of an array of brutal realm-crossing divine hitmen, each having the terrible combination of lethal superpowers and the ability to cross all natural boundaries to use them, sometimes shapeshifting along the way.

Manipulative spirits walk about in the heavens but come sweeping through the earth like wind to pursue their human prey. On earth, the forbidding closed-off room at the far end of the divine House is guarded by fierce composite creatures. An unfamiliar land is filled with giants who are the hybrid descendants of natural and supernatural species. In the depths of the sea, the gigantic and indescribable Leviathan swims with his multiheaded kin. These creatures—the massive and the formless, crossing realms and shifting shapes, with too many wings and too many heads—occupy every part of the biblical universe, their very existence pointing to the god and creator of their world. When we see them, we're confronted with him.

About that *him*: I use masculine pronouns for God in this book. This is because I'm writing about the God who appears as a character in the ancient anthology of texts we call the Bible, in which he's portrayed as male. This is a matter of literary accuracy, not a theological claim. For readers who closely connect that character to a God they believe in today, the gendering of the ancient portrayal of God may be one of many things worth grappling with.

The fifth-century theologian and philosopher Augustine explained that creatures contrary to nature are called "monsters" (Latin *monstra*) because they demonstrate (*a monstrando*) something—and for Augustine, it was something wondrous.[10] Monsters of the Bible can indeed demonstrate something about the nature of the biblical God. But be prepared: God's nature isn't always so benevolent. In fact, this God may be the monster of monsters.

The Biblical God and His Entourage of Monsters

As the biblical monster population comes into focus, one chilling element stands out. The most dangerous of these monsters are in God's employ. They're not his opponents—they're his entourage. He's the one who sends hybrid creatures on the attack, who commands forces of demons and dispatches vengeful spirits, who repeatedly orchestrates the mass slaughter of civilians by his divine hitmen, angelic and otherwise. God is surrounded by bizarre, monstrous creatures, and they commit remarkably violent acts on his command.

In fact, *every single type* of divine being that is shown acting in the service of God in the Bible threatens, injures, tortures, or kills on his behalf. Some are exclusively violent, like the Destroyer. Others have multifaceted roles, like angels, who appear perfectly docile when performing one aspect of their job but create mass carnage when doing another. Each type of divine being in God's service has its own profile, its characteristic set of job responsibilities—and every one of them includes doing the boss's dirty work.

This is the heavenly retinue we'll meet in the first part of this book. Terrifying, serpentine seraphim flap around God's throne and burn a witness with glowing coals. Hybrid cherubim serve as monstrous bouncers and bodyguards. We'll see God dispatch the Adversary, his enhanced interrogation expert, to torture and kill at his behest; we'll watch as God deploys stealthy spirits as psyops specialists to manipulate and gaslight his targets. And as devastating as the demons he sics on the population are, they don't hold a candle to those most lethal shapeshifting soldiers, God's angels, who execute thousands in the blink of an eye, when they're not attacking on a more intimate level. Throughout the Jewish and Christian Bibles, from Genesis through Revelation, God commands an entourage of monsters.

In the second part of the book, we'll meet the monsters of the sea, earth, and underworld. They don't work for God, but they have plenty to teach us about him. The activities of God's monstrous inner circle show us his character from one angle. The intense, heated dynamics between God and the monsters outside of his entourage show us another.

Monsters can be lots of fun—I can grab the remote at any moment and see that I'm not alone in this opinion—but *biblical* monsters can also present some problems that those on the screen don't. So, why choose to look at the biblical monsters and wrestle with such texts? For me, the answer is personal.

A few months after my older brother killed himself, I had a dream in which I was trying to remember which one of us had died. I couldn't figure it out, couldn't wrap my mind around it. As years went by and I ticked off each milestone—now I'm older than he ever was, now I've lived longer with him dead than alive, now I'm twice as old as he ever was—his death became less the focus and more the lens through which I see the world.

His death, and after it my sense of a world spinning out, off its axis, without order, propelled me into a long period of religious exploration, turning over a variety of ideas before finding my way back home to Judaism, the tradition I grew up in. Along the way, I tried focusing on the many biblical passages of comfort and hope, but taken alone, they fell short. Maybe that's why they're not alone. The Bible is rich with comfort, but also chock full of macabre stories, and with their recognition of a troubled reality, they offer something that the safer, prettier texts can't. Hope is all well and good, but acknowledgment of the grim has a comfort all its own.

These monsters that I find so compelling demonstrate something about their world. Monsters have meaning; monsters raise questions; monsters make us think. What are we to make of the menacing monsters of the Bible? Is there room for wonder? Or, seeing that these monsters don't stay put in the *elsewhere* and *beyond*, but break dreadfully into this realm—as monsters do—might they demonstrate something else about the God who deploys them, or about the Bible itself?

The Bible has been domesticated, muzzling its monsters. Sometimes our translations carefully sidestep the brutality of these creatures in the original texts. Later writers cleaned things up a bit, developing some characters in more palatable ways—a troop of hybrid beasties became a serene angelic choir, and the Adversary was safely removed to hell. God, too, has been tamed. But this does a disservice to the original portrayals in the Bible.

The ancient authors understood something about the world. These portraits of God's monsters aren't primitive theological draw-ings over which we can, with relief, superimpose the neater pictures of later theology, where good and evil are clearly distinguished, the heavens are filled with God's goodness, all harm is attributed to another hand, and everyone colors inside the lines. These ancient thinkers recognized that the world can be a sinister and dangerous place. They saw all around themselves the reality of chaos, pain, grief, violence, and fear. They wrote about monsters because they—like us—knew a world that was filled with "monsters" of all kinds. These aren't crude constructions, but poignant expressions of the dangers and afflictions of life.

Far from telling themselves that the presence of God assured their well-being, the Bible's ancient writers had a sense that on the edges of their world, just beyond their own realm, all sorts of monstrous creatures were lurking. Let's meet them now—and the complicated, some might even say monstrous, God who puts them to use.

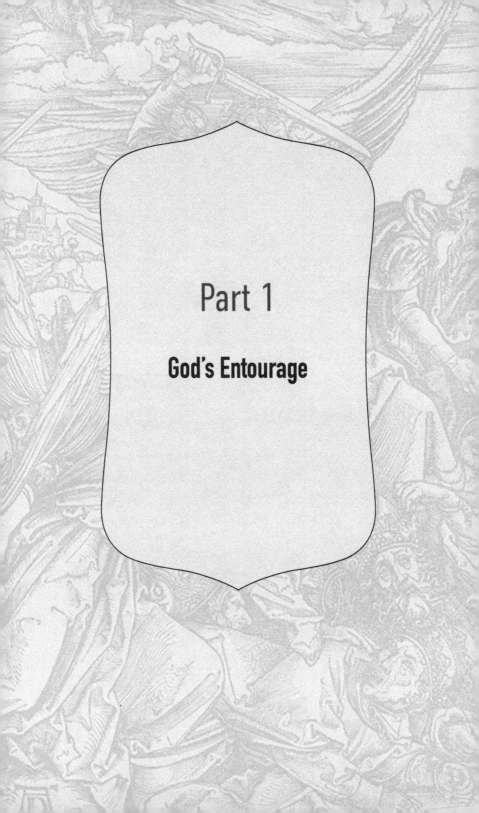

Part 1

God's Entourage

1

Seraphim

On a 110-degree night in July 1945, the USS *Indianapolis* was struck by torpedoes and sank in the Philippine Sea. Among 1195 crewmembers, some 900 made it through the initial disaster, only to end up struggling for their lives in the water. Many died of their injuries, dehydration, and drowning—and then there were the mass shark attacks. Corporal Edgar Harrell described what it was like to see the fins coming toward him in the water, to see a shipmate alive one day and recognize what remained of his corpse the next, to hear bloodcurdling screams cut through the sounds of the wind and sea. By the time rescue came, there were only 316 survivors. Seventy-two years later, when the wreckage was found, Harrell said the trauma lived on.[1]

The crewmembers' ordeal, almost inconceivable in its layered horrors, seems to follow the contours of a story in the book of Numbers in the Bible. The Israelites narrowly escaped Pharaoh's army, only to find themselves dying in the desert, trudging through the scorching heat without water, stricken with disease, with no help in sight. Many are lost (Numbers 11–20). Those who remain lament that it would have been better to die in Egypt, where they had been enslaved. And then come the snakes. Poisonous snakes swarm among them, biting and killing a huge number (21:4–9). From how far away could they see the snakes slithering toward them? Did they witness family and friends attacked and dying? Did they hear screams?

It's easy to blithely bypass the horror of biblical stories. Too often, we chalk it up to being a necessary element of some kind of morality tale. But other great literature of the ancient world doesn't sacrifice meaningful engagement with human drama for the sake of a neat moral. Why expect less of the Bible?

Whatever the Bible means to you as a reader, let's begin with the assumption that this literature, too, is richly textured, filled with the ancient writers' poignant reflections on the human condition. The story of the mass snake attack in the desert is horrifying. The people would be terrified, traumatized. What does a story this appalling reveal of the writers' thoughts about their God?

Wait, you might think, why are we talking about snakes? It's because these particular snakes are sent by God to attack and kill God's people, and these snakes have a special name: *seraphim*.

What's in a Name?

The best-known seraphim of the Bible are the heavenly creatures in the prophet Isaiah's vision of God seated on his throne, surrounded by winged seraphim who cry, "Holy, holy, holy!" (Isaiah 6:1). They're often mistaken for angels, but originally they weren't angels at all. Not only that: they're not even the main type of seraphim in the Bible. They're a small part of a network of related creatures, all called seraphim. Like many famous figures, they have some skeletons in the closet.

The word *seraphim* appears in most English Bibles only in Isaiah's vision. In the original Hebrew, though, seraphim appear in several other texts too—and each time, they're a type of deadly serpent.

Translators of the Bible handle this in a variety of ways, but rarely by using the word *seraphim* as they do in Isaiah 6. This is a glaring example of a principle that my students would tell you I never tire of talking about: all translation is interpretation. In this case, translators decide that Isaiah's heavenly seraphim are unrelated to the deadly seraphim-serpents in other texts—and so they leave the Hebrew word *seraphim* untranslated only in Isaiah 6. Readers then have the impression that these creatures are unconnected. The total disconnect between the celestial and terrestrial seraphim isn't a matter of what's actually in the Bible, but of what we've been taught *about* the Bible.

The earthly seraphim aren't your everyday serpents. In two of the four passages mentioning them, these snakes have—wait for it—wings. And those two passages? Also in Isaiah. Isaiah's heavenly seraphim, which he describes as flying around God's throne, are clearly related to the earthly creatures he calls "flying seraphim," which are explicitly a type of snake. The two stories outside of Isaiah mentioning earthly seraphim (including the desert snake attack) refer to them in Hebrew as "seraphim-snakes," using the two nouns together. No wings are mentioned, so these seem to represent the naturalistic end of the seraphim spectrum (though not entirely natural, as we'll soon see). Recalling that monsters can be naturalistic, unnatural, or supernatural, we see the full range represented in the seraphim family. It's like the spectrum within the scary-canine genre, from Cujo (naturalistic, but not entirely natural) to werewolves (unnatural hybrid creatures on earth) to hellhounds (supernatural monsters residing in another realm).

One thing all of the seraphim have in common is their propensity for a certain form of violence. We see it in every text where they appear, and even in their name. The Hebrew word *saraph* (singular of *seraphim*) suggests burning. That's why the King James Version, not wanting to associate deadly reptiles with heavenly beings, called the seraphim-snakes "fiery serpents." Some modern Bibles stick with this traditional interpretation. (Other translations try to make sense of "seraphim-snakes" by lopping off the interesting bit and just calling them "serpents.") But the Hebrew *saraph* comes from an active, transitive verbal root meaning "to burn [something]." Seraphim aren't passively "fiery," but actively "burners."[2] And I'll give you one guess what they burn.

On earth, they strike people with burning venom; in heaven, with burning coal. And in the Bible's two main stories about seraphim—one taking place on earth, one in heaven—they do their people-burning in God's employ.

The heavenly and earthly seraphim share a cluster of other traits, too—but we'll have to wait to see them. For now, let's tread carefully into the first scene. You may want to watch your step along the way: we begin with the naturalistic end of the seraphim spectrum, the disaster-movie sequence in which God annihilates his people in the desert using an army of seraphim-snakes.

On Earth . . .

Seraphim-snakes headline one show in the Bible. It's memorable, and not just to the modern monster fan—later biblical writers allude to it too. And the clearer the picture becomes, both of that story and of the allusions that follow, the more disturbing it gets.

Snakes on a Plain

This isn't the first time the people following Moses through the desert lament that it would've been better for them to die in Egypt. The previous time, God replied with a diatribe in which he vowed to make them wander for forty years, including multiple versions of,

"Your dead bodies shall fall in this wilderness!" (Numbers 14:26–35). So the people wander on, desperate for water, many perishing along the way.

They grieve for their lives. They have no food other than manna, which we later find out is not all it's cracked up to be. They cry out, "Why have you brought us up out of Egypt to die in the wilderness?" God responds, essentially, "Oh yeah? I'll show you death in the wilderness." He then sends seraphim-snakes to bite the people, many of whom die. Stricken with fear and venom, the people quickly repent and ask Moses to prevail upon God to get rid of the snakes. God responds—but not by getting rid of the snakes. Instead, he tells Moses to "make a seraph" (Moses will turn out conveniently to have some bronze on hand) and pop it on a pole, explaining that anyone lying around bitten and dying will be able to look up at it and live (21:4–9).

God has just performed mass execution by snake. Some people are healed at the end of the story, but for many this divine help comes too late. God offers a way to heal those not yet dead from their snakebites, and everyone lives happily ever after, except for all of the people who just got killed. And their families. And the people who just saw their fellow wanderers killed in a mass poisonous snake attack.

What sparked this lethal act? The people complained, sure—but the appropriate response to that isn't usually mass slaughter. Perhaps it was what they were complaining about? The people lamented that they were dying in the wilderness (and, to be fair, they were). The common defense of God's actions, that the people lacked faith or gratitude, doesn't actually do much in service of God's reputation. This isn't a capital offense. It might provoke a ruler's indignation, though. God lashes out like an oversensitive dictator.

If the people lack gratitude, they have good cause. The broader story of the Israelites' wanderings is traditionally spun as if the wilderness was terrible and dangerous, but God protected them—but in this story, it's God who *made* the wilderness terrible and dangerous for the people. The desert would have been harsh enough without God siccing his attack-snakes on the ailing wanderers.

One of my earliest memories is of attending a school movie night at the age of six, sitting on a blanket on the floor of the gym, terrified out of my mind. We watched *Lost in the Desert* (1969), possibly not the most judicious choice for the event. There's a single scorpion in the film, as I recall all too vividly, and it appears of its own volition, as nonbiblical bugs generally do. The horror in our current story surpasses this: the people lost in the desert are killed when their deity intentionally sends a horde of poisonous creatures to attack them. This divine assault is nothing short of terrifying.

The snakes bear only some responsibility here. They're venomous, and God has sent them precisely for this reason. The mob boss who sends killers out to do a job for him is no less responsible for the outcome than those who work under him. This is not God's finest hour.

But the seraphim-snakes are also monstrous in their own right. God's anger-management issues aside, these frightening creatures act en masse to kill an untold number of people. The coordinated snake attack is like a prototype for *The Birds*, where ordinary creatures appear alarmingly and lethally as an organized group. This isn't just a post-Hitchcockian reading. It's pivotal to the plot that the mass attack is unnatural, happening only because God deploys the army of snakes with their burning venom to accomplish his goal.

In stories featuring the mass attack trope, creatures are often endowed with intelligence and will.[3] When God sends the seraphim-snakes, they don't scatter—they go straight for the kill. Maybe they've been bestowed with intelligence by their mad scientist creator, like the sharks of *Deep Blue Sea* (1999). Even if they're only as aware as trained attack dogs, that's strangely aware for a horde of snakes, and plainly horrifying.

In light of these events, it's startling that God's next move is to offer healing—at least, to those not dead yet—and thus the story is resolved. But what sort of resolution is that?

Kiss the Ring

After orchestrating the mass snake attack, God has Moses fashion a bronze serpent. This is explicitly synonymous with a seraph: "Make a seraph," God says, "And so Moses made a bronze serpent" (Numbers 21:8, 9). God instructs Moses to create an image of the very monster he'd sent to attack the people, and mount it on a pole so that those dying of snakebites could look up at it and be healed.

For some Christian readers, the end of this story might call to mind a comparison made centuries later between the bronze serpent on a pole and Jesus at crucifixion (John 3:14–15). When a writer refers to an older story, knowing that story helps us understand what the later writer has in mind, but not what the earlier writer intended. Faulkner's allusion to Absalom informs our understanding of Faulkner, but not of the ancient story of Absalom. However a Christian reader interprets the New Testament comparison, we need to reckon with what goes down in the Numbers passage itself. The New Testament uses an image from Numbers, but what's the symbolism Numbers is using? Why would a bronze replica of a snake cure its bite?

As it happens, the poisonous snake was a common symbol, and this story reflects a known use of it for protection and healing. The origin of the protective symbol of a venomous snake is the Egyptian uraeus: the image of a rearing cobra, ready to strike, as on King Tut's famous striped death mask. Sometimes these Egyptian uraeus-serpents were winged.[4] Pharaohs wore the rearing cobra image for the protection it gave by spitting "fire" on their enemies. For this reason, one Egyptian term for the uraeus was "flame."[5] Like the Bible's seraphim-snakes, the uraeus—sometimes winged, sometimes not—burns those it bites.

The uraeus wasn't only associated with pharaohs, who were considered semidivine. Deities in Egypt, Mesopotamia, and Canaan were also portrayed with the protective serpent image.[6] By the time the Moses story was written, regional gods had a long history of keeping company with poisonous snakes that were part protector, part avenger.

The uraeus was also used for magical protection from snakebites. In Egypt, a serpent amulet might be placed on a mummy to ward off attacks of underworld snakes, while the living wore snake images to fend off the more usual variety. This is called sympathetic magic, the use of an image to affect the thing it represents. Sympathetic magic was used in ancient Israel, too. There are several biblical examples of it, like when God strikes the Philistines with a plague of mice. The Philistines make five golden mice and find relief from their plagues (1 Samuel 6:4–5). As in the story of the bronze serpent, the creature-feature animal onslaught is resolved through creation of a metal figurine of the creature featured.

Sympathetic magic was familiar to biblical writers—as was the image of the uraeus, which appears in various forms in ancient Israel and throughout the wider region known as the Levant.[7] The magical use of the uraeus—a symbol of a "burner-snake" associated with divine power—in order to heal snakebites is perfectly at home in the Bible.

Figure 1. A four-winged uraeus serpent on a Levantine stamp-seal. Many more uraeus serpents rear up along the bottom register. (Estimated to be from the 8th–7th century BCE.)

What complicates matters is how God uses this image in the story. Returning to the initial question: If the bronze serpent is meant to resolve things, what kind of resolution is that? The raising of the bronze seraph is often interpreted as an act of divine mercy, but after orchestrating the deadly mass snake attack, might God be the one in need of forgiveness? This offer of healing might save those writhing in pain but still hanging on, but does it redeem the God who sent the seraphim-snakes in the first place?

The uraeus was a symbol of protection, and that's how God uses it. But this is "protection" in the mafia sense. These are near-fatal injuries that he's inflicted on the wanderers and is now offering to heal—for a price. Incensed at the people's insubordination, the Godfather sends his heavies to do his dirty work. After the people are satisfactorily beat down, he extorts "protection." Pay homage to me, he says, and I will "protect" you from the deadly assault . . . of those

I sent to kill you. Those who are willing to kiss the ring, to physically show respect to this symbol of Don Almighty's power, will live. The people who capitulate will get "protection" from the boss's goons. As far as we know, the seraphim-snakes are still there when God makes the people this offer they can't refuse.

This isn't usually how we want our stories to end. In any context other than the Bible, it's unlikely that we would consider this ending redemptive. When the villain poisons Indy in *Indiana Jones and the Temple of Doom* (1984) and then offers him the antidote—for a price—we recognize that the bad guy is still the bad guy.

This whole story is full of protection in all the wrong ways. Remember that snakes were associated with divine power because they were thought to protect gods by spitting venom on the divine ruler's enemies. Unfortunately for the Israelites, this is exactly what happens in the first part of our story. When God sees the people as his foes, he sends venomous snakes to kill them. In the face of defiance, he uses seraphim-snakes to protect his sovereignty, and perhaps his honor. In the second part of the story, he uses the bronze seraph to offer the dying survivors a chance for "protection" from his own entourage.

It didn't have to be this way. In fact, within the literature of Israel's Mesopotamian neighbors, another possibility emerges for how a deity might relate to poisonous snakes swarming among his people. Among the tablets recording the military campaigns of the seventh-century BCE Assyrian king Esarhaddon, a scary snake encounter is described. The king reports an arduous journey through the desert where he "stepped repeatedly on two-headed snakes" and "yellow snakes spreading wings." He gives credit to his god for his own survival and for that of his people: "The great lord Marduk came to my rescue. . . . He revived my troops."[8] What Marduk did *not* do was send the snakes in the first place. In general, the Bible takes a dim view of foreign gods. But as the God of the Israelites was preparing to unleash his army of venomous snakes to annihilate his people, maybe, just this once, he could have pondered, "What would Marduk do?"

After these events in the book of Numbers, we never witness another encounter with the deadly seraphim-snakes of the desert—but there are three additional passing references to them, each time in the context of a verbal threat against those who might dare to oppose God.

Live and Let Die

The first of these is in a speech Moses makes to the Israelites. He reminds the people of the great snake attack in the desert, referencing it as a threat to keep them on the straight and narrow. To the reader's good fortune, Moses's speech also gives us some new information: the inside scoop about God's motivations.

Moses begins his speech by exhorting the people to keep God's commandments "so that they may live"—not "so that they may live *long*" or "so that they may live *well*," but merely "so that they may *live*" (Deuteronomy 8:1). Readers today may prefer a softer view, but no survivor of God's snake attack would misunderstand: run afoul of this deity and he might end you.

Moses goes on to remind the people how God led them around the wilderness for forty years in order to "afflict" them (yep, that's literally what the Hebrew word means) and to test whether they would follow his commands (8:2–3). Among the afflictions: God starved them and then gave them strange food. Moses emphasizes the manna's strangeness. As another story explains, the very name "manna" comes from the question, "What is that?" (Exodus 16:15, 31). His blunt recap isn't the comforting tale we often hear, that God guided the people through the desert and provided miraculous food when they were starving. Nope: God led them around the wilderness, starved them, and then gave them weird food—all explicitly in order to afflict them (Deuteronomy 8:16).

I remember the dismay and concern on my young child's face the first time we gave him a taste of baby-friendly strawberry purée. He looked both aghast at the unfamiliar flavor, and confused and hurt that we would betray him this way. This is roughly how Bible-sanitizing traditions make the manna story theologically palatable: that the food was good but unfamiliar, and the spiritually immature Israelites failed to appreciate it. But that's not what happens in the Bible. Everything, from the wilderness-wandering and starvation right down to the manna itself, is all part of God intentionally harming his people.

If we recall that the people's lament about starvation and strange food was what sparked the mass snake attack in the first place, it's beginning to look an awful lot like they had good reason to lament.

As Moses wraps up his reminders of Israel's afflictions at the hands of God, he issues a warning: watch yourself, lest you neglect the commandments and forget the God who "led you around in the great and terrible wilderness, with seraph-snake and scorpion" (8:15). Otherwise, Moses warns, God will destroy you Israelites just like he destroys other nations who don't obey him (8:19–20).

This threatening reminder of the seraphim-snakes, bookended by blunt reminders of the divinely orchestrated travails that led to the snake attack in the first place, reads like a TV gangster cracking his knuckles to remind you of the last time he beat the daylights out of you. Moses cautions God's people: you'd better not forget the God who afflicted you and then sent snakes to attack you when you lamented about it. Obey God so that you may live. Otherwise, you won't. [*Stage directions: hits lead pipe against palm.*]

Beyond the full story of God's snake attack in the desert and then Moses's threatening reminder of it, two references to desert seraphim appear in the poetry of Isaiah. These lines add a twist: these buggers can fly.

Don't Say I Didn't Warn You

One of Isaiah's references to flying seraphim-snakes reads like a poetic version of Moses's speech, reminding the disobedient Israelites what could befall them in the desert. In this oracle, presented as God's own words through the prophet, Isaiah is warning Israel not to seek military support from Egypt because it would demonstrate lack of trust in God. Moreover, in order to carry payment to Egypt, they would have to make it through the dangerous desert. Isaiah introduces this warning as "an oracle about the beasts of the Negev," and the final deadly beast he names is our old friend. In pursuit of the military alliance that would offend God, the Israelites would need to pass "through a land of distress and anguish, from where come lion and lioness, viper and flying seraph" (Isaiah 30:6)—a reminder that should stop them cold. It's like God is saying, "Remember those seraphim-serpents? I can do that again."

Like Moses's menacing nod toward the seraphim-snakes, Isaiah's also comes with the warning that God will destroy the Israelites if they don't follow his commandments. He begins by threatening that God will besiege Jerusalem and leave the people lying in the dust (29:2–4). Then, immediately after the ominous reminder of the seraphim-snakes, Isaiah accuses the Israelites of being rebellious and unwilling to listen to God (30:8–9). God's aggressive response to being ignored should be familiar by now. God has already committed mass slaughter by poisonous serpent, even as he keeps these seraphim-snakes in his arsenal, reminding the people what Very Bad Things can happen to them in the desert.

Weapons of His Rage

Then, in the midst of a long series of so-called "oracles against the nations" (where a prophet rails at one nation after another about all the terrible things God will do to them), Isaiah warns the people of Philistia not to get too comfortable. They've got one oppressive ruler down, says Isaiah, but more—and worse—will come: "Do not rejoice, all you Philistines, that the rod that struck you is broken, for from the root of a snake will come forth a viper, and its offspring will be a flying seraph" (14:29).

We could write off this one-liner, the flying seraph-snake serving as a metaphor for the harshest of rulers (the deadliest of three snakes), except that these oracles are all about the violence *God will do* to each nation. The details are gruesome. It's like Keyser Söze's imposing emissary going around the room, telling each member of the crew in turn about the particular horrific consequences they'll face for not complying with his feared commander (*The Usual Suspects*, 1995).

It begins with Babylon: God summons armies, the "weapons of his rage" (13:5), against the Babylonians. Their hearts will melt, they'll be seized with pain like they're in labor, and they'll look at each other in horror, their faces aflame (13:7–8). Agonies await each nation—Assyria, Philistia, Moab, one by one around the room. The final oracle is against the Egyptians, who will be like women "trembling with fear before the raised hand that the Lord of Hosts swings against them" (19:16). It would be bad enough to say that the people are like beaten women cringing in fear—but in this analogy, God's the wife beater.[9] Throughout these oracles, the horrors that befall each place are acts of God. And this is the Bible, so we're not talking insurance company "acts of God," but actual violence attributed to the deity. The "flying seraph" in Isaiah's oracle is only a metaphor, but it's a metaphor for a weapon of God's rage.

God's motive isn't spelled out in each oracle, but only because it doesn't need to be. The assumption at the core of every series of oracles against the nations is that those nations merit punishment because they don't revere the God of Israel. The flying seraph coming for Philistia is God's penalty for the people's failure to capitulate.

God doesn't settle for just conquering nations. Going characteristically above and beyond, he turns each place into an uninhabitable wasteland. It's like his signature flourish after a good conquering. (Pay attention: we'll see this theme again in Isaiah's vision of the heavenly seraphim.) Babylon will become a desert with ostriches all a-wander, owls nesting in the houses and hyenas howling in the forts; in Moab, the waters will dry up and all vegetation will die; in Ethiopia everything will be left to birds of prey. This is all God's doing: he'll sweep with the broom of destruction and send lions to finish off survivors (14:23; 15:9). Israel's not exempt from God's trademark flourish. Its strongest cities will revert to wilderness. In this case, God's rationale is stated explicitly: the people forgot him (17:10). It's a sore point, but we all have our triggers.

As we'll see, it's no accident that in a series of oracles about God turning everything into uninhabitable wasteland, Isaiah hits upon the metaphor of the "flying seraph."

Did You Order the Code Red?

The seraphim-snakes of the desert never just happen by. Each time they appear, it's in the use or threat of divine violence. Each time, the perceived affront that triggers God is the people's insufficient trust in and reliance upon him. God reacts to this with fierce threats and punishing force.

Yeah, God seems to say. "You're goddamn right I did."

With this pattern in mind, let's return for a moment to the scene of the bronze seraph. The symbol of healing is a bit sinister, given the extortion angle: if the victims of God's mass snake attack want to live, they must acknowledge his divine symbol. Otherwise, no dice. But there are so many places in the Bible where God *does* heal selflessly and *does* show mercy! This text stands out precisely because it's so unlike those more comforting passages. The bronze serpent is disconcertingly in keeping with the consistent pattern of the use of seraphim-snakes to intimidate the people into greater reverence for God.

Another theme links the seraphim-serpents, and it's one we will see again. All of these seraphim are tied to the lethal oppressiveness of the desert. First, God sends his deadly creatures to kill his people in the desert, where they've wandered near death for years. Then, Moses and Isaiah's harsh reminders of the seraphim-snakes both emphasize the brutal setting: "the great and terrible wilderness," Moses calls it, or as Isaiah puts it, "a land of anguish and distress" (Deuteronomy 8:15; Isaiah 30:6). Finally, throughout the oracle series in which the metaphorical flying seraph appears, God turns nations and cities into desolate wilderness filled with all manner of desert creatures. In the first story, we see God making the desert dangerous; in the last oracles, we see God *making* the dangerous desert.

The seraphim-snakes, forever linked to death and wilderness, point to God's promise to destroy the disobedient. This isn't just about the earthly seraphim. These themes also reverberate through Isaiah's vision of the heavenly seraphim. We see a seraph in God's company commit a violent act in response to human sin, and prepare the way for God's threat to turn the entire world into nothing but wilderness and wasteland. In his vision of the celestial seraphim—far from offering a kinder, gentler portrait—Isaiah will up the ante through a brilliant twist on an old tale.

As It is in Heaven

Among the larger seraphim family, with so many appearances of the earthly cousins, the heavenly seraphim of Isaiah's glorious vision are the outliers. They are, let's say, one species, best understood in view of the genus as a whole. Once we've gotten to know the seraphim on earth, we can better understand those in heaven.

They Live!

Isaiah, the same prophet responsible for the two oracles featuring dangerous flying seraphim-snakes, had a stunning vision of God sitting on his throne in the Jerusalem temple. Isaiah's only further description of God is this: the bottom of his robe alone filled the entire temple (6:1). In other words, God is *enormous*. Deities throughout Canaan and Mesopotamia were generally imagined this way—there was even a Syrian temple with three-foot-long footprints, thirty feet apart, engraved into the ground outside to represent the massive deity walking in—but Isaiah describes actually seeing the gargantuan God.[10] And yet, even with God sitting right there, the rest of Isaiah's description of his vision is devoted to the seraphim. And understandably so:

There was God, Isaiah explains, sitting on his throne, being enormous—and seraphim were standing above him! Each one had six wings. With two wings they were covering their faces, with two they were covering their feet, and with two they were flying all about. These fantastic hybrid monsters can remain stationary in the air above God like helicopters or hummingbirds, or flap around—with just two of their six wings, since the other four are occupied. And what about their bodies?

As in Isaiah's other two references to winged seraphim, these creatures are serpentine. He doesn't need to spell this out, since this is what *seraphim* already means, including in Isaiah's own mentions of earthly winged snakes, as we've just seen. While the stories in Numbers and Deuteronomy use the double noun *seraphim-snakes*, Isaiah never does. In his oracles referring to the winged snakes of the desert, he simply calls each a "flying seraph." These heavenly seraphim have bizarre *additional* features that he needs to describe, but their basic serpentine nature isn't one of them, because that part's a given.

In addition to the biblical texts, we've already seen archaeological evidence showing the broad regional popularity of the uraeus—which, in Egypt, was pictured standing (as in Isaiah's vision), and sometimes had hands and feet in combination with its serpentine body.[11] There's even evidence of the use of the flying serpent image specifically in and around Jerusalem during Isaiah's period.

Archaeologists have uncovered stamp seals and seal impressions featuring winged serpents from eighth- and seventh-century Judah, including one uncovered in excavations at the Western Wall (also called Al-Buraq Wall) in the Old City of Jerusalem, and several from nearby Lachish.[12] All of this evidence, together with Isaiah's repeated use of *seraphim* for earthly flying snakes, tells us that Isaiah's heavenly flying seraphim, too, were serpentine.[13]

Isaiah's vision continues: the seraphim call out to one another, and this is no serene choir. At the sound of their voices, the doorposts shake. These thundering voices signal divine identity, like the voice of God that breaks cedars and shakes the desert (Psalm 29). Let's not blithely pass over the fact that these hybrid creatures speak at all. I'm reminded of the Roman scholar Pliny's leucrocotta, a monster with the body and tail of a lion, legs of a stag, head of a badger, and a mouth gaping from ear to ear—and if this mouth weren't eerie enough, out of it comes the imitation of a human voice.[14]

Figure 2. Stamp impression of a four-winged uraeus serpent on a jar handle excavated at Lachish (near Jerusalem).

And what do the seraphim call out? "Holy, holy, holy is the Lord of Armies! The whole earth is full of his glory!" (Isaiah 6:3). We usually hear "Lord of Hosts," but the Hebrew word *tzeva'ot* means "armies," and is rendered "hosts" only in phrases like "Host of heaven" and "Lord of Hosts." These are military terms referring explicitly to the "armies of heaven" and to God as their chief. Isaiah doesn't see Hallmark angels cast in a pale glow singing about some vague heavenly multitude. He sees bizarre, hybrid winged serpentine-humanoid creatures flapping wings over hands and shouting about God, the commander of the heavenly armies. Even before the real action unfolds, we're faced with the monstrosity of these divine creatures.

"Woe is me," cries Isaiah, "I'm done for!" No doubt. "I'm a man of unclean lips, and I live among a people of unclean lips, but my eyes have seen the king, the Lord of Armies." The situation grows more alarming. One of the seraphim flies over to him—how terrifying that alone would be! In its hand is a glowing coal that it's taken from the altar with tongs. The seraph reaches out toward Isaiah's face—*oh God*—and burns his mouth with the glowing coal.

So, in addition to all those wings, the seraph has hands and the use of common tools. Even its hands are oddly hybrid: the seraph uses tongs to pick up coal from the blazing altar, but it can then hold onto that coal nice and tight in order to burn the human interloper. The multiwinged serpentine seraph then turns out to be able to express independent, rational thought. After burning Isaiah's mouth with the live coal, the seraph helpfully explains the logic of this assault: it's to get rid of Isaiah's sin.

This idea of purification by fire has become metaphorical, softened through poetry and theology, but burning is a violent act. We see it here envisioned literally, as a man is burned by a strange and powerful hybrid creature who presses a hot coal against his face. With wings flapping, voices shaking the temple, and a superhuman hand outstretched in a brutal act, the seraphim of Isaiah's vision should prepare any prophet for a disturbing message.

Then, finally, God speaks. He asks, "Whom shall I send? Who will go for us?" He's not talking to himself. Some texts portray God as head of a divine council painted in broad strokes (e.g., Psalm 29:1; 82:1, 6; 89:5–7), and other texts zoom in on the cast of characters, as we'll see later. A few times in the Bible, God's use of the word *us* hints at the presence of this council. In Isaiah's vision, God is surrounded by divine attendants and asks, "Who will go for us?" This time, the *us* is no mere hint. The referents are standing right there flapping their wings.

And what is God's message, the great prophecy that called for this alarming drumroll of the monstrous seraphim? It's to say to the people of Israel, "Keep hearing, but don't understand! Keep seeing, but don't perceive!" God tells Isaiah to "make the heart of the people indifferent, their ears dull and their eyes dim, lest they should see with their eyes, hear with their ears, and understand with their hearts, and turn and be healed." Isaiah, presumably (or hopefully) appalled at this, asks how long he should keep this up. God answers, "Until cities lie waste without inhabitant, and homes without people, and the earth is laid waste and desolate!" (Isaiah 6:11).

If this terrible message rings a bell, it's because we've just seen virtually the same thing in the series of oracles against the nations that includes another flying seraph. The seraphim are always associated with death and divine violence in the desert. Heavenly or earthly, winged or not, the creatures of the seraphim family are tied to this vision of death and desolation.[15] You can take the seraphim out of the desert . . .

Once again, the seraphim aren't the only monsters on the scene. Like in the great snake attack in the desert, they answer to a higher authority. These seraphim are shouting about God, chief of the heavenly armies, and sure enough, the chief is announcing his plans to lay waste to the earth, leaving homes and cities with no remaining human life. This should terrify Isaiah, and probably the reader. The deity's ferocity even terrifies the seraphim. These celestial seraphim—divine, winged serpentine figures surrounding the throne of God—are precisely the image of the uraeus serpents who protect the divine throne. But what do they do in Isaiah's vision? Let's recall what they usually do: they stand with wings outstretched to protect the god or divine king on his throne. But here? With two wings they shield their faces, and with two wings they shield their feet. The heavenly guard are protecting themselves from their savage commander.

Shielding your face is a common enough self-defense move. Shielding your feet is an incomprehensible gesture—but "feet" in the Bible is often a euphemism for genitalia (famously in the book of Ruth). Suddenly, the gesture makes more sense. This is quite the defensive pose. Instead of stretching out their wings to protect the one enthroned, the seraphim cover their most sensitive body parts, apparently needing to protect themselves *from* the one enthroned. Even these bizarre, composite monsters shield themselves from God.

Nechushtan in the Rearview Mirror

When last we met the bronze seraph, it was in Moses's hand, raised for those dying of snakebites to pay homage to and be healed. During the time of Isaiah, there's a bronze serpent in the Jerusalem temple that's said to be the very same one, now known as *Nechushtan*. Not every prophet had connections to the palace and temple system (which were related), but Isaiah did. He even advised the king during the period when Nechushtan was in the temple. Isaiah would have been familiar with the bronze seraph in the temple when he had his vision of the living seraphim in the same spot.

In ancient Southwest Asian religious thought, a deity's earthly temple was seen as a reflection of the god's cosmic abode. The physical throne in the temple represented the god's heavenly throne. In Isaiah's vision, the throne room of the Jerusalem temple is projected into the heavens, bronze seraph and all. The symbolic throne on earth becomes the giant heavenly throne on which God is seated—and the bronze serpent, projected heavenward, becomes the living seraphim flying around the throne.

Nechushtan ultimately comes to be seen as an idolatrous symbol, with the people treating it as an object of worship rather than a mere instrument of God. To put an end to this, King Hezekiah smashes it, an ur-Pete Townshend gloriously destroying the very object of prior glory, even as the people still look upon the instrument with awe (2 Kings 18:4). As we'll see, though, Isaiah understood quite well the symbolism of the bronze uraeus.

His *use* of its symbolism is another story. His cosmic projection of Nechushtan—the bronze serpent believed to be the very one Moses held up in the desert—highlights how alarming his prophetic message is. Isaiah is making a pointed comparison.

In the story of the desert snake attack, the seraphim-snakes "burn" people with their venom. The people, begging for their lives, acknowledge the reason: "We have sinned, for we spoke against God" (Numbers 21:7). Isaiah recounts this as the central action from his vision: he confesses that he's doomed, as a "man of unclean lips," and one of the seraphim burns those sinful lips. But there's no obvious sense in which he's spoken in sin. Isaiah's making an allusion to the story of the desert seraphim, casting himself as a representative of his people. The people (first the Israelites, then symbolically Isaiah) sin with their lips, so the seraphim burn them.

But this isn't where either story ends. In the desert disaster sequence, God then instructs Moses to raise the bronze seraph so that the wounded can turn and look to it and be healed. In Isaiah's vision, God's message to the freshly burned prophet is to actively *prevent* the people from being able to turn and be healed. "Make the heart of the people indifferent, their ears dull and their eyes dim," God thunders, "lest they should see with their eyes, hear with their ears, and understand with their hearts, and turn and be healed!"

Back when we were thinking only about the horrors of the desert attack, God's refusal to heal those who didn't pay homage seemed monstrous. Those were happier times. In Isaiah's vision, healing is no longer simply restricted to those who look to God and acknowledge his power. Now, the very option of looking to God has been taken off the table. God has moved from a limited refusal to heal *some* people to a preemptive refusal to heal anyone at all.

Isaiah projects the bronze seraph, this ancient symbol of healing, into his celestial vision, and it emphatically does not heal. The juxtaposition is no fluke. The central message of his vision comes clear: the people will no longer have the chance to be healed. What they'll get instead is destruction "until cities lie waste without inhab-itant, and homes without people, and the earth is laid waste and desolate"—death and wasteland, the familiar territory of the desert seraphim.

Isaiah harbors no illusions about his God. The later impulse to tame the divine, to present the commander of the heavenly troops as kind and user-friendly, is not an impulse Isaiah shares. He knows God's mercy, too—the hope for deliverance! the light of the Lord!—but not *only* that. When confronted with the terrifying seraphim of God's entourage, he bewails his fate. When Isaiah calls God by the same military term the seraphim used, "the Lord of Armies," he means it.

The seraphim, in all of their magnificent variety, are monstrous members of the army of the Lord of Armies. This network of crea-tures—a family descended from the uraeus, that sometimes-winged burner snake, protector of the gods—all perform related functions in God's entourage. From the naturalistic to the supernatural, the seraphim-serpents and serpentine seraphim strike and burn, remaining in God's arsenal as signs ever pointing to his annihilation of those (ostensibly) without eyes to see and ears to hear. On earth, they're levied as threats against the disobedient. In heaven, they're heralds of God's message of destruction, as he sends Isaiah—"for us"—to declare God's intentions to turn the world into wasteland. Even where a bronze seraph is held up as a symbol of healing, it represents the threat God holds over those who have to acknowledge it in order to be healed. And let's not forget those who *can't* turn to be healed, having died of their wounds when God wielded the seraphim-snakes as lethal weapons in the first place. The famous heavenly seraphim only heighten the horror, as Isaiah flips the script of the old story of God dispatching his seraphim to burn those who sin with their lips, and then raising the bronze serpent to offer healing . . . back when he afforded that option to the survivors of his destructive rage.

Every mention of the seraphim is tied to frightening people into obedience—a classic function of monsters, to reinforce behavioral boundaries and social norms. Don't venture into the woods, explore the lost island, intermingle with strange new people. But it's not always so blatant. Monster theorist Jeffrey Jerome Cohen describes this common monster function in terms that scream seraphim: the "monster of prohibition polices the borders of the possible," warding off challenges to cultural norms, to "call horrid attention to the borders that cannot—*must* not—be crossed." To transgress those behavioral boundaries is "to risk attack by some monstrous border patrol."[16]

In the case of the seraphim, this is their primary function in God's entourage, and he employs them flagrantly for it. At first, they seem to be simply God's attack dogs. He sics them on the crowd when the people become too vexing, a celestial Montgomery Burns murmuring, "Release the hounds . . ." But from the first seraphim-snakes in the desert to the coal-wielding seraph in the sky, these monsters serve to intimidate people into submission to God.

What does this troop in God's company of monsters reveal about their divine commander? This God employs a behavioral border guard to keep people in line. The various appearances of the seraphim highlight different facets of their god—he's the mad scientist who orchestrates a coordinated attack of poisonous snakes, the destructive giant surrounded by a heavenly regiment of hybrid monsters—and throughout, he's the mob boss who uses his heavies to threaten everyone in the neighborhood, extorting deference on pain of death. As lethal and frightening as these serpentine monsters are, they're a mere reflection of the source of greater danger.

Moses had warned the Israelites to obey God, "who led you through the great and terrible wilderness, an arid wasteland with poisonous snakes and scorpions." Not a minute earlier in his speech, Moses had used precisely the same description, "great and terrible"— but that time, it was about God. As with the seraphim themselves, translators often render these phrases differently to reflect their theological interpretations. The NRSV mentions the "great and terrible wilderness," but "a great and awesome God" (Deuteronomy 8:15; 7:21). Moses makes no such distinction. The god he speaks of is as great and terrible as the wilderness itself. The people have been lost in the desert—wandering, hoping, trying to find life in the Great and Terrible, succumbing to its lethal dangers.

Even in their connection to the danger of the desert, the seraphim reflect the danger of the god they serve. Is there room for wonder in response to these monsters? Can one marvel at the sight of the heavenly seraphim, in view of the snakes? Or read the cry of the celestial monsters, "Holy, holy, holy is the Lord of Armies!" and set aside what the divine commander threatens to do?

We could try to find reassurance in the fleeting moment when God also extends the chance for a cure. Does the bronze seraph, raised high in the hand of Moses and higher still in the vision of Isaiah, remind us that God once offered healing? Or that God offered healing only once—and then sent Isaiah to shroud the eyes, ears, and hearts of anyone who might otherwise turn and be healed?

This tension lingers beneath the surface throughout these divine vignettes, and so many other biblical passages. God uses the bronze seraph in the desert only to heal the injuries he himself caused (which seems a bit backhanded, as healing symbols go). Later, just a few lines after Isaiah's final seraph-snake oracle, he provides a similar snapshot of God's m.o. with a declaration about "the day when the Lord binds up the injuries of his people, and heals the wounds inflicted by his blow" (Isaiah 30:26).

Earlier I questioned whether the offer of healing through the bronze seraph was enough to redeem the God who sent the seraphim-snakes in the first place. Let's not rush to a verdict. There's more evidence to come.

2

Cherubim

I am visiting the home of a friend's grandmother. I see an assortment of delicate figurines on her mantelpiece: a child praying, a small white horse, and a beatific winged baby. I look out the window. Across the street, I see a church with fantastically horrible gargoyles grimacing and snarling from its rock face. The winged baby is the figure we call a "cherub" today, but it's nothing like the original cherubim of the Bible, which have more in common with the creatures I see across the street, the strange and frightening guardians of sacred space.

Like so many biblical monsters, the cherubim have been tamed over the centuries. Their case is especially severe: they've been literally infantilized. Cherubim are imagined now as happy, fat angel-babies. To the writers of the Bible, this image would be unrecognizable. They knew cherubim as something far more beastly, and far less friendly.

Before they were conflated with angels and later shrunken into flying babies, the cherubim were something else entirely. The original cherubim were part of a wider phenomenon, a type of hybrid guardian monster found all over ancient Southwest Asia and the Mediterranean. The route from classic monstrous guardian to twee ceramic figurine was long and complex, but in their original state, the cherubim were quintessential composite monsters.

Composite creatures appear often in both mythology and iconography as guardians for the gods. There's logic to this. The fiercest creatures should serve as guardians for the gods, and what could be fiercer than a monster composed from the most powerful parts of other creatures? The raw strength and ferocity of a lion, the talons or wings of an eagle, capped off with that lethal asset, the intellect represented by the head of a human being—with such dangerous parts, these composite monsters were the most menacing guards imaginable.[1]

Hybrid monsters are frequently stationed at gateways. Some sit before earthly gates, like the entrances to Assyrian palaces, where giant sculptures of human-headed winged bulls and lions were carved into stone.[2] More often, the "gates" are cosmic borders, openings between realms. In the Epic of Gilgamesh, scorpion-people stand at the gate of the sun to usher the sun god, Shamash, through on his daily journey.[3] Since a border guard must be ready to fight should the need arise, we sometimes see hybrid creatures in action as monstrous soldiers for a divine commander. In the Babylonian Epic of Creation, the sea monster-goddess Tiamat has hybrid infantry at her beck and call.[4]

Even now, we know the dangerous power of the hybrid. Just ask anyone who's had to fight Wolverine, with his animal strength, retractable claws, and even a heightened sense of smell (the better to track you with). Guardian figures with lethal combined assets appear in the literature, art, and architecture of Israel's neighbors in every direction. Egyptian sphinxes were giant human-headed lions guarding tombs and temples, and small carvings from ancient Syria show similar creatures built into thrones as permanent security guards. In Greek myth, Cerberus, the three-headed dog with

Figure 3. A human-headed winged lion (*lamassu*) from the gates of the palace of the Assyrian king Ashurnasirpal II (r. 883–859 BCE) in Nimrud. One of a pair. The other, seen in figure 4, is a human-headed winged bull.

wriggling snakes protruding from his body like living tentacles, guards the gates of the underworld.

Like these creatures to the north, south, east, and west of Israel—in mythology and statuary alike—the cherubim of the Bible are hybrid monsters who stand sentinel at sacred and crucial sites.

Even the term *cherubim* may draw on a broader tradition. The Hebrew word *keruv*, "cherub," is related to an Akkadian term for a type of hybrid monster.[5] The cherubim are ancient Israel's unique expression of the hybrid guardian monster. They serve a powerful deity, and as we explore their character profile, we uncover something about his.

Guardians of the Gateways

The cherubim appear as living beings in mythological scenes and prophetic visions, and as statuary in descriptions of Israel's symbolic architecture. They stand guard over sacred space, and like God's own Secret Service, they also shuttle away the deity and handle weapons when necessary. To understand their roles as guardians, let's follow the cherubim through several primary locales on earth, and then up into heaven.

The Garden of Good and Evil

Once upon a time, God planted a garden, positioned two especially appealing fruit-bearing trees in the middle just so, showed them to his first human creations, and told them not to eat. It did not go well. The story ends with the eviction of the couple and the deployment of the heavenly guard to the entrance of the couple's former home.

While God has a full company of monsters in his service, the cherubim, as guardians of the gateways, are the natural choice for this job. Their appearance isn't described here, but they're implicitly fierce enough to secure the garden forever. They're not ushers, gently pointing people in alternate directions; they're bouncers, promising violence if their line is crossed. These guardian monsters are there to prevent reentry to Eden at all costs.

God stations the cherubim to guard the gateway to Eden at the end of the story, but from the very beginning the garden is filled with divine danger. Everything is leading up to this moment, this divine decision to threaten humankind with supernatural violence. The fairy tale you are about to hear is less Golden Books, more Brothers Grimm.

God creates Adam from the dirt of the ground (Hebrew *adamah*, "ground"), and then Eve, "mother of all living" (*Havah*, from *hai*, "living"). Adam and Eve—or, as they're known in my classes, Dirt Boy and Life Girl—have had a trap laid for them from the start.

God commands Adam not to eat from the tree of the knowledge of good and evil, claiming, "*on the day you eat from it* you will surely die" (Genesis 2:17). The snake, who's not labeled as evil, just the most "astute" of all creatures, levels with Eve: they won't die, it's just that God knows that "*on the day you eat from it*, your eyes will be opened and you will become like divine beings" (3:4–5).

They eat, and sure enough, their eyes are opened, and even God admits that they've become like divine beings (3:7, 22). In a twist of expectation, God lied and the snake told the truth. God wasn't just talking *eventual* death. The people were created mortal and were always going to die eventually, as we see when God worries that they might next eat from the tree of eternal life and *therefore* live forever, and kicks them out of the garden to prevent that. Both God and the snake explain what will happen "*on the day you eat from it*," and God's version isn't the one that happens.

God's lie has come to light. The people's eyes have been opened. Having eaten from the tree of knowledge, they now "know good and evil" (3:22). He's none too keen on them being able to discern what's good and what's evil. It begins to sound like that last part refers to God.

When God realizes things haven't unfolded as he expected, he curses everyone in his path—first the snake, that whistle-blower who exposed his lie, then the woman, the man, even the ground itself.

He's like Walter White in *Breaking Bad* putting down everyone who sees through his innocent façade.

In a disturbingly typical abuser move, God shows just enough care to keep the people convinced of his love, making them clothing and even dressing them himself. This tender act is almost enough to make you forget that he just lied to them about their lives being in danger if they dared disobey him, then decreed suffering for them, and is about to throw them out of the garden, all while laying the blame solely at their feet. He even alters the story: he misquotes himself to Adam, telling him he's cursed because he ate from the tree "about which I commanded you, saying, 'You shall not eat from it'"—and God ends his quotation there, omitting the false part, "for on the day you eat from it, you shall surely die" (2:17; 3:17). God has just gaslighted the first humans.

In the moments leading up to God's deployment of the monstrous guard, he lies to his human creation, promises them a painful future, and gaslights them. No wonder they hide from him behind the trees. After this, stationing monsters at the door looks less like a new security feature warranted by the people's actions, and more like the next threatening move of a controlling figure whose m.o. now includes bringing in thugs to do his dirty work.

When God stations his hybrid guardian monsters at the gateway to Eden, it's the culmination of a story of divine danger. The garden of Eden, where the deity strolls among the trees as the human beings hide behind them, contains *more* danger than the world outside. Even in Eden, there is no Paradise.

Lord, Have Mercy

We pick up our story after significant developments on the human plane. As the Bible tells it, the descendants of Adam and Eve created civilization, civilization was terrible, God addressed this by drowning

everyone except for Noah's family, and Noah's descendants' civilization was also terrible but some interesting things happened. People
became clans, tribes, nations. The spotlight lands on one family in the
land of Canaan and their descendants who come to be called Israel.
They end up enslaved in Egypt, and a divinely tapped leader with a
tendency to fly off the handle gets them out. We met this character
when he was leading the people on a forty-year detour through the
wilderness, and the people protested to God, who sent seraphim-
snakes to kill them. It's during this period that we next encounter the
cherubim.

On the long road to Canaan, the people need to establish a home
base for God. The everywhere-ness of God is a relatively late idea on
the theological scene. In ancient Southwest Asia (including Israel),
deities needed a landing spot, a place to touch down and call their
home on earth. At that sanctuary, their worshippers could approach
their holy presence.

On the human side, this is hard to accomplish when you're
wandering hopelessly through the desert for decades at a stretch.
In the biblical imagination, God solves this problem by instructing
Moses to build him a movable sanctuary, called the tabernacle. This
portable temple-in-a-tent isn't just a house of worship as modern
readers might think of it. It's God's new residence: he tells Moses to
build it "so that I may dwell among you" (Exodus 25:8). The Hebrew
word generally translated "tabernacle" literally means "dwelling
place." God asks Moses for a mobile home to call his own.

More specifically, God will dwell in one specific location within
the tabernacle, a carefully designed spot in the back room. This room
is God's home, the new holiest spot on earth. It's called the "holy of
holies," and it's where the ark of the covenant resides. God's instructions for building the tabernacle actually begin with the ark, because
his new home is the space just above it, around which the entire

tabernacle is built. The tabernacle isn't just the logical place to store the ark. It becomes sacred space *because* the ark is there. The heart of the tabernacle is the ark's cover, the so-called mercy seat. This is the holy *X* where God will touch down, the precise spot where he says his presence will dwell: "above the mercy seat."

He's got his own Spot. Nothing in the Bible makes me relate to God more. Me, God, and Sheldon Cooper. I didn't feel truly settled in my home until I had a Spot. My husband Jack and I renovated a Victorian row house (mostly he, though I sanded my share of crown molding). When we were finally ready to put together my Spot in a tucked-away corner of the top floor, we designed the room around it: my grandmother's coffee table with the broken drawer, a painting by my grandfather with a shade of blue you can't imagine, a corner for the violin. My Spot reflects who I know myself to be.

God's also got detailed design specs for his Spot, and its core elements reflect an awful lot about who he is. The mercy seat is no simple platform. Built into the top of it, one on each end, are two golden cherubim, spreading out their wings above the ark, over-shadowing the mercy seat. As at Eden, God stations cherubim to guard the gateway to the holy. These golden cherubim are signs, welded into their post to permanently ward off any improper human approach to the ark and to that most sacred space above it where God dwells.

Never one for subtlety, God also commands that cherubim be embroidered into the partition separating the "holy of holies" from the rest of the tabernacle, and yet more into the tabernacle's outer curtains, blocking off the sacred space of the entire mobile sanc-tuary from the outside world (26:1, 31–33). God has even worked cherubim into the very structure of the tabernacle at each gateway, guards at every checkpoint. God's Spot includes a string of built-in bouncers.

There's still more detail to the description of the golden cherubim, though. One at each end of the ark, they spread out their wings over it—and they face each other and look toward the mercy seat. Picture that: the cherubim atop the ark face in and down. It's not just the ark or the divine presence they're protecting. It's not only the people they're keeping away from the ark, but the One on the mercy seat they're keeping *in*.

"There I will meet with you and speak with you," God had told Moses, "from above the mercy seat—from between the two cherubim" (25:22). Suddenly God seems hemmed in, contained between the hybrid guardian monsters.

This reveals another aspect of the role of the cherubim. Their job isn't simply to keep a lookout for enemy approach. It's to prevent passage between realms—in both directions. This is often part of the job description of hybrid guardian monsters, like Cerberus, who guards the gates of the underworld in Greek mythology so the dead can't escape and the living can't enter. The cherubim serve as a safeguard against unauthorized movement between realms.

Good thing there are so damn many of them in the tabernacle. If the golden cherubim poised over the mercy seat aren't enough to contain the sacred danger of the deity, there are plenty more sewn into those partitions at each crossing, more than just embellishments in the curtains of twisted linen. There's an army of cherubim prepared to meet anyone—or anything—leaving the holy of holies.

The presence of God is dangerous even within this contained space. When the ark is first brought inside and God alights on that holy X, a cloud covers the tabernacle like some dark fog over a rickety castle in a horror film, and even Moses can't safely enter (Exodus 40:34–38). The moment when he finally can—only because cultic sacrifices have made it safe enough—we see the vital role of the cherubim. From that time on, when Moses entered the holy of holies, he would hear the voice of God speaking "from above the mercy seat, which was upon the ark of the testimony, from between the two cherubim" (Numbers 7:89). Moses can now approach, but God still speaks from that spot between the cherubim keeping watch forever in both directions.

While modern readers might be startled at the danger that lies within the tabernacle, no one within the story is surprised. Shortly beforehand, when God landed on top of Mount Sinai, he rendered the entire mountain lethal. He warned people not to even touch the foot of the mountain or he would "break out against them" and they would die (Exodus 19:12–22). When God is on the summit, even base camp is deadly. The warning not to approach isn't about protecting God, but about protecting people from the nearly uncontainable danger of the divine presence. It's no different in the holy of holies.

The cherubim guard that new most sacred spot on earth: the mercy seat, where God dwells, and one can't approach without risking death. The mercy seat isn't a place of mercy, but a plea for mercy. The Hebrew term (kapporet) is rooted in the word for atonement. But this atonement wasn't the cozy notion of restoring "right relationship" that you hear sometimes today. It was to ask for clemency in the face of the deadly divine.

The "mercy seat" is a place of terror, approachable only by the select few, and even then only with every possible safeguard in place. This sacred space, so full of the divine presence that cherubim must be permanently built into it, is a place of peril, a continual reminder to beg for mercy or risk the wrath of a very dangerous God.

At the gateway between sacred space and the world at large, the cherubim stand guard, fending off improper human approach and hemming in the lethal divine presence. And hell betide us when that boundary is crossed.

Interlude: The Ark Offensive

For one brief season, the ark was let out of its cage—and wreaked havoc. The Israelites had tried to harness and exploit its power, but like the T. rex of *The Lost World: Jurassic Park* (1997) escaping its chains and going on a rampage through San Diego, the ark could not be contained, bringing death and destruction wherever it went. Though created by human hands, the ark could never be fully secured under human control.

We fast-forward to a time long after the ark's creation, and after the wanderers finally made it to their destination. The Israelites and the Philistines had each settled some parts of the land, and the two do not see eye to eye. At this point (as the Bible tells it), the ark has already long been housed in Israel's main sanctuary in the city of Shiloh.

The plan seemed solid. The Israelites, facing battle with the Philistines, bring out the ark to use as a sort of magical weapon. But magical weapons tend toward unpredictability. The Philistines fight hard, and the ark doesn't come through for the Israelites. The Philistines slaughter thirty thousand soldiers in this battle, and capture the ark (1 Samuel 4:1–11).

But this means the Philistines now have the presence of God in their midst—and that can't be good. In a story begging for Transformers-style animation, the Philistines place the ark next to the statue of their god Dagon in his temple. (Not making it better, people.) In the morning, Dagon is facedown on the ground in front of the ark. They prop him back up, but the next morning he's been laid out in the ring again, this time with his head and hands cut off.

Once the power of God is done knocking Dagon around, he hurls plagues at the Philistines. They panic and try to unload the ark. There follows a game of lethal hot potato as the ark is moved from one Philistine city to another, with residents dropping like flies in each place. The Philistines resolve that the ark needs to be returned to Israel (5:1–12).

But when the ark is dropped back in Israel's lap, the equal-opportunity power of God kills a slew of Israelites. The surviving townspeople pawn the ark off on another town (6:19–21). Things go all right for a while . . . until someone decides to move it again.

King David wants to bring the ark to Jerusalem. As his men are carting it there, celebrating and dancing in the streets, the ark starts to topple. One of the men, poor Uzzah, reaches out to steady the wobbling ark to keep the sacred object from crashing to the ground. For this, God strikes him dead.

David then fears for his own safety and sheds the ark fast, sending it off to a man's home. But the ark is unpredictable, and suddenly its presence provides that man with the blessings people had hoped for all along. Naturally, David therefore wants the ark back, though he's still tiptoeing—he watches to see that the people carrying it this time have safely gone six steps, and then, with relief, resumes his dancing (2 Samuel 6:1–15).

The "cursed object" horror genre has a venerable history. But from the classic monkey's paw to every cursed antique safely locked away in the vault on *Friday the 13th: The Series* (1987–1990), none of these deadly magical objects has got anything on the ark of God. The body count left in its wake is enormous. Every city, town, and army that tries to keep the ark ends up a pile of human wreckage. Israelites and Philistines alike, these are the cocksure contingent who try to employ the power of the dinosaurs in every *Jurassic Park* installment, only to learn their lesson in the jaws of a velociraptor. The ark cannot be contained. It will not be exploited.

This is the lethal divine power that requires monstrous guardians. Each of these two major episodes of the ark saga opens with an ominous nod to the cherubim. Each time, it's not just "the ark" that people foolishly try to harness, but the ark of "the Lord of Armies, who dwells among the cherubim" (1 Samuel 4:4; 2 Samuel 6:2).

The stories don't spell out the role of the cherubim, but we might imagine how their interrelated functions are at play throughout the ark's tour of destruction. First, they're the monstrous soldiers fighting under God's command. Like the divine Tiamat who sends her army of hybrid creatures into battle for her in Mesopotamian myth, the God of Israel has a monstrous infantry when he hits the battle-field. Not for nothing is he called the Lord of Armies.

Next, the cherubim are the permanent guardians of the ark. Perhaps this havoc is what fury they unleash as they protect it from human contamination. This is why the catastrophic blows land on the Israelites as much as on the Philistines. The divine danger of the ark is why the Israelites bring it into battle in the first place, sparking the whole fiasco, but they forget that the destructive power isn't theirs to wield. The guardians of the ark will protect it from *all* unauthorized contact.

Finally, the cherubim are meant to guard the gateways in both directions, like supernatural referees holding back both the chaos of humanity and the overwhelming danger of the divine presence. Throughout the ark saga we see acutely why this is necessary. The boundary between sacred space and the messy tumult of human society has temporarily dissolved, and all hell breaks loose. And it won't be the last time.

Urban Paradise

After David gets the ark to Jerusalem, his son Solomon builds a temple to house it. This first Jerusalem temple, which stood for four centuries until its destruction by the Babylonians in 587 BCE, was seen as the very house of God. The holy X that had been a moving target in the days of the tabernacle was now meant to be a permanent touchdown site for God's home on earth. At this point, the role of the cherubim as guardians of the gateways is literally built into Israel's most concrete expression of God's presence.

The temple is similar to the tabernacle in some key ways, though what's inside is different. The Bible describes the temple as having multiple gates and chambers to pass through before entering the innermost sanctuary, the holy of holies, where the ark of the covenant is kept. It's like a theological *Get Smart* (1965–1970), where only special agents can pass through all of the doors to enter the secret headquarters. This is where the ark will remain for centuries, closed off deep within a house for God, built of stone, wood, and gold.

And it's here, in the holy of holies, that Solomon puts two massive statues of cherubim.

The temple cherubim are fifteen feet tall, made of wood and overlaid with gold. Each cherub has a fifteen-foot wingspan, and standing side by side, touching wingtip to wingtip, their wings fill the room (1 Kings 6:23–28). Unlike in the mobile sanctuary, which required portable cherubim, the temple cherubim are enormous statues suitable for a great stone building meant to be permanent. They stand on the ground on each side of the ark, and they now face forward. (The mercy seat isn't mentioned.) The forward-facing temple cherubim are reminiscent of the pairs of winged bulls and lions that stood guard in Assyrian palaces, and of the sphinxes of Egypt and Syria, positioned in pairs with one on each side of a human or divine king.[6]

But the temple cherubim, with wings extended across the room, don't look quite like any of those other hybrid creatures. We can deduce a little more about their form, too. Each cherub has a wingspan of fifteen feet, and each wing is seven and a half feet long.

Figure 4. The pair of winged *lamassu* from the Assyrian palace in Nimrud, displayed in imposing form at an entryway. The lion-bodied creature is on the left and the bull-bodied on the right. Note the paws and hooves.

This leaves no space between the bases of the wings, which means their wings must come out of the center of their backs, not out of their sides, unlike the sphinxes and Neo-Assyrian hybrid guardians. Beyond this, unfortunately for the modern monster fan, there's a lot lacking in the description. Do they have the bodies of lions? Bulls? Something else entirely? Do they have human heads, like so many other hybrid guardians?

And yet, one thing that's made utterly clear is the precise position of the cherubim's wings. Their wings are outstretched and touching one another to fully cover the ark. This configuration isn't

Figure 5. A ram-headed winged lion paces through the palmettes. (Phoenician ivory plaque, ca. 9th–8th century BCE.) Supernatural hybrid winged animals came in countless varieties.

merely a design element. It's the crucial safeguard making the entire temple possible. When the temple building is finished, there's a celebratory ritual that points to this like a flashing neon arrow. Solomon and his company process with the ark, and this is the culmination of the grand event: "The priests brought the ark of the covenant of the Lord to its place—to the innermost room of the temple—to the holy of holies—to underneath the wings of the cherubim. The cherubim spread out their wings over the place of the ark, and the cherubim covered the ark" (1 Kings 8:6–7).

The hybrid guardians form a wing-to-wing police wall between the human and the divine, secured deep within the most sacred space of the temple. One function of this pose jumps out: with a protective gesture over the ark, the giant cherubim face forward, ready to pounce, threatening any who might dare come within reach of the ark without appropriate cultic preparation.

But isn't there something odd about this position? You enter the temple. You make it through to the holy of holies. You reach for the ark. You're maybe five and a half feet tall. The cherubim, looming at fifteen feet, shroud the ark—from above. You still have perfect access. You can reach out and touch it, if you dare after the object lesson of Uzzah and so many others. If the cherubim were there only to protect the ark from unsanctioned human entry into the holy of holies, they should screen it from the front, not form an obstacle above it. Unless we're to imagine that they're protecting the ark from demons crouching on the ceiling ready to swoop down, which has great on-screen potential but (unfortunately) no basis in the text, this wouldn't be a logical angle of approach. It would, however, be an exit. Ever the guardians of the gateways preventing passage between realms, the cherubim covering over the top of the ark are also, again, keeping something *in*.

This is what all of that cultic preparation is for, after all—it's a life jacket in a stormy sea. Even the priests who carry the ark into the holy of holies can't remain in its presence once the glory of God touches down (8:10–11). The great theme of the ark stories, from its first home in the tabernacle through its catastrophic period on the loose to the temple years and beyond, is the grave danger it represents to human life. According to one talmudic tradition, when the temple was facing Babylonian attack, the ark was hidden beneath a storage room. One day a priest noticed a mismatched floor tile. He began to tell someone and immediately dropped dead.[7] The memory of Death By Ark never fades.

And so, when the ark is brought into the holy of holies, it's ensconced beneath the outstretched wings of the cherubim. As in the tabernacle, there are additional cherubim at each checkpoint between the holy of holies and the world outside. There are cherubim engraved on the walls, the doors that shut off the holy of holies from the central area of the temple, and the doors between that and the foyer (6:29–35). But in the temple, there's an added element to the design. The engraved cherubim are interspersed with palm trees and open flowers, in an apparent garden scene. We've seen cherubim in such a place before.

The Eden symbolism in the temple has been recognized, though it's often explained as representing something to do with creation.[8] But that's not what the cherubim in Eden signified. Creation is *never* what cherubim signify. They don't guard the tree because of God's creative power, but because of God's punishing acts. The cherubim and trees carved into the walls of the Jerusalem temple are a reminder of Eden as the place of ultimate danger to human beings. It's where God lied to them, gaslighted them, and decreed for them misery and hardship all the days of their lives. He threw them out and slammed the door behind them, stationing the cherubim at the gate, and the future of humankind was altered forever, for the worse, and by God's own doing. Reflections of Eden fill the Jerusalem temple, but Eden wasn't a safe space for humankind. In the temple, this urban Paradise, the memory of Eden is engraved like a scar.

The echoes of Eden reverberate around the temple, where the core activity is that of the sacrificial system, through which God offers abundant blessing—but only under certain circumstances, with dire consequences for mistakes (Leviticus 7:18; 19:5–8). God is the provider the people rely on, but he threatens to cut them off if they displease him. This dynamic rings of that first garden, where God showed just enough tenderness to reassure the frightened couple hiding from him behind the trees, before tossing them out and posting his henchmen at their door. We saw it again as the ark, that magical high-stakes roulette wheel, veered between blessing one man and showering destruction upon others.

Even taking into account these indications of divine danger in the temple, though, it seems less emphasized than in the tabernacle, where we're on high alert as the cherubim perch on top of the mercy seat, facing inward and down. There's a disturbing reason for this. The Bible, as an organized anthology, paints a picture of a chronological development from Eden to the tabernacle to the temple, yet the stories weren't written in this order. The history of ideas behind the anthology follows a different trajectory. Though scholars usually can't pin down the precise date when a biblical text was written, relative dating is far more certain. The description of the massive forward-facing cherubim in 1 Kings was actually written earlier than the tabernacle texts. When later writers penned the description of the tabernacle, the cherubim turned to face the mercy seat, the source of peril.

The turning inward of the cherubim expresses an increased concern with the danger God poses to his own people—and this reflects a pattern in the Bible. While we witness God's violence through all periods of biblical writing, there's an alarming development following the devastating Babylonian siege of Jerusalem, destruction of the temple, and exile of the Jews: these horrors are attributed to God's violence against his own people. Postexilic writings like Lamentations 2, a gut punch of a poem about God ruthlessly thrashing his people, show why survivors might crave any possible protection from divine danger. That protection never comes. The image of the violent deity isn't more "primitive," as it's often brushed off as being. It's the development of people who, having survived horrors, reflect greater understanding. The eyes of the people are opened to know good and evil.

The Perfect Storm

Jerusalem is conquered, the temple is destroyed. Many Jews are deported and sent to live in forced exile in the land of their Babylonian conquerors. The prophet Ezekiel is among them.

Ezekiel reports stunning visions of God abandoning the temple and burning Jerusalem to the ground. His visions are at once incredibly detailed and oddly impenetrable. Ezekiel describes what he sees in the glow and haze of heaven and dreams, grasping at the ungraspable. As his first vision dawns, he sees a windy storm coming in, swirling with fire—and in the midst of the storm, four living creatures. These turn out to be none other than our old friends, the cherubim, in fantastic new form.

He paints a vivid picture of the cherubim. At first it seems we could almost visualize them. Their bodies appear humanoid, but they have four wings, straight legs with the hooves of a calf, and under their wings, human hands. Each cherub has four faces: those of a human being, a lion, an ox, and an eagle (Ezekiel 1:5–10). So far, we might be able to follow him on this. But when he sees them again later, the four faces are those of a *cherub*, a human being, a lion, and an eagle (10:14, 22). The shift is incomprehensible. If each cherub has four faces, what's that first "face of a cherub"? Is it some new indescribable visage? Or the quartet of faces from his first vision, and now each cherub has one face that comprises those four faces, one of which comprises those four faces, and so on into kaleidoscopic eternity? Every possibility seems impossible. Ezekiel's a damn fine writer with a particular knack for the poetic gesture at the ineffable. Maybe we're not meant to be able to nail down the appearance of these baffling divine creatures.

Then Ezekiel spots something else. Between the cherubim are burning coals (1:13).[9] This is Chekhov's gun—when it appears in the first scene, you brace yourself for its deadly use before the final curtain.

The near-psychedelic images continue to bloom. Wheels appear alongside the cherubim: four gleaming wheels and wheels within wheels—and eyes in the wheels. In the next picture, the eyes seem to have crawled onto the bodies of the creatures themselves. Their bodies, sparkling like bronze, and their hands and wings and wheels, are *all* covered with eyes all around (1:7, 15–18; 10:12).

Above the cherubim and the wheels, Ezekiel sees what cannot be seen: God enthroned in the temple. He couches everything: there's *something like* a dome, over which is *something like* a throne, and upon it, the *appearance* of the *likeness* of the *glory* of God, with splendor all around. Throughout, all is like stormcloud and fire and amber and sapphire and lightning zapping back and forth and crystal and thunder and glory (1:15–28).

The pieces of the picture start to come together. Each cherub extends two of its wings so the cherubim are touching wingtip to wingtip (1:8–11). With this hint of a familiar position, the hybrid creatures with wings outspread in the holy of holies have come to life in all their vivid monstrosity. But these aren't the frozen statues of Narnia simply regaining life and movement. The *"living creatures,"* as Ezekiel keeps pointedly calling them, have burst into a new dimension, wildly beyond anything we could have imagined, let alone built. Hands and hooves and many faces, wheels alongside and fiery coals in their midst, the heavenly monsters radiate incomprehensible divine life that could never have been captured in mere statuary. With their two new wings they cover their bodies in the presence of the living God.

Finally, as something like a shining throne appears over the cherubim and the wheels, a new image comes into view. These creatures, hooves and wings and wheels and all, now form a living chariot.

This supernatural vehicle is as unfathomable as the cherubim themselves. The semi-animate wheels, filled with eyes all around, move in every direction in perfect alignment with the cherubim, because, as Ezekiel says repeatedly, "the spirit of the living creature was in the wheels" (1:20, 21; 10:17). The cherubim were already menacing monsters. They've now shapeshifted by annexing multi-eyed wheels, and with their spirit in the wheels, they move together as one being—one sentient, powerful vehicle. The gleaming '58 Plymouth Fury that crushes and burns people to death in *Christine* (1983) has got nothing on this living chariot.

The cherubim still use their wings to move, though. The noise is overwhelming: the rustling of their wings is like the sound of rushing waters, like the voice of Shaddai, a tumult like the sound of an army (1:24). These aren't arbitrary examples of loud things. The phrase "rushing waters" (*mayim rabbim*, literally "many waters") is associated with God's victory over the monstrous sea, and his enthronement over it and all divine beings (Psalm 93:4; 29:1-3; Habakkuk 3:13-15). The ancient name "Shaddai" is associated with God as the head of the divine council.[10] The "tumult like the sound of an army" is barely an analogy: the cherubim are literally part of the heavenly "host," that sanitized translation of "army," serving the Lord of Armies. All three descriptions of the sound of the cherubim's wings conjure images of God in battle and as head of a divine entourage.

Then God speaks. As Ezekiel hears the voice of the Almighty in the temple, the terrible reason why God needs a chariot must be dawning on him (Ezekiel 1:28-2:10). God is leaving.

And God does not go in peace. A spirit—this is a surprise to Ezekiel as much as to the reader—yanks Ezekiel up on his feet like a marionette, and God launches into a series of promises of catastrophe for Israel, all setting the stage for his sweep of the cape

(3:1–7:27). Intermittently, marking an ominous progression, Ezekiel witnesses God's gradual steps toward the cherub-mobile, and sees and hears the cherubim as they prepare for takeoff:

Ezekiel hears the rustling of the cherubim's wings and the rumbling of the wheels (3:12–13).

The spirit drops Ezekiel back down by a riverside, where he sits stunned (3:14–16). God unleashes a stream of threats against his people: he'll ravage them without pity and flood them with his rage until he's finally sated (4:1–7:27). God yanks Ezekiel up by the hair to show him a vision of the temple, where Ezekiel sees people committing idolatry (8:1–18). God summons six divine executioners to take the people out, brandishing weapons to smash and destroy (9:1–2).

Suddenly, Ezekiel sees that the glory of God has risen from its place in the holy of holies and has just moved to the threshold of the temple (9:3).

Among the heavenly armed killers is a man in linen who initially performs the merciful slice of God's hit order (though he won't for long), marking the foreheads of those to be spared while the rest of the hit squad slaughters the entire remaining population of the city (9:6). While the squad is busy reducing the city to carnage, the horrified prophet cries out in shock at the divine massacre. God explains that the people have accused him of forsaking them, immediately after which he says he'll slay them without pity (which is not *not* forsaking them).

Now, Ezekiel looks up. Above the cherubim, he sees something like a sapphire throne (10:1). The divine chariot awaits!

Cue Chekhov's gun: God tells the man in linen to grab handfuls of the burning coals that Ezekiel had spotted between the cherubim in his first vision, and to throw them down onto the city (10:2). God isn't just abandoning Jerusalem; he's leaving and setting fires behind him. He's going to burn it all down.

At this point, the cherubim rustle their wings so loudly that the sound can be heard even outside of the temple (10:5).

Then a cherub stretches out a hand from beneath one of its four wings, reaches into the fire that burns between the cherubim, and passes glowing coals to the man in linen (10:7).

Wait, what just happened here? God told the man in linen to grab the coals, but he doesn't get them himself from the fire, he gets them from the cherub. The cherub isn't taking over demolition duty (which it could do efficiently, chucking burning coals over the city as it flies off), only the duty of handling the weapons. The final destruction is not its job. Its role—one we'll see reprised later—is to secure the instrument of destruction and hand it to the appointed executioner. In this moment, the cherub becomes the weapons master.

Ezekiel must think this is the final act.

Center stage, the glory of the Lord, last seen pausing at the threshold of the temple, moves to stand above the cherubim, mounting the living chariot. The cherubim lift their wings and rise up, wheels and all, starting to carry their passenger away (10:18–19).

But at the east gate of the temple, the cherubim pause one last time. The spirit lifts Ezekiel up and brings him in visions to that very gate. The prophet despairs that God is annihilating the remnant of Israel (11:1–13). God, as tenderly as when clothing his first human beings in Eden, offers words of hope and reassurance—and then abruptly abandons the temple.

The cherubim lift their wings and wheels, with the glory of God above them, and whisk God away (11:22–23).

It's all been leading up to this. From their first appearance at the gateway to Eden, the cherubim threatened some unnamed violence. As their menacing images stood welded into the mercy seat in the tabernacle, they signaled the divine danger at hand, warning all to beg for mercy. In the temple, their images were etched into every wall in a repeated garden scene on all sides—a continual reminder that even in what seems to be the safest and most blessed space, we are surrounded by divine danger. Now, with the return of the living, otherworldly creatures in Ezekiel's visions, the threat is realized. Now it becomes clear what that divine danger was: violent, bloody, fiery mass destruction. God orders the deaths of every adult and child throughout the entire city, and the cherubim do what their job has been all along. They're the henchmen. When God says to burn it all down, they grab the glowing coals.

We should have seen it coming.

Divine guardians are effective because they represent a real threat. Sometimes this means they must serve as soldiers for their divine commander, like the hybrid monsters of Tiamat's army. As guardians of the gateways, the cherubim prevented the havoc created by unsanctioned contact between realms as long as they could. But now it has come, the storm when divine chaos and human chaos meet.

It seemed for a time that we might hope the cherubim would protect us from the wrath of God. Didn't they perch over the ark in part to keep something *in*? This isn't how the story was supposed to end. But those were only statues, after all, able to do no more than symbolize the danger triggered by illegitimate contact. What they ward off eventually breaks through. Ezekiel witnesses the abominations in the temple, right there where the stormfronts meet. God responds with complete destruction, and the cherubim do their job. They've stood guard for God, and now they evacuate him, turning to fire on the perpetrators as they go, like a divine Secret Service shielding a brutal leader. This is the horrific reminder that the cherubim's role of guarding against passage between realms didn't mean they were neutral. They have always been in God's employ.

The One Who Dwells among the Cherubim

A handful of times, God is referred to as he "who dwells among the cherubim." This is usually taken as evoking God's glory in some general sense.[11] But you know the cherubim by now. Now that we're more attuned to their role, we'll see a pattern emerge. This epithet is used in three stories and two psalms—and each time, it's in a moment of anticipating, invoking, or celebrating divine violence.

We've come across the first two stories already: this phrase appears in both major parts of the saga of the ark's path of destruction. First, the Israelites bring the ark of "the Lord of Armies, who dwells among the cherubim" into battle to fight for them, and later, David brings the ark of "the Lord of Armies, who dwells among the cherubim" to Jerusalem, and doesn't get far before Uzzah is struck dead for trying to steady it (1 Samuel 4:4; 2 Samuel 6:2).

Next, the epithet is used in the prayer of King Hezekiah. Halfway through the first temple period, Hezekiah's kingdom is facing a dire threat from the Assyrian empire. The Assyrian king Sennacherib taunts Hezekiah, and God himself. Sennacherib claims that no gods have ever been able to save their people from Assyria, rattling off a mocking "Where are they now?" list of defeated deities, adding that

God won't be able to protect his people either (2 Kings 18:29–35; 19:9–13). Panicked, Hezekiah invokes God "who dwells among the cherubim," asking him to prove his divine might (19:14–19). God comes through—sending another member of his entourage, an angel, who promptly kills 185,000 Assyrians (19:35).

Raising an eyebrow yet at the emerging pattern? The cherubim emanate divine danger. Narrators and characters alike whip out this phrase when God's destruction is on the horizon. The cherubim are such recognizable warning signals that the epithet is like sounding an alarm: Danger approaches! It's those foreboding two notes you hear in *Jaws* every time the shark is on the move.

The alarm-bell function of the epithet is equally glaring in the psalms, where it might be easiest to gloss over it as generic praise. The first poetic use of the phrase is within yet another request for divine force against a perceived threat: "Dweller among the cherubim . . . stir up your might!" (Psalm 80:1–2). The second use is bookended by reminders that people should be afraid of God: "Let the peoples tremble! He dwells among cherubim; let the earth quake!" (99:1). The poet then reminds readers that God sometimes takes vengeance on his own people.

The cherubim formula never appears in a neutral context. It's always used to introduce, request, or celebrate divine violence, pointing to a God with a fearsome divine army. People keep trying to beckon the cherubim to fight on their side, but there's no predicting how God will deploy them in battle next.

Cherubim II: The Reckoning (Or, So You Thought the "Old Testament" Was Violent)

Back in the home of my friend's grandmother, I blithely mention—because I cannot seem to bite my tongue on this subject even when it would clearly be the appropriate choice—that the cherubim on her shelf, wide-eyed in white ceramic, are actually ferocious and terrifying.

"Well," she tells me, "maybe in Judaism." [*Esther looks at camera.*]

A lot of people still buy into the old notion that divine violence is a thing of the "Old Testament." First, a word about terminology: it's only the "Old Testament" if you're defining it against the New Testament. "Hebrew Bible" is a good, standard, neutral term to use instead. Next: comments like "maybe in Judaism" forget that Judaism didn't freeze when Christianity began to grow. In reality—wait for it—both the Hebrew Bible and the New Testament include divine violence and divine mercy, and both Judaism and Christianity developed ways of distancing God from *some* types of violence.

The New Testament achieves this in part by jumping on the dualistic theology train (already in motion), in which cosmic good and evil have distinct and opposing realms and rulers. The Adversary, originally part of the divine cohort, leaves the company of God and becomes the evil ruler of his own domain. In the New Testament, God is distanced from that member of his violent entourage—even as other members remain. And they sure don't get any nicer. God's remaining entourage still commits mass slaughter, and it's still explicitly on God's behalf.

Remember how in Ezekiel's first vision, he identified the cherubim as "four living creatures"? Those "four living creatures" reappear in the apocalyptic visions of the book of Revelation, but now they've morphed into a conflation of cherubim and seraphim, becoming hybrids of hybrids, and have also taken on some exciting new features.

Rather than each one having four faces, they each resemble a different animal: a lion, a calf, a human being, and an eagle. If that seems like too normal a starting point, their bodies are still covered with eyes. In Ezekiel's vision, the wheels of the cherubim-chariot were also full of eyes, but now the throne is in heaven, so there's no chariot, and no wheels. Each creature now has six wings, like the seraphim of Isaiah's vision. They also sing an adaptation of the lines Isaiah heard the seraphim calling to one other: "Holy, holy, holy is the Lord God Almighty, who was and is and is to come" (Revelation 4:6–8).

This heavenly chorus, drawn from the seraphim tradition, reflects the most famous role of the living creatures in Revelation: to sing God's praise. As we'll see, though, they perform three functions—and the other two draw from the most terrifying aspects of the cherubim tradition.

But first, the innocuous role: heavenly worship. In several scenes in Revelation, the living creatures praise God alongside thousands of angels (some with momentous roles to play, but that's a story for another chapter). They sing hymns and worship God in ways that might feel familiar enough to some readers that we could forget that these aren't humanoid beings. But when they fall down in worship, it's with hybrid, eyeball-covered bodies; when they say "Amen," it's out of beastly mouths. They hold harps and golden bowls, so it's a safe bet that they also have hands (5:8–9; 15:7). The role of the living creatures as singers of praise is often attributed instead to their two divine ancestors in biblical tradition, the cherubim and seraphim, like in the famous Christian hymn, "Holy, Holy, Holy." One verse of the hymn alludes to Revelation 4 and includes the line, "cherubim and seraphim falling down before thee." Cherubim and seraphim, indeed—but in one body. Our two composite creatures have merged to create a next-generation divine being.

But praise is the only pleasant act of these next-gen creatures. Their second function is upon us in the blink of an eye. The moment they've given their first "Amen," the apocalyptic prophet, John of

Patmos, witnesses the breaking of the seven seals of a scroll (5:14–6:1). This being a divine scroll in an apocalyptic vision, breaking the seals doesn't just allow for some light reading, it releases the infamous four horsemen, who bring war, starvation, and all manner of horror and catastrophe to the earth. The final horseman alone, Death itself upon a pale horse, is given the authority to kill a quarter of the earth's population. But the horsemen can't cross between realms willy-nilly, riding from heaven into the earthly domain as they please. There is a gateway—and we have come to know the guardians.

Sure enough, each time a seal is broken, John hears one of the living creatures say, "Come!" One by one, each living creature beckons one of the horsemen, standing at the checkpoint and waving them through (6:1–8).

Their third function is no kinder. After an onslaught of various divine disasters, John sees another sign: seven angels who unload the seven final plagues on humankind. Each plague is held within a golden bowl, and the angels are to "pour out on the earth the seven bowls of the wrath of God" (16:1). Everything they pour their plague-bowls onto becomes weaponized. One angel pours its bowl into the sea, which becomes like blood and everything in it dies. Another angel pours its bowl onto the sun, which burns people alive. When the seventh angel pours its bowl into the air, the very atmosphere becomes a deadly weapon, with lightning and the most violent earthquake that has ever been. All the cities of the world fall, the islands and mountains are demolished, and hundred-pound hailstones drop out of heaven and crush people.

And how do the angelic executioners acquire their weapons of mass destruction? From the weapons master, naturally. John explains: "One of the four living creatures gave the seven angels seven golden bowls full of the wrath of God" (15:7).

Members of God's entourage until the end, the living creatures have shifted shape, taking on some traits of the seraphim— fortunately the six wings and the praise, not the deadly venom—and keeping the gateway post and weapons-wrangling power of the cherubim. Unfortunately for humankind, they have now expanded their turf. It's no longer the city of Jerusalem or the region of Judah. It is now the entire doomed earth.

From the mythical realm of Eden to the apocalyptic visions of Revelation, cherubim stand at gateways of sacred space. These divine monsters are stationed at each new post as it becomes the most sacred spot on earth, tracking that holy X from the garden to the tabernacle to the temple. When God abandons the earth, the cherubim whisk him away into the sacred realm above. In the end, they stand at the gateway one last time to usher divine destruction back into the earth.

The cherubim guard against hazardous contact between realms, wings outstretched to hold human and divine chaos back from one another. Any unauthorized person entering the holy of holies would do well to heed the warning of their presence. When something violates the cosmic boundary, the results are catastrophic. God warns people not even to touch the foot of his holy mountain or they'll die. We see what transpires when the ark is unconfined. The kill response is indiscriminate. One man reaches out to steady the ark and is struck dead. Entire cities fall.

Sacred space is always dangerous. Even as the cherubim ward off unsanctioned approach, they hem in the lethal power of the deity. Maybe even at that first gateway, as they stand guard to keep people out of Eden, we should wonder what they're keeping *in*. (This could be why the flaming sword in Genesis 3:24 is whirling in *every* direction.)

But in the end, they serve at the pleasure of a divine commander, "the Lord of Armies, who dwells among the cherubim." If he wants to wreak havoc, his cherubim do their part. When God decides to peace out, the living cherubim-chariot carries him off. They're his bouncers, bodyguards, and getaway drivers.

When God places the hit on Jerusalem, they become the divine weapons handlers, in the New Testament graduating from burning coals to bowls of wrath. By that point they're no longer trying to keep anything in; they beckon the horsemen through the cosmic gate, letting them loose on humankind. Like Heimdall, guardian of the Bifröst bridge between earth and Asgard, realm of the gods, the cherubim occupy a position of great responsibility. But these hybrid guardians are loyal to God, not to us, and when the time comes, they shepherd God out of the human realm and divine warriors in. Maybe the real marvel of these monsters is that we've made it this far.

Surely God is due some credit for stationing his cherubim to prevent such havoc, though? That is, until he doesn't, and deploys them against us instead. By now we recognize the m.o. How many times has God shown just enough tenderness to reassure his people, before flipping the switch? After gaslighting and cursing his first human creations, he clothes them with care before evicting them from their home and posting cherubim at their door. He blesses the Israelites with the ark and then slaughters them through its presence. He provides them with the sanctity of the temple and then rains down fiery coals upon it. From the divine tragedy of Eden to the destruction of humanity, the cherubim stand as a reminder that humankind is at God's mercy.

This is not reassuring.

So far we've met two of God's monsters. The seraphim, cousins of the cherubim, are also hybrid border guards. Their jurisdiction is behavioral: they reinforce social and cultural norms. The jurisdiction of the cherubim is physical. They enforce the boundaries of sacred space. It's no wonder the two, policing their physical and behavioral borders, are eventually conflated. As different as they are, they're the complementary forces of God's border patrol, and both participate in mass killings in his service.

The rest of God's entourage is made up of altogether different monsters. We now leave behind wings and hybrid guardians. As we move on to meet God's enhanced interrogation specialist, we also set aside mass slaughter.

The torturer-in-chief in God's employ—who only in later Christian theology comes to rule his own evil domain—is a precision worker, never engaging in the astounding level of depopulation that the cherubim and seraphim commit. (But don't get too comfortable; we'll witness mass carnage again when we come to the angels.) On, then, to the peculiar relationship between God and the Adversary.

3

The Adversary

He towers above all others, black-horned with skin so red it could burn you, dangerously magnetic with a glorious evil laugh (*Legend*, 1985). He's the colossal monster deep beneath the ground ("The Satan Pit," *Doctor Who* S2 E9), the Dark Lord clomping on cloven hoof through the night forest (*Chilling Adventures of Sabrina*). In human form, he's a man of wealth and taste (*Lucifer*; *The Devil's Advocate*, 1997). He shivers with pleasure at wickedness (*Supernatural*). From *Faust* to *South Park*, and with all the diverse images in between, you'd know him anywhere.

Anywhere, except maybe the Bible.

Satan can cloud your judgment. Not *the* Satan, but the word, *satan*. When you meet a character called "the satan" in the Bible, it's hard not to think of *that* Satan. But the familiar figure developed over centuries, not reaching his fully fleshed-out form as Lucifer, the fallen angel, until after the Bible was written. By the time of the New Testament, Satan shows up as the archenemy of God, but even there he's never called an angel. Satan "*masquerades* as an angel of light" (2 Corinthians 11:14), and like God, Satan commands warrior angels (Revelation 12:7–9), but he himself isn't an angel, and never had been. Not in the literal sense—and sure as hell not in the collo-quial sense.

Before he becomes God's nemesis, he's already vicious and malignant—while acting as a member in good standing of God's monstrous entourage. The eventual figure of Satan who rules his own evil empire isn't a good guy who went bad, he's a bad guy who went solo.

Satan wasn't originally a name. The word *satan* is a Hebrew noun meaning simply "adversary," and it can refer to human adversaries too. It's used for divine beings in just four texts in the Hebrew Bible. First we'll see the word describe a function, when one of God's divine hitmen acts "as an adversary." Then we'll see a divine being step into the role as a permanent appointment, identified by his title, "the Adversary." Finally, the word becomes a name: Adversary, or Satan. Even then, he's not the same as the Satan of the New Testament, who's also called *the devil* (and a few other choice names). In the Hebrew Bible there's no devil or hell. None. Zip. Devil-free terri-tory. No punishment in eternal fire. But the devil will get plenty of air time once we hit the New Testament. We have later writers to thank for that. At every stage of his development, though, the Adversary is a disturbing character. On the one hand, the early appearances of a lower-case, workaday divine *satan* shouldn't be blurred with the later character of Satan. On the other hand, even in these early texts, we see a divine figure particularly gifted in the crueler arts, in light of which the Satan trajectory makes perfect sense.

The Hebrew Bible is skimpy on the details where the *satan* is concerned. In view of the monstrous Satan coming down the pike— imagined as a "great dragon" and serpent in Revelation 12:9, later often standing red-tailed and pitchforked—you might expect to find vivid descriptions of the Adversary. What strange and frightful form

Figure 6. Medieval French "Prince of Hell," a handy reminder that the Bible sets no limits on how to imagine the *satan*. (From a 15th century illuminated manuscript.)

will we stumble upon as we read these early tales? Well . . . none, really.

Unlike the monstrous hybrid seraphim and cherubim, the physical form of the divine *satan* is never described. The appearance of the figure in God's entourage on his way to achieving ultimate monster status is nothing compared to the blatantly monstrous forms of those creatures who remain forever in God's inner circle, later to be domesticated and beautified beyond recognition. Those terrifying hybrid monsters get housebroken somewhere along the path from the Bible to the greeting card. Satan gives a wave as he passes them traveling in the other direction, going from nondescript heavenly bureaucrat to full-on red dragon.

While the Adversary remains ambiguous in form, he demonstrates some classic monster traits we haven't yet encountered. We met seraphim-snakes on earth and saw a vision of seraphim in heaven, and we watched cherubim leave the temple and fly off toward heaven, but we haven't yet witnessed a proper realm-crossing. We soon will. And when we see the Adversary crossing back and forth between heaven and earth, he's doing so in order to use his multiple lethal superpowers against his human victims.

Not *his* victims, precisely: he works on behalf of Another.

At Your Service

Of all the members of God's entourage, the Adversary eventually gets tenure as the torturer-in-chief—at which point, safely theologically extracted from the company of God, he's so broadly understood as a monster that he gains horns, hooves, and tail. But make no mistake, he's monstrous long before leaving God's entourage. From the start, the divine *satan* performs his corrosive duties thoroughly in service to God. He is God's monster.

Whose Adversary?

We first meet a divine adversary in the story of the prophet Balaam. Balaam is a colorful character, a freelance diviner and prophet who finds employment in the cursing of his customers' enemies. He's not an Israelite, but he defies a high-profile client, the king of Moab, by delivering oracles of the God of Israel instead of the curses he was hired for. He plays the buffoon in our story's key scene (Numbers 22:22–35), but he's the hero throughout the rest of the story (22:36–24:25).

Balaam is attacked by a divine being who comes after him "as an adversary." Reading in translation, you'd never know the word *satan*

is used here. This isn't the case with any of the other texts referring to a divine *satan*. And why? Translators (who are, as always,
interpreters) seem to find it very important to separate this character from the others—because this divine *satan* is the angel of the
Lord.

Here's what happens. King Balak of Moab sends messengers
to hire Balaam to go with them and curse Israel. Balaam says he'll
sleep on it, and consults the God of Israel (a surprising move for a
foreign diviner). The next morning he declines, having discussed the
matter with God, who told him not to go. The king tries again, and
this time Balaam vows that even for all the king's riches, he'll say only
what God tells him to. With this foreign professional curse-thrower
expressing remarkable faithfulness to the God of Israel, a reader
might anticipate a twist, a moment of weakness from Balaam, but it
doesn't happen. His last word to the messengers is that they should
cool their jets while he waits to hear from God again. And here's
where the twist comes. The next thing God says to Balaam is, "Go
with them," and so, obediently, he goes—at which point "the anger
of God burned because he was going" (22:1–22).

There's no cure for the whiplash. God gives Balaam a direct
order, Balaam obeys, and God is enraged at him for it.

And God doesn't tend to stop at *feeling* rage. As we've become
accustomed to expect, he sends a member of his entourage to take
care of the problem. The divine bait-and-switch is startling even
before you know that in Hebrew it says that an angel of the Lord
takes his stand against Balaam "as a *satan*."

The term *adversary* isn't used lightly. The angel is armed and
licensed to kill. It stands in the road, drawn sword in hand, blocking
Balaam's way as he rides his donkey toward Moab. It repeatedly tries
to kill Balaam. Like other monsters of the "invisible-to-some" type—
the hellhounds of *Supernatural*, Vecna of *Stranger Things*—the angel

is invisible to Balaam, but not to the donkey. Three times, the donkey sees the armed angel blocking its way and tries to escape. The first time, the donkey veers into a field. The second, the angel stands in a narrow alley, and the donkey scrapes itself along the wall trying to get by. When the angel moves ahead and finds a spot so tight there's no getting past, the donkey flat lies down. Each time, Balaam hits the donkey, not realizing the donkey is saving his hide (22:23–27).

God finally lets Balaam in on the situation. He zaps the donkey with the gift of speech, at which point the donkey and Balaam promptly have an argument. Next, God grants Balaam the more dangerous gift, true sight. Balaam sees the divine monster standing before him, announcing that it has come as a *satan*. The angel emphasizes that it would have killed Balaam right then and there if the donkey hadn't kept foiling its plans (22:28–33).

The angel gives Balaam a final word of advice. (Warning: if you feel some resurgence of hope for a satisfying explanation for the attack, best temper it.) The angel tells Balaam to go with King Balak's men (*as Balaam was already doing*) and to speak only what God says (*as Balaam was already doing*). Balaam is already on the road when the angel attacks him, so in his understandable confusion, he even offers to head back home if that's what the angel wants, but it tells him to continue on with the officials. The scene concludes, "So, Balaam went with the officials of Balak"—*as he was already doing* (22:34–35). This story reads like a time loop, a very dark *Groundhog Day*. God directs Balaam to go with the men, and so Balaam goes. God erupts in rage over this and the angel tries to kill Balaam . . . and then directs him to go with the men, and so Balaam goes. Balaam must be bracing himself, hoping it turns out better this time around.

In a three-chapter story praising Balaam for his faithfulness to God, this brief attack scene clearly takes the prophet down a notch:

even the donkey can see what the seer can't. (Balaam isn't alone in the takedown: Israelite prophets get lampooned too, as in the book of Jonah. The ancient authors knew as well as we do that those with Very Important Things to say sometimes merit an eyeroll.) This scene goes beyond playing with the "blind seer" trope. It's a comment on the man's limits—but it's also a comment on the monster. Sure, the donkey's awareness of the angel threatening Balaam's life emphasizes the seer's lack of sight, but Balaam's not the only one who comes off looking sketchy compared to the donkey. The donkey's sympathetic character also highlights the angel's malevolence.

In the argument between Balaam and the donkey, Balaam accuses the animal of mistreating him, swearing, "I wish I had a sword in my hand! I would kill you now" (22:29). Compare this to the angel, who *does* have a sword in its hand, and swears it would kill Balaam now if not for the veering donkey (22:33). Meanwhile, the donkey calmly points out that it's never done wrong by Balaam. The donkey is the only rational, nonviolent character here. The awkward contrast is unavoidable. The donkey might never harm Balaam, but the angel sure gives it a go.

The angel doesn't stop at physical assault. Every bit the apprentice in God's studio, it does a bit of gaslighting. When first gifted with speech, the donkey had asked Balaam, "What have I done to you, that you hit me these three times?" The angel now asks Balaam in virtually the same words, "Why did you hit your donkey these three times?" But then the angel adds that it came "as an adversary [*satan*]," as if this were *in response to* Balaam hitting the donkey, explaining that he would have killed Balaam on the spot if the donkey hadn't been so damned wily (22:28, 32–33). Sounds legit, if you conveniently forget that Balaam was only angry at the donkey in the first place because it swerved to escape the angel, who was already there to kill him.

The donkey asked a legitimate question, but when the angel repeats it, it's spun to imply that this attack from a divine adversary was the consequence of Balaam's actions—when it was the cause!

When the divine being who comes as a *satan* is an angel of the Lord, it's not a kinder, gentler *satan*. This divine adversary is brutal and unfair, stopping an obedient prophet in his tracks, committing assault with a deadly weapon and attempted murder, and demonstrating dominance for its own sake.

"Satan" can't cloud our judgment on this one, where even the title "the *satan*" isn't used, let alone the proper name. There isn't a remote glimmer of possible confusion with the later character. Take away the character eventually named for the function, and all you see is the function. Later on, Satan will become God's opponent, but that's not what "*satan*" indicates within the entourage. The role of a *satan* is not as an adversary to God—but as an adversary to people, on God's behalf.

The Balaam incident is important because it paves the way for the other appearances of a divine *satan*. Removing Satan from the equation, what remains is a stark picture of a divine employee whose God-given job is to oppose people who are being obedient and faithful. The attack on Balaam, who obeys God and is then assaulted for it, is a setup. This turns out not to be a fluke. When God works with an Adversary in his entourage, the team play is entrapment. And the next innocent man targeted doesn't get off as easy as Balaam.

The Job Experiment

The book of Job tells the story of a man who endures unspeakable suffering as the direct result of closed-door conversations between God and a member of his entourage. A traditional summary of the story is that Satan tests pious Job. The entire story hangs on the fact that Job is authentically faithful. But it's not Satan who goes after him, and it's not quite a test.

The stage is set on two planes. It's like a classic upstairs-downstairs story, only with less charm and more sadism. The opening scene takes place downstairs, with a portrait of the man and his life. From the first line, it's emphasized that Job is innocent: "That man was blameless and upright. He feared God and turned away from evil" (Job 1:1). We're then introduced to his family. He has ten children, and his sons take turns hosting meals for all of the brothers and sisters. It's a beautiful family picture. Job also has great wealth, in the form of enormous numbers of oxen, donkeys, sheep, and camels, and a huge staff of servants (1:3–4).

We zoom out and pan up to the scene taking place upstairs, where God is meeting with the divine council. All the heavenly beings come, one of whom is called "the Adversary." This isn't Satan, who doesn't exist yet—satan is still simply a common noun, not a name. Where the Balaam story featured a divine being acting "as a satan," this story introduces a divine being with the job title, "the satan." It looks like originally, this was a function any decently violent member of God's inner circle might fill, and at a certain point, someone well suited for the job took it on as a permanent post.

As the role of "the Adversary" becomes a fixed position in the heavenly administration, the job description is fleshed out. There's a heavenly court, where God is judge. And in God's court, the Adversary serves as the divine prosecutor.

As the scene upstairs begins, the divine beings are gathering. God checks in with the Adversary, asking him where he's coming in from. The Adversary says he's been "roving through the earth and walking all around through it" (1:7). God isn't surprised, and doesn't need to ask the Adversary what he was doing. Apparently, the Adversary regularly crosses back and forth between heaven and earth. It's part of his job. One of the Hebrew verbs implies patrolling for information, like a kind of divine surveillance system.[1] The Adversary gathers intel. The angel of the Lord had also implicitly crossed over to appear on earth as a *satan*, but in this story the Adversary's repeated realm-crossing is highlighted as a plot element. It's how the divine prosecutor does his job of looking into people.

Then comes the fateful moment. This is the bad backroom deal caught on video, the tweet that should end the politician's career. (It doesn't.) God turns to the Adversary, maybe cocking his head toward an unsuspecting father of ten busy on earth worshipping God: "Have you considered my servant Job?" (1:8).

Hold on. Let's rewind the reel. The judge has just prodded the prosecutor to look into an innocent man. God isn't naively trying to elicit the Adversary's admiration for Job. The judge knows his court, and he has just prompted the prosecutor to turn his attention to Job. Professionally.

God doesn't suspect Job of any wrongdoing. He actually makes sure the Adversary knows that Job is completely innocent, explaining: "There is no one like him on earth, a blameless and upright man who fears God and turns away from evil" (1:8). These are virtually the same words used by the narrator in the opening verse of the book. Job's authentic blamelessness is literally the setup to the entire story, affirmed here out of God's own mouth. God is just baiting the Adversary further with the tantalizing fact of Job's innocence, because the Adversary *wants* to go after an innocent man— like the angel who came "as an adversary" did with Balaam, and like we'll see again later. For the judge to prod the prosecutor to scrutinize anyone would already be shady. Here, the judge is deliberately targeting someone he knows to be innocent. This is the very picture of corruption.

The Adversary takes the bait. And of course he does; the prosecutor is just doing his job. It's the corrupt judge who provokes him. Given his role, his response to God is precisely what the reader—and God—would expect. The Adversary has been asked, in his professional capacity, to consider a subject, and it is his professional responsibility to comply. Knowing Job is blameless just makes it more delicious.

God tempts the *satan*, and the *satan* succumbs. He suggests that Job might not be so blameless if God were to attack him rather than bless him. After all, as he asks, "Does Job fear God gratis?" The Adversary presents his case: so far, God has protected Job. "However," the *satan* reasons, "stretch out your hand and strike all that he has, and he will curse you to your face" (1:9–11).

The judge and the prosecutor aren't trying to establish whether Job is blameless. They know he is. They're trying to find out if they can make him *stop* being blameless. They're working out a plan to put Job in a situation in which he's likely to transgress. This is textbook entrapment.

Entrapment alone is pretty bad, but the most horrible part of this is their "trying to find out." They're not angling to entrap Job because he's done wrong and they want to make sure they can put him away for something, using unjust means to a just end. No, God and the Adversary hatch a plan to see if they can get Job to sin— because they're intrigued by the question.

The deal God makes with the *satan* is often understood as a bet, but God never offers a view contrary to the Adversary's. The Adversary claims that Job will curse God, and God never claims otherwise. He says, essentially, "Hey, let's find out." This is something worse than a bet: it's an experiment.

God, having instigated the probe, now gives the Adversary the green light to begin. God is still the one overseeing this, the police captain behind the one-way glass viewing the interrogation room.

The Adversary has just acknowledged that God is in charge of the enhanced interrogation: "Stretch out your hand and strike all that he has," and God responds by giving the go-ahead. Cool-headed in the viewing room, God tells the *satan* that he can go after everything Job has.

God places one limit: no harming Job's body. This is no act of mercy, though. God allows the Adversary to kill all of Job's children. Insisting that it's merciful to keep Job alive and well enough to endure the snuffing out of his family ignores the psychological torture at play. The limit God places is part of the experiment. At what point will Job cave?

And so it begins. Back downstairs, there's a rapid-fire series of assaults on every person and animal introduced in the story's opening verses. Each bloody loss must be reported to Job for the sake of the experiment, so each time, one servant is strategically left alive to report more lives lost, cattle destroyed. The pace quickens as each time, the lone survivor of one attack is still speaking when the next rushes in: raiding Sabeans have stolen all of Job's oxen and donkeys and slaughtered the shepherds tending them! All of Job's cattle and the shepherds with them have been burned to death! Marauding Chaldeans have made off with Job's camels, slaughtering the servants with them too!

This scene had opened ominously on a day when Job's children were all gathered together; now comes the horrific culmination. While the third survivor is still speaking, another comes in with the devastating news of the final assault. All of Job's children are dead. The record screeches; time slows down. Job hears how all his sons and daughters were sharing a meal at one of their homes. What a thing for our enhanced-interrogation team to take advantage of! A great wind swept in from across the desert, destroying the house. It fell on top of the "young people"—we seem to hear this from Job's perspective—crushing them all to death (1:18–19). Phase one of the experiment has ended.

What have God and the Adversary learned? The hypothesis was that the subject of the human experiment would curse God. Finding: unconfirmed. The narrator concludes, "He did not ascribe wrong-doing to God" (1:22). Well, of course not—because he doesn't know that God was the one who instigated these wrongs. The narrator told the reader what transpired in the heavens, but no one told Job. If only Job knew how it all went down—but no one else was in the room where it happened.

The reader, however, learns a lot from the Job experiment—not about Job, but about the pair curiously poking and prodding him from the heavenly lab. First, the Adversary can incite people to do what he desires, as with the Sabean and Chaldean attackers in the first and third stages of the experiment. The Adversary can also control the elements, as in the second and fourth stages. The lone survivor of the second attack tells Job that "the fire of God fell from heaven" and burned the servants to death (1:16). The shock here isn't just that the Adversary can control lightning, but that this is explicitly a divine instrument of destruction, "the fire of God." Not only does God give the Adversary the go-ahead, he provides the weapon. (You'd almost expect to see a cherub in the scene, handing it over.) The fourth attack also hinges on the Adversary's control over the elements, as the great wind strikes all four sides of the house at once, a tornado zapped from a divine hand, killing all of the children.

God instigates this gruesome experiment and supplies the deadly tools. By this point in the story, we could at least hope this would satisfy God's curiosity. It doesn't. In God's estimation, the experi-ment on Job is not complete.

Back upstairs, the divine council meets again, and God and the Adversary greet one another as they did before. The Adversary has crossed back into the heavenly realm for this meeting, again telling God that he's been patrolling the earth. Had this all been a bet, God could now say he's won. Instead, God incites the Adversary a second time, doubling down on his initial suggestion to look into Job, and even repeating his affirmation that Job is definitely innocent—which, of course, is what makes the experiment intriguing. This time, God adds, "He is still holding on to his blamelessness. And you incited me against him, to engulf him gratuitously" (2:3).

"Wait," you can almost hear the Adversary saying, "*I* incited *you?*" We've seen God do this before. God alters the story to shift the blame, as in Eden—despite having just repeated his initial prompt to the Adversary! In Eden, God subtly misquoted himself to Adam to alter the story. This time, God blurs his own words with the Adversary's. He accuses the Adversary of enticing him to attack Job "gratuitously." This is the same Hebrew word the Adversary had used when he questioned whether Job worshipped God "gratis" (1:9). God isn't just playing on the Adversary's words, but on his memory, using the Adversary's own phrasing with a slight twist. Kudos to God—this is quality manipulation.

Playing right into God's hands, the Adversary cannot resist the temptation, and suggests that God up the ante in order to achieve the desired outcome of the experiment: "Stretch out your hand and strike his flesh and bone, and he will curse you to your face" (2:5). It's nice that the Adversary again recognizes God's authority in all of this, even acknowledging that the proposed assault will come from God's hand. God responds with equal recognition of the Adversary's work, handing the human subject over to him and giving him the go-ahead to do anything short of killing him. If you're going to be in a partnership doing torturous human experiments, this is a nice model for teamwork. There's an inspirational poster in here somewhere.

Commence phase two of the Job experiment. The Adversary, again sent to handle the business end of things, strikes Job with horrible boils from the soles of his feet to the crown of his head (2:7). Job is left sitting in ashes, scratching his inflamed boils. This is pretty inventive, as torture goes. The Adversary's work on Job isn't a spiritual test. Between the psychological torment and gruesome murders of phase one and the painful physical ordeal of phase two, this looks more like the torture-glee of the disturbing Mr. Blonde in *Reservoir Dogs* (1992). The man in charge bore responsibility for bringing Mr. Blonde onto that job. God, too, knows what to expect from the torturer he brought on board for this task.

The Adversary's work is done. He isn't mentioned again and the rest of the book focuses on Job's experience. The whereabouts of the Adversary are left to the reader's imagination. He must be invested in the outcome of the experiment, though, and we see in 1:1 and 2:1 that the divine council meets on the regular. I picture God and the Adversary up there together watching the whole thing go down. One year, I had the students in my Job course put on a dramatic interpretation of the book, a performance in the round under a marble spiral staircase. We staged the divine council scenes on the second-floor balcony, where God and the Adversary remained for the rest of the performance, looking down together from the great VIP box in the sky as Job suffered his various torments at the foot of the marble staircase.

While the Adversary leaves the scene, God shows up one more time in the book. Job moves through waves of grief and anger, alternately begging and challenging God to talk to him. But when God finally answers Job out of the whirlwind, it's to interrogate him. Bracketing the cruelty of this, it's just unfair: God asserts that Job knows nothing, and then hurls upwards of fifty questions at him, most of which are rhetorical to emphasize God's own power. When Job can't answer, God somehow takes this as proof of guilt. Justice is not the operative principle in these proceedings.

God turns on Job with this interrogation: "I will question you, and you will inform me!" (38:2–3). Halfway through, he pauses to demand that Job answer, and Job cowers, saying he has no answers (40:2, 4–5). But as with the experiment itself, God is *still* not satisfied. He launches in again, repeating, "I will question you, and you will inform me!" (40:7). The Adversary may be in charge of torture techniques, but the interrogation is all God's.

The religionists and scholars who defend God in Job often point to the "resolution" at the end of the book, where in their perception God makes good. But the brief epilogue is every bit as inhumane as the prologue. God replaces Job's wealth and children. You heard me: replacement children. New children to replace dead ones— murdered ones—whom God himself had the Adversary kill (42:7– 17). This is not a happy ending. There's no softening the loss of ten children, unquestionably innocent victims of this divine experiment. No matter how hard we might try to wrest a spiritual justification out of the divine treatment of Job, there's no tempering this for the ten dead children.

What was it all for? God and the Adversary torture a man they mutually avow to be innocent, and for what? This isn't crucial intel they're gathering. It's to satisfy God's curiosity: Can the innocent man be corrupted? What's his breaking point? Curious to find out, God instigates each phase of what happens. He prods the prosecutor to look into Job, and when he sends the Adversary to do the wet work, he sets the rules. Phase one: don't kill Job, but feel free to murder his children. Phase two: don't kill him, but feel free to torture him to within an inch of his life. The story repeatedly emphasizes that Job "feared God and turned away from evil" (1:1, 8; 2:3). Job might turn away from evil, but God brings evil right to his door. "You have turned cruel to me," Job laments to God. "When I hoped for good, evil came" (30:21, 26). No wonder Job fears God.

The sadistic experiment begun in strategy sessions between God and the Adversary rings of the same abuser psychology we encountered before.[2] "How much do you love me? Would you still love me if I did *this*? How about *this*? If you really love me, you'll stay."

But God isn't the one who poses those questions. Prompted by the curious deity, the Adversary articulates the key question. In that first discussion with God, he asks, "Does Job fear God gratis?" And it's this question that sets the *satan* apart from the other monsters of God's entourage, what sets him on the path to promotion to become a malevolent ruler in his own right: not just that he tortures, but that he ponders. Among all the company of heaven, he alone is a true conversation partner for the Almighty.

Too bad they're both in it to torture and kill the humans, though. Long before the dawn of Satan, the *satan* performs his role as prosecutor in the divine court by roaming the earth to gather intel, having backroom meetings with the corrupt judge, and aiming to ensnare Job by any means necessary, from torture to murder. And he does it all fully and faithfully in God's service. The fact that his inventive use of torture is all to satisfy God's curiosity is less a reflection on him than on God.

The book of Job is often described as a reflection on why innocent people suffer. But Job doesn't suffer *despite* his innocence. He suffers *because* of it. When the angel acting "as an adversary" went after Balaam, while the man was doing precisely what God had instructed him to do, it wasn't a fluke. It is the job of the Adversary to go after the blameless and obedient—on God's command. This divine prosecutor specializes in targeting innocent defendants.

Let's see, then, what happens when the Adversary actually encounters someone guilty.

In Defense of the Prosecution

In another divine council scene, we get to see the divine court in action. This isn't one of the many placid pictures of the heavenly court that focuses on God as judge, leaving the rest of the divine beings in the blurred background ("God stands in the divine council; he judges in the midst of the divine beings"; Psalm 82:1). This scene is painted by the prophet Zechariah, who had a series of bizarre visions—the four horsemen, a flying scroll, a woman in a basket—and, fortuitously for our interests, this play-by-play of the fully staffed divine court. Through Zechariah, we get to see other main characters step into the spotlight, if only for a moment.

Zechariah's vision opens the doors to the heavenly court in session. Joshua, the high priest, is on trial. Two divine beings stand in service, each to make his case: the Adversary for the prosecution, and the angel of the Lord for the defense.

The Adversary stands at Joshua's right to accuse him, just like the human "adversary" (also *satan*) in another courtroom scene (Psalm 109:6–7). The Adversary is doing his job, but God silences him: "The Lord rebuke you, Adversary!" (Zechariah 3:2). Given God's rebuke of the prosecutor's intent to prosecute, you might expect to find out that the defendant is innocent. This is not the case. The angel of the Lord, in defending Joshua, acknowledges that the defendant is guilty. Here's how the scene plays out:

Joshua is wearing "filthy" garments, as many translations will tell you. The Hebrew is more graphic. He's wearing "shitty" garments. Wearing shit-covered clothing is pretty extreme for anyone. For the high priest to appear in the heavenly court in clothing smeared with feces brings this to another level entirely. In the divine courtroom, the angel of the Lord recognizes these soiled and ritually impure garments as symbolic of Joshua's guilt. The angel orders the assembled divine beings, "Take off his shitty clothes!" He then turns to Joshua, explaining, "See, I have removed your iniquity from you, and will clothe you with pure garments" (3:3–4).[3]

The guilt Joshua bears is never specified, but it represents the guilt of the people, since as the high priest he takes on their iniquity (Exodus 28:36–38; Numbers 18:1). Maybe he is wearing their sin, or simply the defilement incurred through living in exile in Babylon.[4] Further clouding any insight into the accusation, Zechariah's vision comes from a context where different Jewish communities had very different views, including about Joshua and the priesthood. Some Jews had been living in exile in Babylon and returned with ideas that came from weathering that storm, while other Jews never had to leave Judah. It's like the core group of survivors on *The Walking Dead* versus the people in the Alexandria community who never had to survive on the outside. There was real friction, and we don't know whose views we're seeing get set up and knocked down in Zechariah's vision, so we can't pinpoint the charge against Joshua.

Considering the tensions between Jewish communities at the time, Zechariah's vision is all the more striking. Even while attempting to defend Joshua against the views of an opposing group, with real stakes on the ground, Zechariah *still* envisions Joshua as bearing real guilt. The angel of the Lord, in declaring that he's removing Joshua's iniquity, confirms that the defendant had walked in guilty.

This brings us back to the Adversary, who is right to accuse Joshua. He's only doing his job, and doing a bang-up job at that.

God engages in questionable behavior, though. Acting as judge, God silences the prosecutor, even knowing he's prosecuting a guilty defendant: "The Lord rebuke you, Adversary!" What exactly is this rebuke for? It's not for being the Adversary; that's his job in this court. God elaborates: "The Lord, who has chosen Jerusalem, rebuke you!" The charge against the high priest represents a charge against the people, and God explains that he has already chosen Jerusalem. In other words, the judge silences the prosecutor because the outcome of this case has already been decided.[5]

The Adversary can hardly be faulted for his accusation. The siege of Jerusalem and the Babylonian exile were interpreted as signs of God's own accusation against the people, as we see in so many biblical texts. In Zechariah's courtroom vision, God has apparently changed his mind about Jerusalem, but this can't be held against the Adversary.[6] How's the Adversary supposed to know that God's rejection of Jerusalem didn't take? He's basing his prosecution on God's own accusation.

And so, exonerating Joshua and all he represents, the assembled members of the divine court replace the prophet's shitty garments with a clean turban and fresh clothing. Remembering that Isaiah's purification by divine beings in the heavenly assembly involved having his face burned by a multiwinged serpentine creature, Joshua seems to have gotten off scot-free.

In the previous texts, we witnessed an angel acting "as an adversary" going after an innocent man, and then the Adversary targeting and torturing an innocent man, both times on God's behalf. Now, we see the divine prosecutor finally ready to prosecute a guilty man—only to be silenced by the judge.

All told, this is some spectacular judicial corruption. Though God rebukes him for making it harder to exonerate a guilty man, the *satan* is simply performing his job in the heavenly court. Once again, he is not an adversary against God, but against people, in God's employ. He doesn't use a weapon, like the adversarial angel in the divine setup of Balaam. He doesn't use the elements or behavioral control, like the *satan* in the divine setup of Job. He uses his official position in the heavenly court. He uses the power vested in him by God to do exactly what he's supposed to do, and for this he finds himself on the receiving end of a divine attack, coming off forever the worse for it. In this case, maybe the Adversary is the one who gets set up.

Two Peas in a Pod

And now, we leave the vision of the exoneration of a guilty man, and we return to the safe and familiar territory of the entrapment of another innocent man. Well, familiar territory, at any rate.

The first time Satan appears in the Bible—not "the *satan*," but a character with the personal name, "Satan"—he acts just how you might expect. It's pretty straightforward, as stories of divine manipulation go: "Satan stood up against Israel, and he incited David to number Israel" (1 Chronicles 21:1). We don't know why taking a census is sinful here, but other characters in the story also realize it's a terrible idea. But David succumbs and takes the census, incurring God's wrath. Disaster ensues. This devious act of inciting someone to sin is precisely the sort of behavior Satan becomes famous for later on.

Here's the problem: this isn't the original version of the story as told in the books of Samuel. This is the remake.

Like many remakes, there are a few expansions and deletions and some rephrasing to reflect a later perspective. All of this is characteristic of how the books of Chronicles, written late in the biblical game, retell stories from the older books of Samuel and Kings. But within this largely faithful recasting of the story, the remake has altered one dumbfounding element of the original. Here's the opening line of the older story: "The anger of the Lord again burned against Israel, and he incited David against them, saying, 'Go, number Israel and Judah'" (2 Samuel 24:1).

The divine goal of getting David to take a census is the same. The divine action of inciting him is the same. Even the Hebrew verb for this divine manipulation (*vayyaset*, "incited") is the same. As the story progresses, the catastrophic outcome is the same. The difference? The divine being is switched out.

This is generally the moment when my students freeze in their seats: the quintessential role of Satan in the remake is played by God in the original.

At this point, we shouldn't be surprised to see God's behavior align with Satan's. It's perfectly in character. God and the Adversary have a history of working as a team. This time, instead of seeing them target someone together, we watch two versions of the story, performed in split screen by God and Satan in perfect unison.

The remake might feature Satan doing what he gets famous for, but it's the original, featuring God alone, that includes the m.o. we've seen when the team's working together. God had told Balaam to go with the Moabite king's men, and then sent his angel "as an adversary" to kill Balaam for doing so. God prodded the Adversary to target Job specifically because Job was blameless and faithful to God. Now God incites David to do something—and then punishes him for it.

All told in the Bible, David does a lot of terrible things. He's not big-picture innocent, the way Job is. But even so, in this story he gets set up. Unlike in the later version where Satan instigates and God punishes, the original is a story of entrapment. This m.o. isn't the Adversary's. It's God's.

God's actions as the story unfolds (which are nearly identical in the two versions) are also in keeping with what we saw when God and the Adversary were working together . . . only worse. When God told the Adversary to go after Job, a lot of innocent people in Job's life were slaughtered. For David's divinely inspired census,

God's punishment includes the gruesome deaths of seventy thousand people. *Seventy thousand.* God has a high tolerance for collateral damage.

God's punishment is like something out of a crime thriller. He makes David choose between three horrible ordeals. This is right *after* David repents. Each option is an ordeal for the entire nation—years of famine, months of enemy attack, or days of pestilence (2 Samuel 24:10–13; 1 Chronicles 21:8–12). This choice isn't an act of inscrutable mercy, as if at least David can select the catastrophe to come. It's part of the punishment. David must bear the burden of deciding what special kind of suffering his people will endure.

I can't read this story without thinking about the Joker's affinity for forcing people to choose between deadly options—kill the accountant or the hospital gets blown to smithereens, choose whether hundreds of people on that ship die by your own hand, or by mine and you along with them (*The Dark Knight*, 2008). This isn't getting to decide, it's being forced to participate. The mass casualties are secondary; the primary aim is to torment the person who now has agency in the death of others foisted upon them.

God gives David three options. Imagine David's dread upon hearing God's menacing conclusion: "Choose one of them, and I will do it to you" (2 Samuel 24:12; 1 Chronicles 21:10). "And that's the point," says the Joker, "you have to choose."

David chooses door number three. For people who've lived through the COVID-19 pandemic, a few days of pestilence might sound pretty doable. An awful lot can happen in three days, though; this is less COVID and more *Outbreak* (1995). But pestilence seems like the best bet to David, too. He gambles that falling into God's hands will be preferable to falling into human hands. He might rethink this later.

Choice made, the pestilence is delivered by an angel, stretching out its hand to destroy throughout all of Israel. (We'll witness the Destroyer's acts up close in the next chapter.) The remake includes a sword in the angel's hand, but the effect is the same in both. Over those three days, seventy thousand people die. It's only when the angel stretches out its hand to destroy Jerusalem that God grows remorseful, and commands the angel, "Lower your hand" (2 Samuel 24:16; 1 Chronicles 21:15). But God's just putting his angel on standby. It's the tactical hand signal of a closed fist: "Hold your fire." Even now, remorseful for the carnage, God doesn't actually stop the pestilence.

With the angelic soldier holding fire, David begs God to punish him rather than all of those innocent victims. He urges God, "Let your hand be against me and my father's house" (2 Samuel 24:17; 1 Chronicles 21:17). "Lower your hand," said God to the angel. David essentially now turns to God and says, "Lower *yours*."

This story that began with Satan's first waltz onto the biblical stage contains no reference to hellfire, horns, or any number of other later ideas. Satan does not yet rule his own evil domain. In fact, his grand entrance, his debutante ball, contains no reference to Satan doing evil at all. It does, however, refer to *God* doing evil. When the angel stretches out its hand to destroy Jerusalem, what prompts God to call out, "Hold your fire!" is that he regrets "the evil" he has done (1 Chronicles 21:15; also 2 Samuel 24:16).

This isn't the later concept of "evil" as a cosmic force opposing "good," but it's getting pretty damned close. The Hebrew word *ra'ah* has a range of meanings—evil, wickedness, depravity, devastating harm—and the choice of how to translate it in any given instance is a matter of interpretation.[7] Most English Bibles shy away from referring to God's "evil," even if they translate the same word as "evil" when it applies to human beings—and even in the same verse.

Check out how the NRSV sanitizes a verse from Jeremiah in which God refers to his own "evil" alongside that of people. The italicized English words are both translations of the Hebrew ra'ah: "If that nation . . . turns from its *evil*, I will change my mind about the *disaster* that I intended to bring on it." (The King James doesn't shy away: "I will repent of the *evil* that I thought to do unto them.") In the next verses, God even juxtaposes his "evil" with his "good," and confirms that he is indeed planning "evil" against the people (Jeremiah 18:8–11). This isn't an aberration. References to God's "evil" are all over the Bible.[8] Wherever one places it along the depravity spectrum, two points stand out. It's suspect to translate the word as "evil" when it refers to people but to soften it when it refers to God; and the word is used to refer to the actions of God, and God alone, in a text in which Satan appears.

The sole appearance of capital-S Satan in the Hebrew Bible shows him inciting someone to sin, honing the craft that later puts him on the map. When Satan was still cutting his teeth on some fairly rudimentary work—enticing a man with enormous power to use it wrongly is low-hanging fruit on the temptation tree—God was already a pro, having done this in the older version of the story. In both versions, God follows this up with mass extermination with a biological weapon. The question of whether God or Satan incited David might not matter to the people on the wrong end of the angel. God has them wiped out with pestilence either way. But as we watch the synchronized performances of God and Satan in these two versions of the story, it might matter to us.

In the Hebrew Bible, the developing *satan* figure is almost always in God's employ—through attempted murder and assault with a deadly weapon, the killing of a man's children and many other people, human experimentation and psychological torture. Even when God silences the Adversary, it's as the judge to the prosecutor within God's heavenly courtroom. In Chronicles we see a single moment of Satan acting independently as he inaugurates his classic later role of inciting the innocent to sin. Later, in Christian theology, Satan becomes the ultimate adversary of God, rather than being the adversary of innocent people on God's behalf.[9] Most references to Satan in the New Testament demonstrate this new direction—but not all. Old friendships die hard.

Still Crazy after All These Years

"Old friends, old friends, sat on their park bench like bookends. . . ."

By the time the writers of the New Testament were getting to work, Satan had been distanced from God, excised from his entourage—mostly. But despite what many New Testament readers might hope was solely a Hebrew Bible collaboration, there are scattered hints of ongoing teamwork between God and Satan.

In the Gospel of Luke the Job dynamic resurfaces. When Jesus anticipates his disciple Peter's denial of him, Jesus warns, "Satan has obtained permission to sift you all like wheat" (Luke 22:31). In other words, Satan's going to give them one hell of a good shake, and we'll just see who makes it. Almost like an experiment. But what's this about him having "obtained permission"? Even translations that try to soften this can't mask the core dynamic. Satan wants to harm people, but he can't just go off half-cocked. He still needs to ask for divine permission. And he gets it.

The apostle Paul also alludes to God and Satan's continued cooperation. With a characteristic flair for the dramatic, he writes that God has given him a thorn in the flesh in order to keep him humble.[10] Here's the snag. Paul also says that the metaphorical thorn God jabs in his flesh is "a messenger of Satan to torment me" (2 Corinthians 12:7–9). The instrument of Satan afflicting Paul is given by God to achieve his divine purpose.[11] God uses Satan to cause Paul pain.

It's too bad we don't get to see the conversation between God and Satan this time around. In the book of Job, the narrator opened the curtains onto the scene upstairs. This time we know far less. How did they work out the deal to torture Paul? Then again, at least Paul knows what Job and his friends didn't: that his suffering is a result of teamwork between God and the Adversary. As we saw in the early days of their relationship, the *satan* here is not the adversary of God, but the adversary of an innocent person on God's behalf. These two are still good team players.

This isn't the first time in Paul's letters that Satan shows up as a destructive instrument of God's salvation. At one point, Paul writes about a certain sinful man who is apparently shtupping his father's wife. In the first letter to the Corinthians, Paul instructs the people to hand this man over to Satan so that his flesh may be destroyed, and his spirit saved (5:5). The same principle is at play in 1 Timothy, in a passing reference to a couple of unfortunate characters who've been turned over to Satan so they'll learn not to blaspheme (1:20).

Whatever exactly it means to turn someone over to Satan—the phrase resembles known ancient curses, and could involve physical harm or even death, or exclusion from the community—the implications about our dynamic duo are stunning.[12] It's one thing to suggest that in some general sense God *can* use Satan's torments for a higher purpose. These texts go further. In each letter, people want to sic Satan on their naughty friends *in order to* achieve God's purpose. As far as these Christian writers are concerned, Satan is still in God's service.

And then we come to the book of Revelation, with its great swirling visions of beasts and dragons and divinely wrought catastrophes. Through most of the book, Satan is conceived of as God's ultimate foe. And yet, even here, there's a hint of a behind-the-scenes working relationship between the two.

Part of Revelation is a series of messages to different churches. The writer, John of Patmos, says these words are straight from Jesus. The message to the church in Smyrna reassures people regarding what some of them are about to suffer at the hands of Satan (here called the devil). Although the people are comforted that the devil's torment will be followed by their salvation, there's no explicit statement of cause and effect, unlike in the previous texts. No one's overtly seeking out Satan's work in order to help God achieve his agenda this time. The oddity in this case is different. John writes that this is the message of Jesus: "Do not fear what you are about to suffer." [*So far, this is heartening.*] "Beware, the devil is about to throw some of you into prison so that you may be tested"—[*Maybe a bit worrisome, but more to the point, how does Jesus already know what the devil is about to do?*]—"and for ten days you will have affliction" (Revelation 2:10). [*Okay, now this has gotten awfully specific.*] Jesus has just revealed detailed knowledge of Satan's next move. The divine lines of communication are still open. The followers of Jesus aren't talking about turning someone over to Satan this time. Satan's torture seems to be simply his own plan in the making—but Jesus is already in the loop.

Eventually, God and Satan will no longer be seen sitting on their park bench together. But that's at a further point along the Satan trajectory. In the New Testament, God still employs Satan to achieve his own goals, relying on his old operative's advanced torture skills to get the job done. Maybe this is why, where the goals are Satan's, Jesus can know what Satan is plotting and let it slide, just this once . . .

Before going out and forging his own path in the world, eventually becoming the archenemy of God, the Adversary acted faithfully in God's service. The later Satan mythology gets that part right, but not because the Adversary was ever remotely good. From the start, the Adversary served God by going after the human target of God's choice. Even at his worst, tormenting Job to such ruthless effect that the work is commonly credited to the devil, he hashes out the plan with God at home in heaven—looking down at the earth from above, not up from below. The Adversary gradually individuates and uses his sadistic skill set for his own purposes, rather than God's, but he doesn't achieve full independence for a long time to come. Satan is still at God's beck and call at several points in the New Testament— and God still becks and calls.

After teaching Christian seminary students for nearly twenty years, I understand how difficult it can be to see the spotlight fall on this violation of the expected neat distinction between God's blessing and Satan's harm. My students often find that they can wrap their minds around divine violence as long as it's safely in the Hebrew Bible, but struggle when they encounter it in the New Testament. But it's there, spotlighted or not, and sometimes it's better to know what's lurking in the shadows.

Monsters don't simply scare us with their toothy grins and growls. They terrify by shaking our sense that we know what our world contains. Just as physically hybrid monstrous creatures disrupt our fundamental framework of the categories of distinct species, the morally hybrid monstrous upsets our comfortable moral binaries.[13] Is the *satan* prosecuting the guilty man in service of the heavenly court "good" or "bad"? What about when he tortures a blameless father of ten, at God's prompting? The latter case seems clearer—but if the Adversary is somewhere on the depravity spectrum in that case, then the God who repeatedly prods him, guiding each phase of the experiment, must be further along that same spectrum.

The seraphim and cherubim, for all their violence, at least have an undeniable majesty. There's some glimmer of hope to cling to there, some beauty comingled with danger and terror. Maybe, even after witnessing the seraphim and cherubim perform their duties in God's entourage, it's possible to hold onto some sense of security about the biblical heavens being a place of benevolence and wellspring of mercy. But if so, how that must crumble as we watch the *satan* come into his own under God's tutelage . . .

If only this breach of our security came from the *satan* alone. Cherubim and seraphim, a person might choose to bracket as wonders of ancient storytelling. The Adversary, some will always choose to view through the lens of much later clear-cut dualism, no matter what these Hebrew Bible and New Testament texts say. But the next monsters we meet throw the whole system into confusion. As a supernatural species, they never leave heaven for a newly conceived hell, and they never grow to be called evil. They are God's angels, morally ambiguous in their violent splendor, remaining cherished in popular thought and praised as God's close companions even as tales of their horrific massacres remain in plain view. Satan is no angel, but this turns out to be not much of an upward comparison.

4

The Destroyer and Other Angels

Watch yourself, we're heading into new territory now. This might be the most dangerous part of the safari—because it *appears* to be the safest.

If you know one angel by name, it's got to be Gabriel. As a Jewish kid with no personal connection to Christianity but seemingly a thousand school Christmas pageants behind me by the eighth grade, I knew Gabriel as well as I knew Superman. Or at least, I thought I did.

As Luke tells it, God sends Gabriel to tell Mary that she'll give birth to Jesus. After the baby is born, an unnamed angel appears to a group of shepherds. Luke describes the spectacular scene: "An angel of the Lord stood before them, and the glory of the Lord shone around them, and they were terrified!" The angel tells them not to be afraid, announcing, "I bring you good news of great joy!" A multitude of the heavenly host appear, praising God (Luke 1:26–38; 2:8–15).

How marvelous it all is! Who are these wondrous divine figures? They follow a long line of benevolent angels in the Hebrew Bible. An angel calls to Hagar from heaven and saves her and her son, Ishmael (Genesis 21:17–19; 22:11–12). An angel leads the Israelites through the desert, guarding them along the way (Exodus 23:20–22). Good news of great joy! If we don't look too closely, these tame moments could make it seem like angels are on our side.

What, then, of all the times angels go around slaughtering people?

This is the problem with angels. Yes, they're God's messengers, bringing words of comfort, rescuing people from danger and distress. From Genesis through Revelation, they seem the most benevolent figures in the company of God. But they're not just messengers and helpers. They're also the most ruthless of God's soldiers, the deadliest of all his divine hitmen.

We've come up against the moral ambiguity of the heavens before. But with angels it reaches a new level. How can these attendants of God—his divine representatives to humankind, no less!—engage in such brutality? How can they do such profound good and such devastating, lethal harm? For people accustomed to thinking of angels as benevolent and benign, it might be as hard to see their ugly side as to recognize malevolence in a beloved family member.

The "we need to talk about Kevin" moment comes the first time we see an angel massacre thousands of innocent civilians. Or maybe it's when we see an angel in hard pursuit of a single innocent victim. There are so many slaughters it's hard to choose. The cumulative impact of the angelic history of violence should leave us cold. Excusing the evil for the sake of the good might stem from loving hope, but it also takes a special kind of denial. And it can get you killed. Biblical characters, more often than Bible readers, recognize angels for what they are, and know full well the lethal danger they pose.

No wonder angels so often need to reassure people when they're *not* there to kill them. "Don't be afraid, Mary," says Gabriel. "Don't be afraid," the next angel tells the shepherds, because "they were terrified" (Luke 1:30; 2:9–10). "Don't be afraid," the angel tells the women at Jesus's tomb, while the guards shake with fear till they pass out. The women, even in their joy at the angel's message of resurrection, still leave in fear (Matthew 28:1–5). Because how comforting is it, really, to be reassured that *this* angel, *this* time, won't spell the end of you?

Getting to Know You

"Exclusive: Seasonally Inspired Angels," reads the ad caption beside the porcelain figurine, a winged little girl bedecked in four-leaf clovers, from her pretty dress to the garland in her blonde hair, brought to you by Precious Moments in time for St. Patrick's Day.[1] The domestication of the most terrifying monsters of the Bible is complete.

Television angels show more of a range. Here, we've mostly moved beyond the pure-as-snow and sweet-as-saccharine Roma Downey on *Touched by an Angel*. A recent pinnacle of angelic portrayal is *Supernatural*, which includes Castiel—complex and flawed, but noble at his core—but also countless angels whose sadistic violence is far closer to biblical portrayals than Downey's role ever was. Because really, you don't want to be touched by an angel.

But across the spectrum of modern representations, from wide-eyed figurines to TV sadists, one common feature stands out: angels usually look like people with wings. Remember that the image of each monster we've encountered so far has been altered dramatically through time and tradition. It's no different with angels. In the Bible, angels sometimes look like people, sometimes look not at all like people, and spoiler alert: they never, ever have wings.[2]

Everyone we've met so far—the seraphim, the cherubim, Satan—all eventually get subsumed under the angel heading. But before becoming a catch-all category, angels were a specific supernatural

Figure 7. NOPE.

species. Biblical angels vary in appearance, but you'd never mistake them for cherubim.

In some biblical stories, angels show up looking human. Sometimes this is followed by a flashy reveal: *Kablammo! I'm an angel!* Sometimes it's not. One human-looking angel ends a conversation with a fiery flourish, but another angelic visit and shared meal ends with the angels simply walking away (Judges 13:20–21; Genesis 18:2–22). And note: when angels look like people, they don't look like white people. The characters aren't white, the authors aren't white, a Middle Eastern appearance would have been assumed as the norm, and yet no one ever mentions that an angel appears foreign or oddly pale. It takes a serious prior commitment to the notion of the whiteness of angels to come away with the sense that they're white, but that biblical writers and characters alike uniformly fail to mention such a surprising trait. Angels sometimes wear white garments (Matthew 28:3; Mark 16:5; John 20:12). Not white skin.

Angels occasionally glow, but it's no warm Hallmark situation. When an angel appears to the apocalyptic prophet Daniel, body like gemstone with arms and legs gleaming like burnished bronze, face like lightning and eyes like flaming torches, Daniel nearly faints with fear. Even bystanders who can't see the angel instinctively run and hide (Daniel 10:5–8). But at least that's a vision. Another angel with an appearance like lightning shows up at Jesus's tomb, and this time the bystanders keel over from fright (Matthew 28:2–4). Because unlike Daniel's Goldyloins vision, everyone can see this holy terror.

Angels also take other forms altogether as it suits their purpose. An angel leads the Israelites through the desert in the form of a pillar of cloud when it's light out, and a pillar of fire when it's dark (Exodus 14:19–20). So practical! The Israelites follow the same rescue signals you'll find on a wilderness survivalist website: smoke by day, fire by night. In some stories, formless angels speak as disembodied voices calling from heaven (Genesis 21:17; 22:11, 15). Even when an angel shows up with some implicitly human trait like the ability to hold a sword, it's often in combination with classic monster traits, like terrifying giant size and use of bizarre, lethal superpowers.

There's a word for a creature that takes different forms at different times. The religiously minded may not want to use it. But it's unavoidable already from this first example, for a start: cloud by day, fire by night. There's no way around it. Angels are shapeshifters.

They're also the ultimate realm-crossers. Other divine beings also have the ability to move between realms, like the cherubim

Figure 8. Three angels, shown in both birdlike form and abstract form, conveniently identified by name in each. The image is part of a birth amulet in *Sefer Raziel*, a work of Jewish mysticism and magic (1701).

deployed to stand guard at Eden and the Adversary patrolling the earth before attending the heavenly convention, but angels are built for this. It's their defining feature. Because one of their main duties is divine message delivery, angels are constantly crossing back and forth between heaven and earth as they change form to meet the demands of any given situation. The famous image of "Jacob's ladder" shows Jacob, the early patriarch, dreaming of a ladder reaching from the earth up into the heavens, with angels climbing up and down it (Genesis 28:10–12). In some biblical stories the realm-crossing is simply assumed. God sends Gabriel (from heaven) to a particular town. Gabriel chats with Mary and then leaves—presumably Destination: Heaven, but the story doesn't bother to mention it. Elsewhere, we get to witness the moment of crossing over, like when a glowy angel descends from heaven, rolls the stone away from

Jesus's tomb, and instead of instant ascent, takes a seat (Matthew 28:2). Moving in the other direction, the angel who predicts the birth of Samson ascends to heaven in flame after the announcement (Judges 13:20).

Angels dwell in the *elsewhere* and *beyond*, but their functions involve infiltrating this realm. They serve as messengers, sure— meaning that when God wants to send a divine emissary to earth with an overt verbal message (as opposed to covert ops like we'll see in the next chapter), he uses an angel. But that's not all God sends angels to do. He also deploys them, unfortunately, on other missions altogether.

There's a centuries-old Hebrew song traditionally sung on Friday evenings as Shabbat rolls in, called "Shalom Aleichem," meaning "Peace Be upon You." It's sung to the angels. It begins like this:

> Peace be upon you, ministering angels . . .
> May your coming be in peace, angels of peace . . .

It's a beautiful song—but the repeated insistence on peace, which continues throughout the song, begins to sound like a worried plea. These writers knew a thing or two about angels.

The Destroyer

In the previous chapter, we met a member of God's entourage with a distinctive title: the Adversary. Unlike seraphim and cherubim, who are referred to only by the name of their supernatural species, the Adversary has a title that reflects his role. We now meet another member of the entourage with an ominous title: the Destroyer. It's the Destroyer's role to execute acts of mass destruction on

God's behalf. While the Adversary is eventually extracted from the company of God and identified as evil, it's funny the Destroyer isn't. As we'll see, this figure is no safer for God's human prey.

The Tenth Plague

Of all the horror stories the Bible has to offer—and God, there are so many—this one seems most unspeakable. (Would that it had never been spoken!) It is the horror of horrors: the divinely ordered slaughter of all the firstborn children of a nation. The wet work will be done by God's aptly named appointee, the Destroyer. But the bloodshed isn't the whole story. There's an intense buildup before the monster of the hour emerges from the darkness.

Back when Moses was asking the Pharaoh to let his people go, God decided to manipulate Pharaoh's mind on the matter—but not to get Pharaoh to agree. Instead, God "hardens Pharaoh's heart" so he *won't* let the Israelites go. That way, God can do it, miraculously and violently, himself. When God stretches out his hand against Egypt, as he explains to Moses, *then* they'll know he's God! (Exodus 7:3–5). Have you ever seen a guy pick a fight just to prove himself? God literally explains that he's making the situation more adversarial because he wants a chance to harm Egyptians with his destructive "signs and wonders," also known as the ten plagues.

The plagues are the stuff of classic horror, beginning with images to put the bleeding walls of *The Amityville Horror* (1979) to shame. All the water in Egypt turns to blood—even what's about to be poured from that clay pitcher on the table. Frogs infest houses, jumping through beds and into kneading bowls and onto people, like something out of a 1950s B movie. Next it's lice, then flies. Then pestilence kills the Egyptians' cattle. The Egyptians themselves are next: their skin erupts in boils, so people scratch, burn, and shed like the festering and foul victims of the grotesque body-horror subgenre (think *Cabin*

Fever, 2002). At this point, six plagues in, God points out to Pharaoh that if he'd wanted to kill them all he could've inflicted that deadly cattle pestilence on the people too, but didn't—because instead, he wanted to prove his power (7:14–9:17). God then sends such heavy hail that it'll kill anyone who can't make it indoors in time. Next locusts devour anything remaining after the previous seven plagues, filling houses. Then—darkness. Nothing can be seen, not even a hand in front of your face. It's an amorphous monster, darkness so thick it can be felt on your skin, pressing in on you. Imagine the suffocation. Once more for good measure, God hardens Pharaoh's heart so he won't let the Israelites go (9:18–10:27).

Because, somehow, God *wants* to deliver the tenth plague.

It will happen in the dead of night, God warns: the slaying of the firstborn child of every Egyptian. There will be a tremendous cry throughout the land, like there had never been before and would never be again (11:4–6; 12:12). The horror is ungraspable, the mass trauma unspeakable. The Israelites are instructed to put blood all around their doors—blood, more blood—as a sign to God to spare their families (12:7, 13). They're warned not to set foot outside of their blood-smeared houses until the morning comes (12:22). Because apparently, through this lethal night, God's indiscriminate killing machine won't know an Israelite from an Egyptian, so they'd better take cover till daylight.

And who is this divine killer? God first highlights his own role, telling the Israelites: "When I see the blood, I will pass over you" (12:13). So far, it seems for once he might do his own dirty work. But no—he's the general giving orders to the divine soldier. As Moses then explains, "The Lord will pass through to strike Egypt," and each time he sees a bloody doorway, "the Lord will pass over the door, and will not let the Destroyer come into your houses to strike you" (12:23).

The monster who kills all the firstborn throughout the entire land of Egypt brushes by us in a single verse. We can only imagine how it goes: God and the Destroyer head out on their joint mission, weaving among the houses, God pointing here and there, having his divine hitman slaughter these but not those.[3] In the end, there's not an Egyptian home left without someone dead (12:30).

The Destroyer isn't called an angel in Exodus, and may not have been conceived of as one when it was written. Psalm 78 differently records the plagues. Among other things (bonus caterpillars!), the tenth plague isn't delivered by a single killer. God dispatches a "deployment of evil angels" (Psalm 78:49). This doesn't mean "evil" as a cosmic force opposing God, like in later apocalyptic writing. It means wicked, harmful, destructive—hence common translations like a "band of destroying angels" (NASB, NIV) or "company of destroying angels" (NRSV).

"Destroying angels" is appropriate, but words like "band" or "company" mask one key fact: the Hebrew word refers specifically to a group that is *sent*. This isn't some roving gang, it's a deployment, and someone is the Sender. The "evil angels" are part of the divine army, and God is their commander.

The Destroying Angel

You may remember we've already seen "the Destroying Angel" in action. In the previous chapter, we watched God punish King David through an angel, focusing at that point on the roles of God and the Adversary in scenes presented in two biblical books. We'll now zoom in on the angel itself, sticking with the Chronicles version, where the angel graphics are in sharper focus.

God's punishment of David is three days of pestilence to be delivered by an angel "destroying throughout all the territory of Israel," bearing the lethal "sword of the Lord" (1 Chronicles 21:12). Soon the sword-wielding, pestilence-shooting angel takes out seventy thousand innocent people. At first, this terrible divine soldier is introduced only as "an angel of the Lord," while the narrator flashes variants of the key word like an alarm: destroy, destroying, destruction! When the angel is just about to unleash the pestilence on Jerusalem, and God suddenly regrets the evil he's done and orders the angel to hold its fire, the figure is finally named: meet "the Destroying Angel."

Midattack, God hits pause. David looks up, and there's the Destroying Angel waiting for its next command, "standing between heaven and earth," sword stretched out over all of Jerusalem. (Mythology often has divine beings carry a signature weapon—Thor has his hammer, Apollo his bow. Swords are the weapon of choice for angels of the Bible.) Imagine the terror! The enormous threatening figure hovers high above, armed with a supernatural sword extended over your city. It's like the moment in an alien-attack movie when the UFO floats overhead with hazardous-looking beams of light radiating down, and the people all look up in horror.

The Destroying Angel bridges two categories with which it shares monstrous DNA. On one side, it's related to the Destroyer figure we saw in the tenth plague. On the other side, it's unquestionably identified as an angel. This new character, the Destroying Angel, remains a singular figure. The Destroyer in Egypt is left in mysterious silhouette, and we shouldn't color in its outlines with the later picture of the Destroying Angel. And no other angel is drawn like this one:

This angel is giant, like nothing we've seen before, high above the earth but visible to all, with its proportionally enormous sword covering the whole city—and it's caught in the in-between, a freeze frame of the moment of crossing realms. The Destroying Angel's sword, like its very body, is next-level terrifying. The supernatural weapon is as huge as its user requires, and it's wielded for a divine

act of biological warfare. We don't know the operating specifics—
how the angel uses its lethal superpowers and divine weapon to shoot
deadly plague through the entire land—but, like the terrified survivors looking up at the angel, we know that a supernatural weapon in
the hand of a divine being is very bad news.

It would be easy to focus on the violence here, the ruthless
divine soldier exterminating innocent civilians. But that's not what
the story highlights. In the end, the story doesn't offer exactly
what the Destroying Angel does. And the writer also doesn't tell us
about the dead bodies—seventy thousand of them—or about what it
was like to die of pestilence. There's no mention of families all across
the land in grief. The writer instead tells us about fear.

The story moves directly from the unadorned remark that
seventy thousand people died (21:14) to an expansive description
of the reactions of David and others who see the Destroying Angel
hovering over Jerusalem, from their fear in the moment to the
emotional aftermath (21:15–30). But time has elapsed: in the silence
between verses 14 and 15, these survivors have lived through days
of heaven-sent disease and death all around them. Like that classic
UFO movie trope, we see one person, one group, then another, each
in the moment that they look up and register what's coming.

The first group of survivors the lens focuses on is David and
some important men of Jerusalem. They're all dressed for mourning,
because so much of the population has just been killed. When they
see the Destroying Angel wielding its sword in the sky above them,
they fall on their faces in fear. We then get a close-up of David,
begging God to spare the people of Jerusalem the ghastly fate that
has befallen so many others.

But it's not God, it's the Destroying Angel who speaks,
commanding a prophet to tell David what he'll need to do to stop the

divine plague. David must build an altar to God on the property of one Ornan the Jebusite, currently the angel's ground zero.

The next group of survivors we see are Ornan and his four sons. Ornan is minding his own business when he turns and sees the Destroying Angel. So do his four sons, who are terrified. They hide in fear, like Adam and Eve in the garden. Then Ornan sees David. Ordinarily, the presence of the king on his property would have seemed momentous, but having just noticed a giant sword-wielding angel overhead, Ornan takes David's approach in stride. He bows to the king and quickly agrees to sell him the land. But Ornan doesn't say yes just because it's the king who's asking. David explains that he needs to do this "so that the plague will be withdrawn from upon the people" (21:22). Standing in the line of fire, your children cowering nearby, who wouldn't agree?

David builds the required altar on this plot of land. Later on, according to the Chronicler, this will also be the very spot where David's son Solomon builds the temple (2 Chronicles 3:1). The holy of holies, the place where God dwells, where cherubim guard the gateway between the divine and human realms, warding off human contamination and hemming in the dangerous divine—this is God's spot.

And what made this spot sacred? The first moments of divine-human contact in this space aren't in some future time when the temple is built, the ark is brought inside, and "the glory of the Lord" fills the temple (2 Chronicles 5:14). They're when the Destroying Angel extends its sword over Jerusalem and threatens to exterminate everyone. The first sacrifices in this now-sacred space aren't those of Solomon in his joyful dedication of the temple (7:1–7). They're those of David in his desperate plea to stem the tide of pestilence and death. *This* is God's spot.

Once David has made these sacrifices, God orders the ceasefire, and the Destroying Angel sheathes its sword at last. But the story doesn't end there. The writer finishes the story with a glimpse of the psychological fallout for David. The king is now too afraid to go to the tabernacle to make the usual sacrifices or inquire of God as he'd done before. He's always known the tabernacle as God's dwelling place, and now he can't go back there—because he's "terrified of the sword of the angel of the Lord" (1 Chronicles 21:30).

This story that begins with one monster ends with another. Satan triggers the initial catastrophe, but it's the Destroying Angel who slaughters the masses and leaves the king paralyzed with fear. Odd that after all this the Adversary should be pegged as evil, but not the Destroyer. If this monster wanted to go solo too, the sky's the limit.

In the story of the tenth plague, God's divine Weapon of Mass Destruction is drawn differently than in the story of the sword-wielding angel. But both times, God deploys the Destroyer to kill unthinkable numbers of people—the firstborn of every Egyptian family, and seventy thousand people in Israel. Both times, the victims are innocent. Both times, God sends the Destroyer to kill them merely as collateral damage to make a point to a third party: to prove his power to Pharaoh and the surviving Egyptians, and to punish David. Both times, the Destroyer demonstrates God's terrifying appetite for destruction.

When Angels Attack

If only the "Destroying Angel" were an outlier! It would be nice if angels without this clear warning label could be counted on to be safe and benevolent, occasionally popping down to look in on us like Clarence in It's a Wonderful Life (1946). No such luck. It turns out the bloodthirsty angels of *Supernatural* aren't a creepy twist on the ancient tradition. Clarence was the twist.

Bring in the Big Guns

Seventy thousand had seemed like a lot. Seventy thousand pestilence-ridden corpses strewn throughout the land—how could it get worse?

[*Narrator: It gets worse.*]

Remember King Hezekiah, the one who asks God "who dwells among the cherubim" to prove his divine might against Assyria? God, as we have learned, is not one to pass up an opportunity like this. He answers Hezekiah's prayer with a show of strength achievable only by a divine warrior. An angel of the Lord goes out into the Assyrian camp and slaughters 185,000 people. While they sleep.

This time there's no mention of a weapon, no hint about the angel's appearance, no indication of whether the victims die of pestilence, sword wounds, or some newly imagined horror. Maybe it's like Thor joining the battle in Wakanda, dropping multitudes with one blow to the ground of his lightning-spewing axe (*Avengers: Infinity War*, 2018). However it happens that night, in the morning there are 185,000 Assyrian corpses. This angelic massacre is a one-liner, stunning carnage passed by in a single sentence (2 Kings 19:35).

If God had sent his angel to kill on such a massive scale solely in order to save Jerusalem, we could at least debate the ethics of warfare. But God plainly states his motives. He will save Jerusalem *partly* "for the sake of my servant David" (referring at best to the entire Davidic dynasty, or at worst to the one guy he cut a mutually beneficial deal with early on). But like the smug perps forever incriminating themselves in a *Law & Order* interrogation room, God's not done talking. He will also save Jerusalem, he declares, "for my own sake" (19:34).

Hezekiah asked God to show his might, and God is happy to oblige. As with the ten plagues, God's violence is partly to help the people, but partly to prove his strength. Having seen God, by his own admission, harden Pharaoh's heart *so that* he could prove his power through a series of catastrophic attacks on the Egyptians (Exodus 7:3–5), it turns out this impulse to flex divine muscle can't be put down to special circumstances. It's a behavioral pattern.

"He started it," God could say. The Assyrian king Sennacherib had mocked the gods of nations his armies had defeated, and he taunted Hezekiah about God being equally unable to protect his people (2 Kings 18:29–35; 19:9–13). Facing a direct challenge to his potency, what could God do? Is 185,000 overkill?

The Iceman Cometh

Not every angelic hitman comes to commit mass slaughter. Sometimes the work is more intimate. Some angels come with a single target in their crosshairs.

We've already met the angel who blocks Balaam's way and tries to cut him down in the streets (Numbers 22:22–35). This divine hitman is described in detail, unlike the shrouded killer of Assyrians, but is utterly different from the giant angel standing over Jerusalem. The angel in the road is armed with a sword, but it isn't a supernatural weapon. This angel gears up to slaughter Balaam the old-fashioned way.

The angel's appearance is deceptively modest. Well, when it appears, at least. It does have the monstrous trait of being invisible to some. But unlike the giant angel in the sky, this angel is able to stand on the ground in a spot so narrow that Balaam's donkey can't get past (22:26).

Sometimes the most human horror stories are the most disturbing. The angel is there to take Balaam out. We might read these few verses in a matter of seconds, but within the world of the story, there's an extended pursuit. After each time its attack is averted, the angel shows up again in Balaam's next location—not a few steps later, as in some brief fight scene with a few missed punches, but a field or a vineyard later. This angel hunts Balaam.

In the end, even as the angel apparently gives up, ordering Balaam to do exactly what he was already doing anyway, he throws Balaam a barfight line: *I could've killed you.* Someone's been learning from the Master.

Eaten Alive

We skip forward many centuries now, landing in the New Testament book of Acts. For anyone holding out hope that the amplified violence of the next-gen cherubim in the New Testament was a fluke, I hate to break it to you: that was just the beginning. Angels, too, those most beloved of heavenly figures, are every bit as brutal in the New Testament as in the Hebrew Bible. That is, until they get much, much worse—but you still have a moment to acclimate before we get there.

We come, then, to a story about the death of King Herod Agrippa. He's just called Herod in Acts, but this isn't the same Herod who orders the killing of children in the Gospel of Matthew. Herod Agrippa's done bad things, but not *that* bad. I mean, if someone went around ordering the slaying of a nation's children, of course *they'd* deserve . . . oh, whoops. (Awkward.)

One day, Herod Agrippa comes out to give a public speech. He dons his royal robes, sits on his grand seat, and appears before the people. They greet him as a god. He fails to correct them. An angel of the Lord immediately strikes him down, and he is eaten by worms and dies (Acts 12:21–23).

Eaten by worms. Then dies. Not the other way around.

According to the ancient Roman historian Josephus, Herod Agrippa died after five days of abdominal pain.[4] The Acts story isn't sloppily worded, accidentally implying that the worms precede the death. The writer apparently knows that Herod Agrippa suffered internal pain for days before dying, and provides this gruesome explanation. An angel struck Herod, and he was eaten alive.

The graphic details are new, but the m.o. isn't. When the Destroying Angel killed seventy thousand people in Israel, its method was three days of pestilence. If it worked for seventy thousand, why not for one?

The End of the Age

In the Hebrew Bible, most angelic slaughter happens in straightforward narrative stories, but in the New Testament, the tradition of angelic violence takes on new breadth. It's still found in stories (eaten by worms; then dies), but it also shows up in the teachings of Jesus, in a letter to a church, and in apocalyptic visions. It's sprinkled through every section of the New Testament: the Gospels, Acts, the Epistles, and Revelation.

We move forward in time again . . . far, far forward. It's the end of the world as we know it. This is the setting for the majority of angelic activity in the New Testament—and it turns out the majority is quite unpleasant. The most elaborate picture of the end times is found in Revelation, where the overwhelming picture of angels is of them wounding, burning, poisoning, drowning, and otherwise massacring human beings. And it's not just Revelation. Even before we come to the wild, terrifying visions of John of Patmos, Jesus paints a picture of the end of the age, and it's not pretty.

We might hope that all that previous angelic slaughter had been a means to an end, and that that End would bring peace. But that's not the biblical angel story. Even in the Bible, past behavior is the best predictor of future behavior. After seeing all those angels hunt, terrify, and kill people on earth, we now look to the future—to the End—where looms an escalation and final explosion of angelic slaughter.

May Angels Drag You to Hell

The image is famous: Jesus is teaching by the sea, and so many people gather to listen that he goes to sit in a boat and teach the crowds on the shore from there. It's a favorite scene for Christian bookstore art. It seems so gentle and peaceful—from a distance.

He tells the people parables from his seaside perch. The kingdom of heaven, he says, is like this: someone planted good seeds in his field, but an enemy snuck in and planted weeds. For now, the weeds are growing amid the wheat, but when harvest time comes, the owner of the field will tell the reapers to bundle up the weeds to be burned (Matthew 13:24–30). Then Jesus explains his parable to his followers: the one who planted good seeds is the Son of Man, the field is the whole world, the enemy is the devil, the weeds are his children, the harvest is the end of the age, and the reapers are angels. And at the end of the age, says Jesus, the Son of Man will send his angels out into the world, and the angels will collect the sinners "and they will throw them into the furnace of fire, where there will be weeping and gnashing of teeth" (13:41–42).

Think about that. The parable is about a field, Jesus says, but the *real* reapers are angels. He speaks of burning weeds, but says the *real* fire is the furnace of eternal torment. Some hopeful readers would like to take the whole kit and caboodle as metaphorical, but Jesus's point is that the reapers burning weeds is the metaphor, and what's real is angels burning people.

Jesus hits this last point hard, going on to talk more about the reality of angels tossing people into the furnace, even without any matching metaphor of burning on earth.

He tells another parable, different in every other way, involving a net and the sea and fish of every kind; good fish are gathered in baskets and bad fish are thrown away. But again, he explains: "So it will be at the end of the age. The angels will come and separate the wicked from the righteous and throw them into the furnace of fire, where there will be weeping and gnashing of teeth" (13:49–50). Different parable, same explanation. The angels will throw people into the fire for eternal torment. Reality.

Jesus's first explanation includes another detail: the angels don't come on their own. The Son of Man sends them (13:41–42). Later, sitting on the Mount of Olives, Jesus describes the great chucking of people into eternal punishment as something that will happen "when the Son of Man comes in his glory and all the angels with him" (25:31–46). He doesn't concern himself with detailing the division of labor, but sticks with the big picture of his parable explanation. He and his angels will doom people to eternal agony in fire.[5]

Another New Testament writer draws this in more detail, with the angels as Jesus's soldiers as he leads the charge. The writer of this letter to the Thessalonian church thanks God for the Thessalonians' faith and steadfastness amid affliction, and offers them words of (apparent) encouragement: those afflicting them will get what's coming to them. God will repay such people "when the Lord Jesus is revealed from heaven with his mighty angels in flaming fire, doling out vengeance on those who do not know God and on those who do not obey the gospel of our Lord Jesus. They will be paid back with eternal destruction" (2 Thessalonians 1:7–9). A little schadenfreude never hurt anyone, right? As for the slippage from the afflicters to everyone who doesn't know God—well, details, details.

Jesus heads up the final vengeance (the verb "doling out" is singular), but he doesn't come alone. For this job, he's accompanied by his "mighty angels," or literally, "the angels of his force," connoting both divine power and military strength, because this is precisely what angels are: God's mighty warriors.

One year, in a course I teach on modes of divine-human communication in the Bible, we read this text for "Angel Week." Our discussion period began with unusual silence. Finally a student said, "I sure don't remember going over this one in Bible study."[6]

All Shall Be Revealed

If this is at all uncomfortable, the book of Revelation won't help. Over the years, I've had a number of students tell me (more or less) that their churches discreetly set aside Revelation like Joseph did Mary. And fair enough, it's both terrifying and weird. But Revelation is also where so many treasured images come from: the angels surrounding God's heavenly throne, the Son of Man with a golden crown, the bright-as-crystal river of life!

Here's the catch. Those images are all part of the apocalyptic imagery of the book, and they're inextricable from the brutal and bloody violence. This kind of apocalyptic literature is concerned with supernatural conflicts in which God and the armies of heaven are glorified in their victory over, essentially, the dark side. Trying to hold on to the worshipping angels of Revelation without the context of their epic battles is like thinking you know Leia, Luke, and Han from the Yavin medal award ceremony in the throne room alone. The joy, the glory, the trumpets in the throne room—in heaven, as on Yavin 4—are about triumph in cosmic battle. The shining glory of Revelation is part of a story of violence, and you can't have one without the other. There's no *Star Wars* without the *Wars*.

Another way of handling the difficulty of Revelation is to excuse its astounding violence as entirely figurative. The book is filled with cloaked allusions to historical characters and events, coded references, and strange symbolic images. But some things are literal: God

means God. Angels means angels. At the heart of apocalyptic literature is the conviction that conflict on earth is only one part of the
story, because there are supernatural forces at work battling behind
the scenes, and the forces of God will win out in the end. Their bloody
victory is not symbolic. It's the very heart of the story.

Revelation is like Exodus on acid. Okay, that's an oversimplifica-
tion. Revelation is like Exodus and Joshua and Joel and Ezekiel and
a few other books all on acid together. With horrors that are reminiscent of the plagues but explode into global proportions, the book
draws from across the Hebrew Bible, each image now gone psychedelic. And God's signature is inscribed across it all. The tangled images
of Revelation, with its strange numbered series and jarring interrup-
tions, are defined by his brutality, with angelic violence punctuating
every turn.

In a series of visions, seven seals are opened, each triggering cataclysmic events. The four horsemen are released (ushered through
the cosmic gateway by the next-gen cherubim), the moon becomes
like blood, the skies roll up like a scroll. The first six seals cause devas-
tation and terror, but they're only the prelude to the main event, the
crescendo before the cymbals begin to clash.

I remember going out to see the fireworks on the Fourth of
July as a kid, watching the grand celebration of explosives set to
Tchaikovsky's *1812 Overture*. The *Overture* builds to a finale of brass
fanfare, clanging bells, and cannon fire, meant to evoke military
triumph. The opening of the seven seals is like this. The first six are
already memorable, but the finale's where the real action is.[7] And for
the explosive fanfare of the seventh seal, we need more monstrous
military might. We need angels.

The seventh seal is opened. It doesn't trigger a single event, but
instead blossoms into its own series of seven global catastrophes.
Seven angels standing before God are handed trumpets. Each one

will blow its trumpet, causing its own special brand of disaster and doom. It's the battle of Jericho (where seven priests blew horns and the city walls came crashing down) gone global and psychedelic.

Before the angels blow their seven trumpets of doom, one angel throws fire down onto the earth, creating lightning and a terrible earthquake, as a final divine drumroll building up to these catastrophic halluciplagues (Revelation 8:1–5). If *The Amityville Horror* paled in comparison to the first plague in Egypt, those ten plagues pale in comparison to the angels' hyperplagues. No horror movie holds a candle to Revelation.

The first angel blows its horn. Hail and fire mixed with blood— you read that right—are hurled down onto the earth, burning up a third of the earth and its trees, and all the grass (8:7).

The second angel blows its horn. A fiery mountain is thrown into the sea. A third of the sea turns to blood, killing a third of the sea creatures and destroying a third of the ships in the sea (8:8–9). So far, humankind seems only to be collateral damage. This is about to change.

The third angel blows its horn. A star burning like a torch falls from heaven into a third of the earth's fresh waters, which become toxic and kill people (8:10–11). This would be horrible even if the "star" were just a star—it doesn't matter to the people poisoned— but "stars" sometimes represent angels. We're looking here at God's first use of a fallen angel, a rebel, to kill people.[8] It won't be his last. He tosses the toxic angel, named Wormwood (which is like calling it "Cyanide"), into the water to contaminate it, and everyone who drinks is poisoned. He uses Angel Classic to cue this disaster, and the renegade Cyanide to execute it. God's an equal opportunity employer.

The fourth angel blows its horn. A third of the sun, moon, and stars are struck and darkened, so that a third each of the day and night have no light whatsoever (8:12). Although these global plagues don't track the originals one for one, we should be on high alert now, since the plague of suffocating darkness in Egypt directly preceded the apex of horror.

Angel Five doesn't disappoint. This psychoplague is the most awesomely horrible of them all (9:1–11). When the fifth angel blows its horn, a star that had fallen from heaven is given the key to the abyss. If there was any ambiguity in identifying the first fallen star as an angel, that's gone here: this "star" knows how to use a key. Instead of opposing the rebel, God hands it the key to a locked ward. The renegade angel opens the shaft that goes down to the abyss, smoke pours out as if from a giant furnace—and out of the smoke come locust-monsters. Their locust bodies have scales like iron breast-plates, and they have scorpions' tails, human faces, women's hair, and lions' teeth. They emerge decked out like war horses, and the noise of their wings is like horses and chariots rushing into battle. (This is the prophet Joel's locust vision gone psychedelic; Joel 1–2.)

Your ordinary locust destroys vegetation, like in the Exodus plague. These jacked-up hell-locusts are instructed *not* to harm vegetation—and instead to go after people. They're not to *kill* the people, mind; that would be insufficient cruelty. They're to torture them, using their furnace-powered scorpion stingers to cause people such anguish they'll wish for death. These are the hell-creatures that scurry out of the abyss, and God, the zookeeper, handed over the key. This is the flip side of God's angels breaking the disciples out of jail in Acts. Here, the rebel angel busts the monsters out of their prison to torture people. This, equally, is on God's command.

The sixth angel blows its horn and releases a quartet of killer angels who'd been bound up, "kept ready" for this moment, in order to kill a third of humankind (Revelation 9:13–15). I picture the flesh-craving monsters harnessed by Negan on *The Walking Dead*, pulling at their chains with their single deadly instinct, yearning to attack. There's a tradition of renegade angels being "bound" in chains, so these must be rebel angels too (Jude 6; 2 Peter 2:4; 1 Enoch 54:3–5).[9] There are only two possibilities: either they're rebel angels and God's been keeping them in his arsenal, now employing them to do his murderous bidding, or (best case scenario?) they're among his general crop of angels . . . and yet, God's been keeping them tied up, now employing them to do his murderous bidding.

Figure 9. Four angels hack away at people. The angel on the upper left holds a woman by the hair as she appears to beg for mercy. Next to her are two heads that have been relieved of their bodies. (Portion of The Four Avenging Angels, from "The Apocalypse," Albrecht Dürer woodcut, ca. 1498.)

The final trumpet sounds. The seventh angel blows its horn, cuing heavenly praise and thanksgiving. Wait, praise? Shouldn't we be at peak cannon fire now? Alas, we are indeed—*this* is the praise of the heavenly elders: "You have taken hold of your great power. . . . Your wrath has come, and the time for judging the dead, for rewarding your servants . . . and for destroying those who destroy the earth!" (Revelation 11:15–18).

In other words: "Yippee ki-yay, it's judgment time!" No sooner has the heavenly chorus finished its Ode to Wrath than God's heavenly temple is opened. The ark comes into view, and there's lightning, thunder, an earthquake—and rumblings. John is vague about the rumblings, but let's think about what kind of noise we might expect to hear as the cosmic gateway is opened and the heavenly ark appears. When Ezekiel envisioned God abandoning the temple, being carried across the threshold and up, up, and away, he saw the living chariot in motion. He saw the cherubim, and heard the noise of their wings, like the noise of rushing waters (Ezekiel 1:24). The noise John hears, the rumblings—this is the same Greek word as in the Septuagint of Ezekiel 1:24. The heavenly gates are thrown open, the ark appears, and the noise of the cherubim's wings is heard once more.

Those aren't peaceful signs, as we know. Sure enough, we soon see one of the four living creatures, John's next-gen cherubim, handing the plague-bowls of wrath over to the angels, who pour them out one by one on the doomed earth. Remember how the wrath-powered plagues weaponize everything they strike? With these plague-bowls, one angel targets the sea, another the sun, another the air—the sea turns to blood that kills everything in it, the sun burns people to death, and the deadly atmosphere triggers the most destructive earthquake that has ever been. Every city on earth is destroyed, islands and mountains are demolished, and hundred-pound hailstones crush people to death (Revelation 15:7–16:21).

Mixed in among these last visions is a gruesome picture of what that final judgment looks like. It looks like a harvest—of people. Jesus's parable by the seaside described the end of the age as a harvest where the angels would reap people, and we see it now: An angel emerges with a sickle in its hand. Another angel calls out, "Swing your sharp sickle"—its sharpness is mentioned three times in a row—"and gather the grapes from the vineyard of the earth" because they're "ripe." Ripe, indeed. The first angel swings its sickle over the whole earth and gathers the harvest. Remember the fruit of the harvest? In case you temporarily blocked it out, that's us, human beings. The angel throws the full harvest of people into "the great winepress of the wrath of God." The winepress is then "trampled," and blood flows out from it for hundreds of miles all around "as high as a horse's bridle" (14:14–20).[10] The angels' bloody winepress full of people is nothing short of a celebration of ravaged human remains. This is the Bible's splatter film.

These are the angels of God: angels who throw fire and blood down onto the earth, who poison the fresh water supply and open the abyss to unleash locust-monsters that torture people till they long for death; killer angels tugging at their chains, itching to fulfill their savage calling; angels trampling the winepress full of people until human blood flows like a river; angels hurling their plague-bowls of divine wrath down onto the earth.

Could we hope, at least, that these astoundingly violent angels are a different breed from the rest, and that we can still rely on the benevolence of your average angel? That these vicious creatures can be set apart from angels bearing messages of hope?

The book of Revelation does close with angelic messages of hope. John is shown visions of the "new Jerusalem," in which a "river of life" flows from God's throne through the city streets. But that comes with some bad news. The angel who shows John these beautiful things is one of the seven angels he just saw hurling plagues onto the earth. The angel bringing these good tidings of comfort and joy, restoration and hope, also helps destroy the earth in the first place (21:9–22:2).

The angel of this new hope can't be separated from the story of its brutality. The vision the angel shows can't be extracted from its context: the "river of life" stands alongside another deep flowing river described moments earlier, one flowing with blood. River of life, river of death; the two flow from the same source. The angel who comforts is the angel who kills. In the final chapter of Revelation— the final chapter of the New Testament—we're back to the God of the seraphim-snakes and the bronze seraph, the God who strikes and heals. If this is a new hope, it's the hope of those surviving a new dimension of assault.

Gloria in excelsis Deo! Glory to God in the highest! So praise the angels before the shepherds, in a refrain celebrated in works from Vivaldi's *Gloria* to "Angels We Have Heard on High." What joy! Except, of course, that the shepherds are scared out of their wits.

When a single angel appeared to them moments earlier, the shepherds were "terrified" (Luke 2:9). Understandably so. The angel's attempt at reassurance (yet another "do not fear") probably fell flat when it was "suddenly" joined by "a multitude of the heavenly host," or "the army of heaven" (2:13–14). That's who voices those joyous strains: the divine figures sweetly singing o'er the plains are God's army. Picture the cherubim roaring, the seraphim swishing serpentine tails. Now that's a Christmas pageant.

The angels of the Bible—terrifying, violent, and so widely known for killing that they sometimes start by reassuring people when they're *not* there to kill them—are fully a part of the divine company of monsters.

And yet: gloria! Angels announce, angels call from heaven, angels save! How do we make sense of their profound moral ambiguity? They have the capacity for such good and for such harm.

Among the many monstrous creatures in the biblical heavens, angels are the most like us. They are the most human of monsters, not just in their sometimes-anthropomorphic appearances, but in their characters. They're the best of it all and the worst, the most benevolent and the most brutal. At a certain point they even start getting human names. Gabriel and Michael both show up in the latest texts of the Hebrew Bible and in the New Testament, and they're joined by many more named angels in other ancient Jewish and Christian writing.[11] How appropriate that angels become like winged human beings in later interpretation.

This could begin to explain our Stockholm syndrome. On some level, we identify with angels; we register that they're like us. And maybe we seek to domesticate them in art and song and seasonal decor in order to avoid the mirror image of our own monstrosity.

The self-protective aspect of human loyalty to angels goes beyond this, though. We've developed the notion that angels are supposed to be on protection detail. If it's the Bible we're looking to, rather than *It's a Wonderful Life*, a few scattered verses suggest this. In Psalm 91, the poet writes that God will command his angels to guard people in all their ways, offering the chief example of toe-stubbing ("lest you strike your foot against a rock")—though graver dangers in the psalm are handled by God (91:11–12). In Exodus, God sends an angel to guard the people in the desert—shortly before sending seraphim-snakes to kill many of those same people (Exodus 23:20). There might be enough here to hope for protection, but not to count on it.

The loss of that (false) sense of assurance might be hard to take. Maybe getting through the heist is easier if we believe that, when it comes to it, the guys with the guns will look out for us. We've engaged in a profound collective forgetting of angelic crimes against humanity—and it spares us having to confront our inner angels (demons are no worse, as we'll soon see), as well as having to face the absence of special heavenly protection.

But it's not just about us. As usual, we sanitize the Bible to protect God's image, most of all. In this case, we're looking at the members of God's entourage especially tasked with crossing back and forth between heaven and earth, the divine beings he designates as his go-to representatives to humankind. We have more at stake with this supernatural species than any other. If we face up to their moral ambiguity, it becomes all the harder to deny his.

There's understandable temptation to spin their moral ambiguity into a framework of good angels working for God versus bad angels working for the dark side—but that isn't the picture the Bible shows. God's got malevolent angels in his employ, using one as a giant cyanide pill for the rivers, giving one a key to the abyss so it can liberate the locust-monsters to torture people, and keeping another four bound till it's time for them to kill masses of the human population. These renegade angels aren't worse than, say, an angel hurling a plague-bowl into the sun in order to burn people alive.

Some angels do fight for the dark side. In a brief snippet in Revelation, war breaks out between God's angels (with Michael leading the charge) and Satan and his angels. That's right: Satan's got his own angels (12:7–9). But Satan's angels only merit passing reference, and they don't harm human beings. God's angels, on the other hand, are responsible for some of the worst violence perpetrated against human beings in the Bible.

Clear good guys and bad guys are appealing, but that isn't what we get with biblical angels. Angels aren't good or bad. What they are is obedient. Angels are fierce, powerful divine soldiers, and they fight for whoever leads them. If they're in the army of Satan, they fight for Satan; if in the army of God, they fight for God. They'll deliver a message or a fatal blow. Their interest is in dutiful service, no matter what it entails.

One biblical story even has an angel spelling this out. Joshua, the leader of the Israelites after Moses, encounters an angel facing him down with a drawn sword in its hand. Joshua, presumably nervous, asks, "Are you for us or for our enemies?" The angel says, "Neither! I am the commander of the army of the Lord" (Joshua 5:13–15). You can almost hear the angel enunciating to make sure Joshua gets it: *I don't care about you, little man. I just follow orders.*

And follow orders they do. This doesn't only mean that violent angels are obeying God's orders. It also means that when an angel appears benign, it's because *its current orders* don't involve doing bodily harm. It means that God has commanded the angel, in that particular context, to do something associated with one of the other bullet points in an angel's job description. There's no reason to assume that some angels are harmless while others go around killing people. Like at the end of Revelation, where the angel showing John visions of hope also hurls plague upon the earth, the angel saving in one story could be the same angel slaughtering folks in another. The writers generally didn't specify, because it didn't matter to them. They weren't concerned with making sure we'd still have some nice benign angels to feel comfy with while we mentally bracket the rest. They understood angels simply to be powerful and obedient, and didn't draw a distinction between angels who announce (while people shake with fear) and angels who kill. There's no Angel of Death in the Bible—because every angel who shows up might have come as an angel of death.

Friday night comes around. I sing the words to Shalom Aleichem with tenderness and trepidation. I begin, once more:

> Peace be upon you, ministering angels . . .
> May your coming be in peace, angels of peace . . .

The first part already sounded like a worried plea—do you come in peace? *Oh God, I hope you come in peace.* As I sing the final words, they seem to have an enduring urgency:

> Bless me in peace, angels of peace . . .
> May your leaving be in peace, angels of peace . . .

Go, angels. Leave in peace. Please.

5

Demons in God's Ranks

Paula White, spiritual advisor to Donald Trump, delivered the opening prayer at Trump's 2020 reelection campaign kickoff rally in Orlando. "Let every demonic network that has aligned itself against" President Trump be broken, she prayed, proclaiming that he would "overcome every strategy from hell and every strategy from the Enemy." She prayed for his protection from this demonic network from hell: "Let the angel of the Lord encamp around about him."[1] In a sermon soon afterward, White declared that she was making the White House holy ground by releasing angels and renouncing demons and "every covenant made with Satan," so that every "demonic altar" would burn and crumble.[2] White's declarations, while dramatic, reflect a common notion of warring angels and demons, with demons sent by Satan to attack people and angels sent by God to protect them.

This idea is pervasive from preachers to pop culture and politics. But there's one place it doesn't show up: the Bible.

Demons evolve, like everybody else. As with pitchfork-bearing Satan and his horns and tail, ideas about demons that might feel familiar, or even certain, to many people actually come from points on the demon timeline falling long after the Bible was written.

Demons don't fight angels anywhere in the Bible. Angels fight *each other*, but never demons. Also, demons aren't yet thought of as fallen angels. In the Bible, demons are a distinct supernatural species. Even at the latest stages of biblical writing, they're linked with evil spirits, not with evil angels (and not for lack of evil angels). Demons aren't angels gone bad, and they're not pitted against angels. In fact, nowhere in the Bible do angels and demons have any particular relationship to one another.[3]

And that's not the awkward part. Satan has both angels and demons in his entourage, okay. So does God. Satan uses angels to fight other angels, ultimate warriors that they are, but uses demons against people. God's more flexible. He deploys every type of monster in his entourage against human beings—angels and demons alike.

There's significant demon development within the Bible itself, not just from the Bible to Paula White. By the time of the New Testament, demons are all minions of Satan and usually indistinguishable from one another. But before demons were associated with Satan and hell—because remember, for most of the biblical period, there was no capital-S Satan or hell—demons were a diverse assortment of figures with unpredictable allegiances.

Some demons in the Hebrew Bible are animations of harmful forces. They might be disease-related, like Pestilence or Plague, or weather-related, like Hail. This type of demon was common throughout ancient Southwest Asian writing. For example, Pazuzu, now best known for possessing Regan in *The Exorcist* (1973), was a Mesopotamian wind demon. Some named biblical demons are also known from other regional sources, and some are even gods elsewhere, downgraded in the Bible.

Most of the monsters we've met so far have exhibited classic physical monster traits—giant size, hybrid form, shifting shape—as well as supernatural powers. Only the Adversary lacks physical description, but we witness his repeated realm-crossing in order to use his lethal powers. Once we come to demons, we see even less. There are no bodies to find, physical features to point out. In the Hebrew Bible, demons are simply the manifestation of deadly power. We catch a glimpse of realm-crossing, and they stalk, destroy, even eat—but they're faceless and voiceless. Reduced, they simply are their acts. Their utter lack of humanity highlights how anthropomorphic even the seraphim and cherubim are by contrast. If angels are the most like us, demons are the least.

Unlike cherubim and seraphim, angels and the Adversary, all of whom have complex and varied roles, biblical demons have a single function—no matter who's sending them. They exist to cause harm. In the Hebrew Bible, this often takes the form of plague, pestilence, and disease. In the Gospels, an embarrassment of demons cause all manner of illness and disability. This goes back to Mesopotamia, where demons are low-level supernatural entities whose role is to act upon human beings.[4] From Mesopotamia through the Hebrew Bible and New Testament, other divine beings *can* act upon people, but it's the sole purpose of demons. One difference stands out, though: Mesopotamian demons can be malevolent or protective. Biblical demons are never, ever benevolent—and yet, God freely employs them.

Hidden Demons

Unlike the flashy demons of the New Testament, the demons of the Hebrew Bible are subtle. Most of those with the juiciest after-lives have modest biblical profiles at best. You might know Azazel as the yellow-eyed demon from *Supernatural* or Denzel Washington's demonic foe in *Fallen* (1998), but in the Bible, he has only the briefest cameo. It's in the "scapegoat" ritual, in which a goat is designated "for Azazel" and sent off into the wilderness symbolically carrying away the people's sin—and that's all she wrote (Leviticus 16:8–10). Lilith, for all her fame as an enticing predator in later Jewish and Christian writing, doesn't show up in the Bible at all.[5]

Other demons are hidden, masked in natural phenomena and obscured in translation. These are the demons you should be worried about. It might be easiest to recognize these camouflaged demons when they turn up in a theologically palatable context—that is, where God is protecting people from the demons, rather than sending them.

Psalm 91 is sometimes called a "psalm of assurance," but it's assuring in about the same way as a parent telling a kid, "There is definitely a monster under your bed, but I won't let it get you."

The psalm is full of skulking, creeping things. They've been neutered in translation: "the pestilence that stalks in darkness," and "the destruction that wastes at noonday" (91:3, 6 NRSV). But *pestilence* and *destruction* aren't just common nouns. These are figures we know.

The first is Dever, personified Pestilence. The Hebrew word *dever* often refers to literal pestilence, but in Psalm 91, "deadly Dever" lives, "stalking in darkness." In another text, we'll see him marching into battle in other demon company.

Dever's counterpart in the psalm is Qetev. Qetev appears four times in the Bible, always with another demon. The word never shows up as a common noun, so scholars who try to translate the name don't have as easy a job as they do with Pestilence. One opts for "Destruction," another "the Sting."[6] Others call him by his given name, Qetev, which I figure is the least we can do.

This is the assurance of Psalm 91: God will deliver you from Dever and Qetev, who stalk in the night and destroy in the day. There are

Figure 10. Aramaic incantation bowl showing two bound demons, an image of them being magically prevented from causing harm (5th–7th century). Bowls like this were often pressed into the ground upside-down to trap or ward off demons.

demons on the prowl, says the psalmist, and you need protection from them.

Psalm 91 was understood to describe protection from demons in ancient times, from the Dead Sea Scrolls and Aramaic magic bowls to the Talmud and the New Testament. Given the lines about Dever and Qetev, other verses of the psalm were seen as referring to God's protection from demons too.[7] In Luke, the seventy disciples tell Jesus that the demons submit to them, and in response, Jesus alludes to a line from Psalm 91 (Luke 10:17–19; Psalm 91:13).[8] In other words, Jesus gets that there are demons in that psalm.

Happily, Psalm 91 promises that God will be on the pro-human, anti-demon side of things. It won't always be that way.

We'll soon encounter Dever, Qetev, and their cohort in far less comfortable contexts. Most of these personified forces of

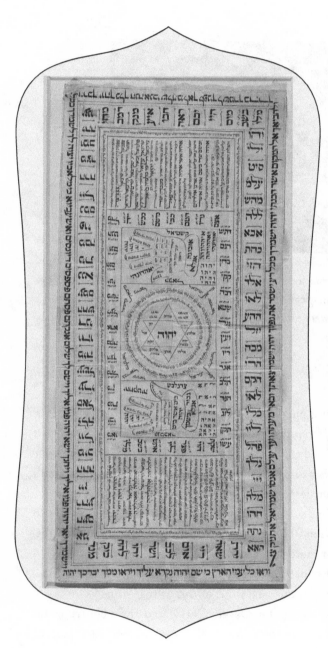

Figure 11. Kabbalistic personal amulet for protection from all kinds of demons and spirits, written for a woman named Farna bat Zafira (whose name is used in the text). The amulet includes all of Psalm 91—that's the tiniest writing in the thinnest inner rectangle—along with other key verses such as Exodus 23:20 and Zechariah 3:2, which arise elsewhere in this book (19th century, possibly Italy).

destruction aren't associated with the underworld, unlike later concepts of demons—but two are, and we'll meet them first. After all, other demons attack selectively. The forces of Death are pertinent to all.

At Death's Door

Death stands tall, black robes alive in the breeze. The knight he's come for challenges him to a game of chess, the man's very life the winner's prize (*The Seventh Seal*, 1957). For those who haven't mastered chess, Battleship and Twister are acceptable alternatives (*Bill and Ted's Bogus Journey*, 1991). Death is personified in the Bible, too, but he has no black robes, accepts no challenges. Then again, you can make a covenant with Death, and even God considers it binding (Isaiah 28:15–18). He's not the Grim Reaper—he's not nearly so human—but he's also not entirely unique.

His name in Hebrew is Mavet ("Death"), and he's very similar to his Canaanite counterpart, Mot ("Death" in Ugaritic). Mavet and Mot are so similar, in fact, that we'll start by taking a quick look at the Canaanite mythological poetry, where we can meet Death in a theologically safer space than the Bible.

Mot dwells in the underworld, and he's always looking for new company. If you're picturing him coming around with a scythe, let that go. Mot's method of bringing people down into the underworld is more personal. He stretches wide his gaping maw—"one lip to the earth, one lip to the heavens"—and swallows them. And he's insatiable. Don't take my word for it; he himself says, "My appetite longed for human beings, my appetite for earth's masses."[9] The best-known story of Mot's voracious appetite is from the Baal myth, where he even swallows up the god Baal. (Don't worry, Baal rises and conquers Death.) Mot can also represent the underworld itself. He opens that gullet and swallows people into Death, and so into the netherworld.

In the Bible, Mavet is pictured similarly with that characteristic enormous mouth and rapacious appetite, and he too casts a shadow as the underworld, called Sheol. Mavet's traits are such a given that they're even used as an obvious illustration of greed: the arrogant man "opens wide his gullet like Sheol; he is like Mavet and cannot be sated" (Habakkuk 2:5). Mavet shows up in a famous oracle in Isaiah too. Isaiah puts a twist on the Canaanite story of Mot swallowing the god Baal: God turns the tables and "will swallow up Mavet forever" (Isaiah 25:8). In the New Testament, this line about God swallowing Death is reinterpreted as referring to resurrection (1 Corinthians 15:54), but in Isaiah, the "swallowing" imagery is graphically physical: God makes a feast of rich food and fine wine for the people (Isaiah 25:6), and then does his own feasting too—on Mavet. Mavet the Swallower is vanquished.

Mavet doesn't seem so bad when he's being conquered. The prophet Hosea even scoffs at him after declaring that God will rescue people from the power of Death: "O Mavet, where are your plagues? O Sheol, where is your destruction?" (Hosea 13:14). Even if Mavet's weapons were just your everyday plagues and destruction, it would be a relief to envision him disarmed, but these, too, are names. Mavet's weapons are known violent offenders, Dever and Qetev, paired once more: "Mavet, where are your Devers? Sheol, where is your Qetev?" Hosea's taunt is, in other words, "Hey Mavet, where are your henchmen now?"

Between Isaiah and Hosea, we're at God 2, Mavet 0. Living Death should be fading fast. There's a slight hitch in the New Testament, when Paul follows up his use of Isaiah's line with a version of Hosea's, forever linking the two in the minds of readers who never knew Mavet was peering out from behind the original texts: "Death has been swallowed up in victory. Where, Death, is your victory? Where, Death, is your sting?" (1 Corinthians 15:54–55). Ironically, for many readers, it's in Paul's triumphant verses that Mavet lives on.

The demon of personified Death in the Bible is easier to stomach when he's cast as God's enemy. The problem comes when he shows up instead as God's agent.

He Came in through the Bathroom Window

As in any good horror movie, the moments leading up to the revelation of the monster grow tense and disturbing. This is the scene in an oracle in Jeremiah as Mavet stealthily approaches, just before we finally see him in action.

God is angry at the people and determined to end them: "I'll feed this people wormwood and give them poisoned water to drink!" (Jeremiah 9:15). (Ring a bell? The New Testament ratchets this up where God uses a rebel angel named Wormwood to poison people; Revelation 8:10–11.) In case poisoning the people's water doesn't do the trick, God says he'll also send the sword after them "until I've finished them off" (Jeremiah 9:16). So, says God, you'd better learn this dirge:

> Mavet has come up through our windows,
>> he has come into our palaces,
> To exterminate the children from the streets,
>> the young men from the town squares. (Jeremiah 9:21)

Mavet is on the prowl. He's coming for the regular folk and the royal, the little ones and those in the prime of life. The liveliest sounds outdoors are silenced. This picture of Mavet sneaking in through the windows and disappearing the children would be creepy enough if the agency were all his. But throughout the oracle, God is crystal clear in taking responsibility for each method of annihilation. *God* poisons the water, *God* sends the sword. And the next Thing he sends is Mavet.

We should have known after the poison that something worse was coming: God never trusts poison alone. It's like murder foreplay. Two other times in Jeremiah, God speaks that same terrible line: "I'll feed this people wormwood and give them poisoned water to drink," and both times he follows up by unleashing an instrument of his destruction—once, his whirling rage-storm, another time venomous snakes (8:14, 17; 23:15, 19). This time, when God spits out the brutal line, he deploys another agent. This time, God sends Mavet.

"People's corpses will fall like dung in the open field," God continues, "like sheaves behind the reaper, but no one will gather them" (9:22). There's no Grim Reaper in the Bible, but here we get our first kernel of a connection between a figurative reaper and personified Death, sent by God, slicing down the people.

Rejoice as you might that God swallows up Mavet in Isaiah. But don't get too comfortable. God's relationship with Mavet is . . . complicated. They're a bit on-again, off-again. In Jeremiah, with one of the most vivid personifications of Death in the Bible, Mavet isn't being defeated. He's being deployed.

In the New Testament, Paul will say God and Death are off-again ("Death has been swallowed up in victory"), but in the end— the *End*-end—there comes John of Patmos and they're on-again. It's the Bible's most recognized picture of Death, as the infamous fourth horseman. Remember, the horsemen are sent by God, with the next-gen cherubim beckoning them through the cosmic gateway. The last to come through is a pale horse: "Its rider's name was Death, and Hades followed him" (Revelation 6:8). Death, trailed by his shadow, the Underworld (like Mavet and Sheol), is given divine authority to kill a quarter of the earth's population. Paul might say it's over between God and Death, but John shows them thick as thieves till the End.

Abaddon Rises

In a few scattered verses of the Hebrew Bible, Abaddon is simply another name for the underworld, the Hebrew word indicating (a place of) Destruction or Ruin (Psalm 88:11; Proverbs 15:11; Job 31:12). In a couple of other texts, we see the first glimmers of Abaddon's growth into a living—and deadly—entity.

"Sheol and Abaddon are insatiable," begins one proverb, depicting the personified underworld in twin shadows sharing the familiar trait of Mavet (Proverbs 27:20). In Job, we catch a glimpse of Abaddon among a small group of mythological creatures. God slays the sea monster, and every Thing around cowers before God, from the shades of the dead to the underworld itself: "The shades writhe," the poet says, "Sheol is naked before him, and Abaddon has no covering" (Job 26:5–6, 12–13). All of these monsters are vulnerable before God—including Abaddon. In these first signs of personification, Abaddon and Sheol both seem poised to develop into independent beings. Only one of them makes it.[10]

Abaddon begins to stir. His most creaturely appearance in the Hebrew Bible comes soon after the snapshot of him among other monsters in Job. He's in more elite company now. The poet asks where wisdom can be found. The answer begins: "The Deep says, 'It is not in me,' and the Sea says, 'Nor with me.' . . . It is hidden from the eyes of all living, and concealed from the birds of the sky" (28:12–14, 21). Wisdom's not in the Sea, not on the earth, and not above. But what about below? Surprise: "Abaddon and Mavet say, 'With our ears, we have heard a report of it'" (28:22). All humankind is in the dark, but Abaddon and Mavet have an inkling. The next line completes the picture: "God understands the way to it and knows its location" (28:23). In contrast to every other living being, three figures know something about where wisdom can be found: God, Mavet, and Abaddon.

We see these tantalizing moments in the Hebrew Bible, but it's in the New Testament that Abaddon comes into his own. In Revelation, when the seventh seal is broken and the seven angels blow their trumpets of doom, the fifth trumpeter cues a scene you might find filed under Torture Porn next to *Saw* (2004). God gives a renegade angel the key to the abyss, where lion-toothed, scorpion-tailed, human-faced locusts have been locked away. The locust-monsters swarm out and are "given authority" on earth and instructed to torture people with their superpoison until the victims long for death. Finally, we find out that the mutant locusts have a king. He is first called by his title, the "angel of the abyss," and then by his name: Abaddon (Revelation 9:1–11).

Don't miss the shift: Abaddon has become an angel. He's not a fallen angel who became a demon, as in later theology. He began life as the personified underworld and grew into an angel. But he hasn't changed his stripes and become any less ruinous. The writer of Revelation makes a point of giving Abaddon a Greek name alongside the Hebrew: Apollyon, still connoting Destruction or Ruin. The writer newly identifies Abaddon as an angel, and in the same breath affirms his role as Ruin.

In this horror scene, God commands every creature. He sends the renegade angel down with a key to the abyss, and he deploys the locust-monsters—who are the subjects of Abaddon. There's nothing to indicate that Abaddon is playing for the other team. He's got a fresh "Angel" stamp and his monstrous underlings follow instructions from God. Abaddon, angel of the abyss, king of the locust-monsters, isn't God's prisoner in that evil domain. He's the warden.

Sole Objective

Death is a certainty, demonically speaking. These next characters might take you more by surprise. They show up in pairs and trios and in varying combinations, so we won't meet them demon by demon, but scene by scene. We'll encounter personified harmful forces and downgraded deities, figures of diverse origins now working together like some demonic Dream Team. But, though their lineups shift and their tactics vary, their mandate is always the same: first, do harm.

Platoon

The brief book of the prophet Habakkuk ends with a violent, cataclysmic poem that paints a picture of God in cosmic battle against the earth and sea. God sweeps in, his glory lighting up the sky. When he touches down, the earth shakes. His mere glance makes the nations lurch. He shatters the mountains, tramples the sea on horseback, and brandishes a bow and arrow (Habakkuk 3:3–15). The poem is full of imagery that rings of mythology shared with Israel's neighbors, describing a divine victory over the personified Sea. God battles the River and Sea, the Deep gives forth its voice and lifts up its hands, and God rides over the "rushing waters" (*mayim rabbim*) of the primeval sea (3:8, 10, 15).

Heading into cosmic battle, it's not surprising that God would show up with some of his entourage. You might expect, say, angels. But "before him went pestilence," says the NRSV, "and plague followed close behind" (3:5). An odd way to describe diseases: each verb has a modest range of meaning—pestilence "walked," plague "went out" or "headed out"—but their agency is palpable even before you know that these aren't just pandemics. They're names.

"Pestilence," as you might have guessed by now, is none other than our friend Dever. God will deliver you "from deadly Dever," wrote the hopeful poet of Psalm 91, so you need not fear "Dever who stalks in darkness" (91:3, 6). Not so lucky now, are we? God's not offering anyone protection from Dever now. He's the one bringing him into battle.

Dever isn't the one who changed. The NRSV treads lightly: before God "went" pestilence. But this is the same verb used for Dever in Psalm 91! Funny how there, the NRSV freely describes how dangerous Dever "stalks"—there, where God is *anti*-pestilence. For the uncomfortable situation we find ourselves in during Habakkuk's battle scene, suddenly everyone's more circumspect. But Dever is the same as he ever was—only this time, he's in God's army. God comes rolling in for battle with his demons-at-arms, and "Dever stalked in front of him."

"Plague," Dever's counterpart in this scene, is a figure we haven't met yet, but he's the bigger celebrity of the two. In fact, out of the whole cast of characters in this chapter, he has the fullest profile in other literature from the region. His name in Hebrew is Resheph, and outside of the Bible, he's a god.

When a foreign god shows up in the Bible, you expect him to be the bad guy, or the fool, like when God wipes the floor with Baal in a miracle contest (1 Kings 18:20–40). There's occasional acknowledgment of another god's power—like when the Moabite king sacrifices his son to petition his god for victory against the Israelites, and it works (2 Kings 3:26–27)—but *most* of the time, other gods play the foil to the God of Israel. But not always. Resheph, a god venerated in many places across ancient Southwest Asia and especially throughout the broader Canaanite region, enters this battle scene marching at God's feet.

Throughout this region, Resheph was worshipped as a protective deity and venerated as a warrior. He's associated with arrows, and is even called "Lord of the arrow" in one Ugaritic incantation.[11] Elsewhere, he's called "Resheph of the army," just as the biblical god is called "YHWH of armies" (using God's personal name in Hebrew).[12] Resheph's other specialty is bringing death through disease. Sometimes he's more of a stealth-assassin, with clandestine methods but unequivocal results: in the Ugaritic Epic of Keret, he "carried off" some children, and an omen text warns that he'll "finish off" or "devour" others.[13]

In the Bible Resheph is downgraded, turned into a harmful supernatural figure subservient to God, but his defining traits are still recognizable. In the battle poem of Habakkuk 3, he shows up as a warrior and is paired with Pestilence: here, he's probably Plague at war.[14] (And if he's using other covert methods, it's no better for the victims.) In another biblical text, we'll see God send Resheph to devour people. His name eventually comes to signify flame and lightning (likely stemming from the image of Resheph causing plague with his burning arrows), and we'll see a provocative use of that too.[15]

Unlike Dever, Mavet, and some other figures we'll meet, we don't know exactly what Resheph's name means.[16] It's often translated as "Plague," but that's a little unfair, since in texts from the region he kills people in *lots* of different ways. Given his changing role and diverse methods of execution, Resheph is Exhibit A for why we should call these masked demons by their proper names, rather than translations. So, in the war poem of Habakkuk: "Dever stalked in front of him, and Resheph headed out behind him."

These two demonic figures accompany God into battle, Dever marching in front while Resheph brings up the rear. And they're not alone. Their agency is unmistakable even in translations that shy away from capitalization, where pestilence and plague still "walk before" God and "go forth behind" him, and their demonic qualities have been recognized for a long time—Jerome even rendered Resheph as *diabolus*, devil, in his Latin translation of Habakkuk 3.[17] But there's another demon in the picture who was in full camo until the discovery of the Ugaritic tablets in the twentieth century revealed him.

Let's go back to Habakkuk's poem to look at the line right before Dever and Resheph march in. We've just heard that God's glory covers the heavens, and the brightness is like the sun. Here's what happens next in a standard translation you might pull off the shelf: "Rays came forth from his hand, where his power lay hidden" (3:4 NRSV). The image of God shooting rays from his hand is awesomely comic-book-ready, but the next phrase appears to have something to do with God hiding power in his hands. He's shooting laser beams from them, so if he's trying to hide his power there, it isn't going well. Consider this translation taking a stab at it: "He has rays flashing from His hand, And there is the hiding of His power" (NASB). What?? But as it turns out, the original Hebrew phrase suddenly makes perfect sense if you've got your registry of Canaanite demons handy—because it contains a name.

The Hebrew word often rendered "hidden" or "hiding" doesn't appear anywhere else in the Bible. As a hypothetical common noun appearing only in this verse, the word is incongruous at best. But used as a proper noun, it reveals a phrase that's entirely harmonious with the next phrases about Dever and Resheph. Travelers, meet Hebyon.

Hebyon, also called Haby or Habayu, has a colorful backstory. He's a Canaanite demonic figure, referred to in Ugaritic literature as "lord of horns and tail," who once debased the high god El, who'd gotten drunk and passed out: "Then Habayu confronted him, lord of horns and a tail; he smeared him with his crap and piss."[18] An incantation from Ebla, also in ancient Syria, refers to binding the demon, using another close variant of his name.[19] This was a ritual intended to do just what it sounds like: to prevent a threatening demon from causing harm. Look back at those bound demons in the magic bowl. That's what the Ebla incantation is trying to do to restrain this dangerous demon, too. [*Somewhere, Hebyon shudders.*]

In Habakkuk, the phrase that leads into the description of Dever and Resheph isn't an inconsistent suggestion that God is hiding his power, it's the first image of the divine regiment accompanying God into battle: "There was Hebyon, his powerful one." This gives us a much clearer picture. God rolls in, shooting laser beams from his hand, and like any good ancient Southwest Asian god, he brings backup. Picking it up from where we've just seen God's glory covering the heavens as he sweeps in for battle:

> The brightness was like the sun;
>> rays came from his hand.
> There was Hebyon, his powerful one.
> Dever stalked in front of him,
>> and Resheph headed out behind him. (Habakkuk 3:4–5)

As God shows up on horseback with bow and arrow, he's got his troops crossing that cosmic border with him—and UN peacekeepers, they're not. God's coming in heavy with his crew of demons.

Zombie Apocalypse

Haby (using the simpler form of his name now) has one other biblical cameo, coming in just about the creepiest scene of the entire Bible:

the rise of the corpses in Isaiah. I would pay good money to see a horror ballet of this scene. Isaiah reflects on the fate of the dead, noting that God's the one who decimated the people in the first place: "The dead do not live, shades do not rise—you have punished and destroyed them, and wiped out all memory of them" (Isaiah 26:14). But hey, he goes on, things will turn around: "Your dead will live! Their corpses will rise! Awake and sing, you who dwell in the dust! . . . The earth will push out the shades of the dead" (26:19).

In a world where the earth pushing out the living corpses of people God has killed qualifies as an improvement, it shouldn't be too surprising that the divinely sent horrors aren't over yet. Isaiah's macabre hope isn't for eventual recovery just from the violence God has *already* done, but from the violence yet to come. Isaiah continues with a warning to the people not dead yet to protect themselves from what God is sending next: "Go, my people, enter your rooms and shut your door behind you—it's Haby!—for just a moment, until the Wrath has passed" (26:20).

Haby's been sent on a solo mission this time, and that power we hear about in Habakkuk is enough to keep people inside with their doors locked. The wrath isn't merely a bad feeling God's having, like maybe we could give him some space till he's more chill. It's a wrath we pray will pass as we hold our breath in the closet. But given what we know of the dread figure of Haby, and the graphic physicality of the image, "the Wrath" is almost certainly an epithet for the demon. Lock up those doors, people, until "Haby, the Wrath" has passed.[20]

The divine m.o. might ring a bell. Another of God's spokespeople issued a warning similar to Isaiah's, instructing the Israelites to stay indoors until the Destroyer had passed. Moses assured the people that God, accompanied by his divine hitman, would see the blood marking their doors and "pass over the door, and will not let the

Destroyer come into your houses to strike you" (Exodus 12:22–23). But there's no sign of blood on the doors to keep Haby out, no way to say, "Oh God, not us!" The only hope now is to shut your door behind you until the divine hitman has passed.

English translations of this Isaiah verse don't recognize Haby's name, and insert a verb like "hide." But in Hebrew, if it's a verb, that verb is a mess, dead wrong on multiple levels.[21] Like "Hebyon" in Habakkuk, "Haby" is a word that shows up nowhere else in the Bible, and translators have interpreted it as a strange (and incorrect) version of the next closest thing. The word as it stands, however, is precisely the Hebrew equivalent of the Ugaritic Haby.

And Haby is entirely at home in this picture, smack in the middle of a cluster of allusions to other creepy supernatural figures. Immediately before this are the "shades of the dead" when they're staying dead, and the living corpses being pushed out of the earth (Isaiah 26:14, 19). In the line right after Haby's appearance, the dead again won't stay underground (26:21).

The imagery of supernatural figures radiates outward, all with roots in the same Canaanite mythological realm as Haby. God swallows Mavet, reversing the roles from the Baal story (25:7). God will slay "Leviathan the fleeing serpent, Leviathan the twisting serpent" (27:1). That's a blatant adaptation of Canaanite mythology too: Leviathan is Israel's version of the sea monster Litan, who's described in the Baal cycle (which predates Isaiah) using precisely these paired phrases.[22] Demons appear in the next chapter of Isaiah too (28:2, 15). There's a stunning concentration of dangerous mythological figures in the ring of chapters around Haby.

Haby's in good company (or bad company, but at any rate plenty of company) in this part of Isaiah, but in one way he still stands out. God wipes out all memory of the shades of the dead; God conquers

Mavet and slays Leviathan—but *deploys* Haby. In this crowd, what's striking about Haby isn't his presence, but his role. The demon Haby is a divine operative sent on a deadly mission. Yet again, God intends to annihilate people en masse, and his executioner this time follows in the grooves cut by another. Haby, unmasked, looks an awful lot like the Destroyer. With this divine assassin coming for them, the people should be scared to death—even if their corpses will yet rise up and walk the earth.

Vengeance Is Mine

It turns out God has demons fighting on the front lines for him too frequently for us to explain it away. One revealing incident occurs in a poem often called the Song of Moses, set after the exodus from Egypt. It tells of how God guided the people during their desert wandering and established them in the land, where they enjoyed milk and honey . . . and foreign gods (Deuteronomy 32:4–18). The poem then details God's revenge, and includes a colorful array of promises of his wrath-fueled violence (32:19–43). As part of this divine payback plan, Resheph strikes again, this time in different demon company. We won't start with that violent climax, though; let's briefly follow the buildup of God's angry rant.

The people have been worshipping other gods, and even making sacrifices to demons (32:17). This is a sensitive issue for the Almighty: "They made me jealous with their non-gods. . . . I will heap evils upon them!" (32:21, 23). That's right, evils. This is the same word as in the story where God sics the Destroying Angel on Israel, and after seventy thousand people die, God repents of his evil (1 Chronicles 21:15). In that story, God (eventually) turns away from evil. Here, he leans in. Worse, this is also the same word used in Psalm 91's reassurance of God's protection against demons: "No evil will befall you" (91:10). The juxtaposition is chilling. Here God whips around and promises, "I will heap evils upon them!" In the psalm, he protected from demons. Now he sends them himself.

As always, major Bible translations mask the demons lurking in the ancient lines. In this case, where in Hebrew two names appear, modern translations will tell you about some combination of plague, consumption, destruction, and whatnot. But these are names you know by now: the people will be "devoured by Resheph and bitter Qetev" (Deuteronomy 32:24).

We've seen demons in a few different configurations at this point—Resheph in battle formation with Dever and Hebyon, and Qetev paired with Dever to stalk and destroy. There's frequent partner swapping within God's cohort of demons. This time, Resheph and Qetev are sent to execute a mission together.

Qetev doesn't have the rich backstory Resheph has, but he's got a bright future. He becomes well known as a demon in later ancient Jewish writing (the Talmud, targums, and midrash), where he's some-times called by his description in the Song of Moses, "bitter Qetev" (qetev meriri), now as a name, Qetev Meriri.[23]

In Deuteronomy, we finally see how the demons attack their victims: they consume them. This isn't the distinctive, character-defining gaping maw and insatiable appetite of Mavet. This is your more generic demonic devouring. It's often how ancient Southwest Asian demons kill their prey.

But sending Resheph and Qetev to devour the people isn't the first phase of God's attack. The people apparently need to get beaten down a little more first. They aren't quite . . . tenderized. First, says God, "I will use up my arrows on them!" (32:23). Then, he lets them starve (another tried and true wartime strategy). When the people are nearly down for the count, God sends his demons against them: "They will be weakened by hunger, devoured by Resheph and bitter Qetev." The paradox is painful. The people are starving—but it's the demons who get their fill.[24] At least God's giving *someone* their daily bread.

He makes no secret of his motives. He's jealous and angry at his people, and this is his revenge. After the attack of his hungry, hungry demons, he at last turns his attention to his people's enemies, and gives a shout that could pass for his personal catchphrase: "Vengeance is mine!" (32:35). God warns, "My sword will devour flesh!" He swears, "I will make my arrows drunk with blood!" (32:41–43). A sword that eats flesh, arrows that drink blood like wine—even God's weapons seem animate, like gluttonous monsters feasting on his people.

By the end of the poem, God's assaulting everyone, and promises to take vengeance on them all. On his enemies, yes; and so too, his people.

This line from Deuteronomy's Song of Moses, "Vengeance is mine," is quoted twice in the New Testament. In Romans, the context is an exhortation to people to "leave room for the wrath" of God rather than taking revenge themselves, because this is a great way to "heap burning coals" on your enemy's head (Romans 12:19–20). In other words, "kill 'em with kindness." Literally. In Hebrews, the quotation from Deuteronomy is used in frank recognition of the character of God: "For we know him who said, 'Vengeance is mine!'. . . It is a horrifying thing to fall into the hands of the living God" (Hebrews 10:30–31). So much for the notion of the vengeful God of the Old Testament, and the kinder, gentler deity of the New. God's love of vengeance is baked into the Bible, through and through.

I'll Blow Your House Down

Back in Isaiah, shortly after Haby's Destroyer-like sweep, the prophet again speaks of God sending his demons to strike human targets. One of his agents this time is Qetev, whom we've seen so far once in cahoots with Resheph and twice with Dever. This time, he's joined by someone new.

Isaiah begins by lambasting the proud rulers of Israel, with their "crown of pride" that will be "crushed" (28:1–3). The smugness of these "arrogant men" (28:14, 22) is emphasized throughout the oracle. These self-important leaders clearly need to be taken down a notch.

God is sending someone powerful and ruthless to conquer them, Isaiah warns—God's "strong and mighty one" attacking them will be "like a storm of Barad, a whirlwind of Qetev, like a storm of mighty overflowing water he hurls down to the earth with his hand" (28:2).

We've met Qetev, that minion of Mavet (Hosea 13:14) "who destroys at noon" (Psalm 91:6), last seen devouring people in the Song of Moses (Deuteronomy 32:24). This time, Qetev is a destructive storm wind blasting through the earth. But Barad (meaning "hail") is a figure we know less about, even as he's well partnered with a known demon. Like dever ("pestilence"), barad often refers to a natural phenomenon, but is also the name of a demon personifying that force. Barad is Israel's expression of a figure known from the region. In texts from Ebla in ancient Syria, the god Barad (or Baradu) was also the personification of hail. Barad appears in this role a couple of times in the Bible. One expert calls this character, in the Ebla texts and the Bible alike, "(big) Chill."[25]

We don't see Barad and Qetev in action in this verse. When Isaiah warns Israel that God is sending something brutal and destructive their way, he looks for an apt analogy, and lands on this: it will be like Barad and Qetev, which God "hurls down to the earth with his hand." Isaiah gives us a vivid picture of what they're like and how God deploys them.

The threats made, now Qetev disappears from view. But Barad shows up again a few verses later. The rulers of Israel have done a Bad

Thing, they acknowledge: "We have made a covenant with Mavet." Then Isaiah uses a *tone*, as my grandmother would have said. He has them add the harsh words he thinks better describe their actions. You can almost see him doing a puppet hand: "We have made falsehood our refuge, we have hidden in a lie" (Isaiah 28:15). The covenant may be a refuge of falsehood, but it's still a binding covenant. God won't stand for it. The pact must be destroyed, and God explains his plan: "Barad will sweep away the refuge of falsehood" (28:17–18). As he does, the covenant with Mavet is annulled.

Each time we've seen God deploy demons, it's been to attack human beings. This time initially seems different. It's demon versus demon, and Barad wins one for God against Mavet . . . right?

But Mavet wasn't God's primary target. The people say they made the pact with Mavet for protection, and God counters: once their covenant with Mavet is annulled, the danger coming will "crush" them (28:15, 18). On the one hand, annulling a pact with Mavet is probably a good thing. On the other hand, God annuls it so that the people won't get the cosmic disaster protection they seek. God sends Barad on the sweep-and-destroy mission against Mavet's refuge, not to protect the people—but to *deprive* them of protection. He wants to see them "crushed."

And why? This is a form of the same word from the beginning of the oracle, when Isaiah warned that the arrogant rulers' crown of pride would be "crushed." God sends one of his own demons to destroy the house that Death built—not to take down Mavet, but to take down the arrogant rulers. God's goal is explicit: he alone will be their "crown of glory" (28:5).

Maybe I was unfair to Paula White for her claim that demonic networks were going after President Trump. It turns out that for all the evolution of demons after the Bible was written, biblical demons do go after smug rulers after all. It's just not Satan sending them.

Shades of Gray

Not every hailstorm is a manifestation of a demon sent by God. And sometimes plague is just plague, pestilence is pestilence, and a cigar is a cigar. But sometimes it's not so clear. Somewhere in between references to natural phenomena (even if supernaturally caused) and the array of named demons in the divine militia, there are passages filled with ambiguity.

In Psalm 148 we meet a roll call of mythological beings invited to praise God (angels, hosts, sea monsters), including *barad* "fulfilling his command" (148:8), but also fire, snow, and storm winds. Psalm 18 is chock full of mythological imagery and supernatural creatures, including Mavet on the attack and God flying on a cherub (18:4–5, 10). In that context, *barad* seems personified, emerging out of God's brightness—but is followed by cracks of thunder and lightning (18:12–14).

In one poem in the book, though, textured layers of meaning are perfect artistry.

Signs of Life

The poetic retelling of the ten plagues in Psalm 78 lifts the story out of its matter-of-fact narration in Exodus and subtly infuses it with demonic presence. First, the early plagues are ratcheted up. The frogs don't just invade homes, they "destroy" them. When God sends flies, they "eat" people (78:45). This is the heightened supernatural landscape when God sends the next plagues:

Common translations will say something like, "He handed over their cattle to hail, and their flocks to lightning bolts" (78:48). On one level, this refers to actual hail and lightning, as in the Exodus narrative. There are layers of meaning, though. The Hebrew word for hail is the same one used in Exodus: *barad*.

This wouldn't raise any demon alarms on its own, in the context of the plagues—but it's not on its own. The Hebrew word used here for lightning bolts doesn't appear anywhere in the Exodus story. The new word this poet chooses is one we know by now: *resheph*.

The double entendre is genius. The word *resheph* does eventually come to mean "flame" or "spark" (e.g., Job 5:7, Song of Songs 8:6) and can legitimately mean "lightning." The poet could have used language from Exodus for thunder or fire alongside the hail, but instead selected the rare word *resheph*, giving the reader the potent pairing of Barad and Resheph.

The poet selects another new word too. In the original story, God "sent" thunder and "rained down hail" upon Egypt (Exodus 9:23). But in Psalm 78, he instead "handed over" their flocks to Barad and Resheph.[26] In Hebrew, this is a specific phrase in which the indirect object is *always* animate.[27] It might be an individual or an entire nation, but in biblical Hebrew you don't get "handed over to" a rainy day.

It's a phrase used, for example, throughout the discussion of whether David will be handed over to King Saul, who wants him dead (1 Samuel 23:11–20). In every biblical use of the phrase, the source of danger is alive.[28] In Psalm 78, the poet introduces *resheph* into the scene where *barad* was already in attendance, suggestively transforming it into a picture of known demons—and then describes God "handing over" the flocks to them. Weaving together these sensitive word choices, Psalm 78 raises the specter of God sending demonic plagues upon Israel.

After this, the poet describes God's violent plans in stunningly physical terms—"He cleared a path for his anger"—and follows this with allusions, in immediate succession, to Mavet and Dever.

In Exodus, God causes literal death (*mavet*) and pestilence (*dever*), but in the poet's hands, they take on new life: God did not "hold back" the people's lives from Mavet, and he "handed over" their lives to Dever, evoking supernatural foes who are coming for the people, and to whom God relinquishes them (Psalm 78:50).

In between these pairs—after Barad and Resheph, before Mavet and Dever—God dispatches his "deployment of evil angels," the pack of destroyers taking the place of the single Destroyer who slaughtered the firstborn in Exodus. These few verses are brimming with life. And not in a good way.

The plagues were monstrous enough in the Exodus story, when God handled most of the dirty work himself. In Psalm 78, the poet takes the already monstrous and knits in monsters:

> He handed over their cattle to Barad and their flocks to Resheph;
> He unleashed on them his burning rage, wrath and indignation and distress,
>> a deployment of evil angels;
> He cleared a path for his anger;
> He did not hold them back from Mavet, but handed over their lives to Dever. (Psalm 78:48–50)

What's a reader to do with this biblical recasting of the traditional story? Every year at Passover, we recite the ten plagues—*dam*, *tzfardea*, *kinim* (blood, frogs, lice), on through the terrible final event—and with each word, we dip a finger into our wine glass and let the drop of wine fall onto our plate to acknowledge the suffering of the Egyptians.

The list we read is drawn from Exodus, but in recent years I've found myself reading it through the lens of Psalm 78, with those eerie new figures flitting overhead as I spill my drops of wine. Which kind of divinely inflicted suffering are we to imagine, I wonder? Should we picture God sending his demons to commit these unthinkable acts of cruelty, or of him doing it himself? Which is worse?

As I contemplate those ten drops of red wine on the seder plate, I suddenly think: the genius of that ancient poet wasn't merely the literary artistry of suggesting the activity of demons; it was also stopping at the suggestion. Because it doesn't matter. It could be God, implies the poet, or it could be demons. Six of one . . .

Until now, God has shown loyalty to his monsters. They're brutal, terrifying, and sometimes a bit twisted, but at least he treats his team well. Enter the New Testament. With the influence of dualistic theology and the growth of apocalypticism, demons become identified as evil, and the complex tapestry of God's relationships within the divine realm gives way to the cosmic battle between good and evil that lies at the heart of both pre-Christian Jewish apocalyptic literature (like Enoch) and the New Testament. By the New Testament period, demons are definitively associated with Satan and are fully excised from the divine entourage. God has banished his demons.

But God only abandons the monsters, not the acts. He's like the corrupt boss who fires people when they get caught doing what he ordered, and once they've taken the fall he shifts that work to other employees. In this case, God transfers the jobs of demons to his most eminent minions: angels.

Where earlier God sent demons into battle against entire populations, and against the earth and sea (Habakkuk 3, Deuteronomy 32), by Revelation, angels are deployed for this. Where God once sent demons of plague and pestilence, in Revelation it's his angels who pour out bowls of plague over the earth (Revelation 15–16). Where God once sent "bitter Qetev" against people, in Revelation he hurls an angel into the water to make it "bitter" and poison people (8:11). Not one drop of the rivers of human blood in Revelation is spilled by demons. Who needs demons when you've got the blood-soaked angels of God?

It's not just Revelation. In the New Testament book of Acts, when a smug ruler of Judea needs to be taken down, it's an angel who does the job (Acts 12:21–23). In the Hebrew Bible, Mavet leaves corpses in his wake "like sheaves behind the reaper" (Jeremiah 9:22), but in the Gospels, Jesus says that angels are the reapers of the human harvest (Matthew 13:39–42). In the Hebrew Bible, God sends Resheph and Qetev to devour the disloyal, crying, "Vengeance is mine" (Deuteronomy 32). In the New Testament, angels are the soldiers accompanying Jesus for "doling out vengeance on those who do not know God," throwing in a little eternal destruction to make the point (2 Thessalonians 1:7–9).

Angels don't ever give us a hand by fighting demons in the Bible—but it's worse than that. They inherit their functions *from* demons. The old demons are gone because their jobs were commandeered and given to angels.

Of all the monsters we've encountered so far, the demons in God's service seem the least explicable. Their roles aren't morally ambiguous like those of angels and other members of the divine company. They have no praise for God, no song, no glorious light. They offer no magnificent, formidable signal of sacred space. They provide no hope, no solace, no communication whatsoever, having no speech for humankind. They exist solely to cause people harm. They are bitter and wrathful, stalking and devouring, and coming for you.

Figure 12. Amulet for protection against plague, pestilence (*dever*), demons, spirits, and more. This popular amulet goes back to the 16th century Kabbalist, Rabbi Isaac Luria, who was born in Jerusalem in 1534 and died in Safed in 1572—of plague.

And yet—there's something poignant in this blunt portrayal of disembodied danger. For all their nightmarish qualities, these demon passages reflect something close to our world, where we often experience suffering with no explanation, harm with no face. When I read these ancient expressions of invisible, impersonal danger, I recognize something in them. I sense in these disembodied personifications of harm, as in the rest of the divine entourage too, that the ancient authors understood something about the precarious experience of life in this world.

But we have yet to encounter the last of the task force. A proper entourage requires a variety of specialists. We've met behavior enforcers and bodyguards, a torturer, and an array of divine hitmen. Let's meet the last of the monsters of the divine entourage, God's experts in psychological warfare: the stealthy spirits who manipulate the minds of their human targets.

6

Manipulative and Mind-Altering Spirits

Not every job requires a hitman. Sometimes all you need is a good disinformation campaign. Plant the lies, and see what havoc blooms. Sow discord. Mess with minds, topple regimes.

It's a tried-and-true mode of attack we recognize all around us. Psychological operations can alter the course of history, from wartime tactical psyops to the dissemination of lies through Facebook. Goals may vary. For one, there's the deliberate planting of a specific idea. The US Army website summarizing career paths in psyops highlights the goal of "missions that convey selected information . . . intended to influence the emotions, motives, reasoning and behavior of foreign governments and citizens in a manner that is favorable to allied objectives."[1] On the other end of the spectrum, there's the control exercised through blocking access to information, like governments filtering Internet content.

Somewhere in between, there's the insidious objective of creating conflict. Alongside the systematic use of fraudulent posts that aim for particular results—say, to an election—Facebook continues to reckon with "state-backed disinformation campaigns" from Iran and Russia in which posts cross "categories and ideological lines, seemingly with no specific intent other than to foment discord."[2]

All three of these agendas also prove useful when conflict goes supernatural. In clashes with both individuals and populations, God has more at his disposal than the blunt force of his angels and overt assaults of the other henchmen we've encountered. God's psychological warfare experts disseminate lies, obscure reality, and sow discord in a manner that is favorable to allied objectives.

Spirits are built for this. Their ethereal form is perfectly suited to covert ops. The Hebrew word for "spirit," *ruah*, also means "wind" and "breath." They're wind, coming and going unseen. An angel in human form might serve as an effective messenger (if it's not there to kill you), but a spirit that can sweep into your body and mind without you knowing it? Now *that's* an agent for divine psyops. As the US Army says, psyops soldiers are selected in part for their "adaptability" and have "unique capabilities . . . that increase their effectiveness in the field."[3] Indeed.

That's not to say spirits have no form whatsoever. In our first story, we'll see a spirit that changes form to accomplish its mission. The prophet Micaiah, who shows up in just one colorful story, has a vision of God on his celestial throne with all the host of heaven "standing around him on his right and on his left." (And if that's not an entourage, I don't know what is.) God wants to kill off a certain king and asks his heavenly army who can get the job done. A spirit comes forward and stands before God—*stands*, like the other embodied members of the entourage in all their splendid diversity. The spirit volunteers to create a false prophecy for the king to get him killed, and explains that it will achieve this by entering the mouths of the prophets—for which it needs to be on earth and formless (1 Kings 22:19–22).

Later, we'll hear a man describe the hair-raising dread he felt when a spirit brushed over his face in the night (Job 4:12–17). It stood right in front of him, and he saw its form. He tries to explain what he saw, but it was unrecognizable to him, indescribable—as classic monsters are so often said to be.

Most spirits don't appear to be shapeshifters, though, and instead retain that other classic monster trait, formlessness. They move into and among their human marks in subtly different ways from one another, ever adaptable, their unique capabilities guaranteeing their effectiveness in the field. The divine disinformation operatives target hearts and minds in ways no other member of God's entourage can.

Stealth and Vengeance

In Micaiah's throne vision, the realm-crossing, shapeshifting "spirit of falsehood" gets its name on the marquee. In other texts, deceptive spirits lurk in the shadows. True to their elusive form, these spirits have largely gone undetected and are interpreted metaphorically, as if the word *spirit* refers to a feeling or frame of mind. Once we get to know the "spirit of falsehood" and some divine colleagues, though, we'll be able to recognize furtive spirits of vengeful deception in a few places where their covers hadn't been blown yet.[4] Because of the trademark stealth of the psychological warfare artists, we sometimes see them best by the cognitive wreckage they leave in their wake.

"A Spirit of Falsehood"

King Ahab was rotten. There'd been some bad kings, but none so wicked as Ahab, who sacrificed his sons, had a man executed on false charges for his own gain, and generally "did evil in the sight of the Lord, more than all before him" (1 Kings 16:30). God, perhaps understandably in this instance, wants Ahab eliminated.

As our story begins, Ahab is considering going to war against the Arameans. He consults the prophets to find out if he would triumph in battle. This story should be like the kind of movie where you start with the final shot and then experience the gradual progression toward that fateful end—

Flash Forward: Ahab does go into battle. He's badly wounded and is stuck propped up in his chariot, bleeding out as the battle rages on. His blood fills the bottom of the chariot, and he dies. When the chariot is washed out later, dogs lick up his blood (1 Kings 22:29–38). As ignominious ends go, this is the ignomini-est.

36 Hours Earlier (well, back to the beginning): When Ahab consults four hundred prophets about whether he should go to war, they assure him he'll be A-OK. One of them, Zedekiah—whom we'll meet again—even makes a pair of iron ox horns to symbolize Ahab's victory, proclaiming that the king will "gore" the Arameans to death (22:12). One lone prophet remains: Micaiah. The king wants Micaiah to predict victory too, but Micaiah demurs: "What the Lord says to me, *that* will I speak" (22:14). This is just like what Balaam said (fresh from the near-fatal attack of the armed angel) when the king of Moab tried to compel him to predict Moabite victory: "The word that God places in my mouth, *that* will I speak" (Numbers 22:38). It's like a warning shot from the prophet as he gears up to deliver an oracle predicting the king's defeat.

With such a declaration of prophetic integrity, you'd expect Micaiah to say, "Don't go, you'll be slaughtered!" Instead, he tells Ahab that he should absolutely go into battle, and that God will give him the victory. Now, you and I already know that this isn't true, and even Bad King Ahab sniffs it out. He rebukes Micaiah for the lie: "How many times do I have to make you swear not to speak to me anything but the truth, in the name of the Lord?" It's only after

Ahab's rebuke that Micaiah admits the truth: he "saw Israel scattered upon the mountains," defeated, slain (1 Kings 22:15–17).

At this point, Micaiah tells Ahab about the vision he'd had: he saw God sitting on his throne, with the army of heaven surrounding him. God asked which of them would deceive Ahab so the king would go get killed in battle. Various members of God's entourage throw out suggestions: "One said this, and another said that—and the spirit came forward and stood before the Lord and said, 'I'll deceive him.'" God asks how, and he answers, "I will go out and be a spirit of falsehood in the mouths of all of his prophets." The vision concludes as God agrees to the strategy and commissions the spirit: "You will deceive him, and you will succeed. Go out and do it" (22:19–22).

A *spirit*—which you'd think should, by definition, be disembodied—comes forward from the group and stands before God. It speaks up and proposes its idea, which God approves. It's only when the spirit crosses into the human realm that it shapeshifts, as if disintegrating into myriad invisible particles that can enter the mouths of four hundred prophets. The spirit isn't inherently disembodied; it dis-embodies itself for the mission.

No one sees it coming. The spirit enters stealthily, does its work, and is gone. Imperceptibility is key to this operation, and as always, God deploys the member of his entourage best suited to the job at hand. The formless monster is a virtuoso in its trademark psyops work. The prophets remain unaware that anything is amiss and faithfully pass on the message they've received.

Talk about a "state-backed disinformation campaign." At least Mark Zuckerberg claims that Facebook is now trying to clamp down on disinformation.[5] Here, God's the one *creating* it.

In case King Ahab hasn't connected the dots, Micaiah explains that the divine plan from his vision was already put into action:

"Look, the Lord put a spirit of falsehood in the mouths of all these prophets of yours." My good man, your prophets predicted your victory because God is *toying* with you. Micaiah makes sure the king fully registers how bad this is, adding, "The Lord has decreed evil for you" (22:23).

Then Zedekiah comes up and punches Micaiah in the face. (Bet you didn't see that coming.) He asks Micaiah which way the spirit of the Lord went when it left him to go speak to Micaiah. Zedekiah's image is absurdly visual, as if he's mocking, "Didja see *that* in your vision too?" Micaiah's retort is just as sharp: when Zedekiah has to go hide from attackers, he'll know Micaiah was telling the truth about Ahab's defeat.

Ahab orders that Micaiah be thrown in prison until he returns from battle in peace. Micaiah gets in one final comment, maybe with a raised eyebrow: Yeah, sure, "if you return in peace, the Lord didn't speak through me" (22:28). Reader, Ahab does not return in peace.

It's a tapestry of deception. Ahab's prophets initially seem like obsequious staffers lying to flatter the king, but it turns out they've been deceived by the spirit of falsehood, and are truthfully reporting the divine message given to them. The logic of the story only works if they would have told the truth, if only God hadn't orchestrated the deception. Micaiah, meanwhile, is the sole character who knowingly lies. He'd witnessed the divine strategy session, and still reassures Ahab that all will be well. Ahab's prophets are deceived; Micaiah chooses to deceive. Moreover, he does so immediately after declaring that he'll speak only what the Lord tells him to—falsely implying that it will be true. Bad King Ahab then correctly accuses Micaiah of lying, exhorting him "not to speak to me anything but the truth, in the name of the Lord." (That last part is some pungent irony.) Micaiah finally tells the truth . . . about God planting lies. Zedekiah, aiming for insult, inadvertently hits on the truth: the spirit of the Lord isn't with him, but with Micaiah.

There's some next-level irony now, as the guy who's been hoodwinked by the lying spirit utters the truth about the spirit of God having left him—the same God who perpetrated the lie. So it makes perfect sense that now, free from the spirit of God, Zedekiah utters the truth.

If you're confused, don't worry. That's the point. The spirit has done its job.

Amid these layers of deceit, two characters tell each other the truth. In the heavenly council, the lying spirit tells God the truth about exactly what he'll do and how he'll do it. In response, God tells the lying spirit the truth about the successful outcome of the operation. Even Micaiah gets the short end of the stick. He knows the truth because he witnessed the meeting of the divine council in his vision—but by involving Micaiah, God makes a liar of him too. (Remember, to go along with God's plan, Micaiah starts off by lying to Ahab.)

God shows his true colors: his primary loyalty isn't to Israel, or to all of those prophets ready to report divine messages, or even to Micaiah. It's not to humankind at all, but to the lying spirit. When push comes to shove, God's loyalty is only to his own crew.

The contrast is night and day. God displays a radical lack of concern for human life. When he wants to get rid of Ahab, his strategy is to entice him to go into battle—but not in an *existing* war. The story's opening line is that there was peace between Israel and Aram (22:1). God hatches a plan to persuade the king to *enter Israel into war*. The spirit proposes the method, but the ruthless core plan is God's. It involves untold casualties. We hear later about how after Ahab is struck by an arrow, the battle rages on so intensely throughout the day that Ahab sits propped up in his chariot in the midst of the chaos until finally bleeding out after sunset (22:34–37). How many others died in that raging battle?

God's disloyalty to humankind, exposed in his scheme of entering Israel into war just to kill off Ahab, is also glaring in his chosen strategy. Kings would often consult prophets before making critical decisions, and Bad King Ahab seeks God's guidance in this customary way. When God responds by sending the spirit of false-hood to plant lies in the prophets' mouths, God's taking advantage of this trusted way of turning to him in a moment of crisis, a stunning betrayal of the human inclination to ask God for help. The spirit plants the specific lie, but the greater treachery is God's.

As head of the divine council, God's authority underlies every plan. The spirit is serving God by figuring out a way to bump someone off, at God's request. We catch a glimpse of the operations of the divine council, with "all the host of heaven" present, as some in attendance propose ideas: "one said this and another said that." (There needs to be a monster midrash filling in the gaps there. What were the suggestions God *didn't* take?) The spirit volunteers for the job and offers a suggestion. It has some agency, but it's limited: the initial request is God's, as is the authority he gives the spirit to do what it proposes.

The dynamic is like another scene of the divine council in action. Both here and in Job, the heavenly beings are assembled and one of them comes into view. God initiates the discussion about the human subject, triggering everything that follows. The monster of the hour proposes an idea, and God gives the go-ahead. The Adversary's more of a "Big Questions" discussion partner for God than the spirit, and shines with depraved creativity—and yet, the Adversary in Job is never called "evil."

But that's not because God doesn't have anyone evil working for him.

"An Evil Spirit" Should Do the Trick

Almost no other spirit appears quite as vividly as the spirit of falsehood in Micaiah's vision, but nowhere are the horrific effects of a spirit's psychological assault more vivid than in the divine attack on Saul, the first king of Israel.

In a trio of vignettes, Saul is tormented by an evil spirit that ravages his mind, sending him into fits of frenzied violence. Could God save him from this terrible fate, perhaps? But nope, God's the one sending the evil spirit in the first place. We know this from the moment the spirit sweeps in: it's introduced as "an evil spirit from the Lord" (1 Samuel 16:14). We might hope that when God sends an evil spirit on the attack, it's at least as punishment for a serious offense. Bad King Ahab, after all, was very bad indeed. But not Saul.

This is Saul's offense: he spares a life. God orders him to slaughter every Amalekite. He comes close, but spares the king—which, as mercy goes, seems unimpressive. But for this, God rejects Saul and chooses David instead (15:3–16:1, 12). David is anointed king in Saul's place, and the spirit of the Lord enters David (16:13). Saul has been rejected and replaced. Shouldn't this have been enough?

It wasn't enough. "Now the spirit of the Lord departed from Saul, and an evil spirit from the Lord terrorized him" (16:14). This is the *Fatal Attraction* end of the breakup scale. Saul is wildly agitated by the evil spirit from God, to the point that his servants bring someone in to play the lyre to soothe him (16:16).[6] The solution is temporary. The evil spirit from God keeps coming back. Whenever it comes upon Saul, the musician plays and soothes him, and the evil spirit departs from him again (16:23). For the time being.

The musician the servants find, by the way, is David—David, whom God has chosen to replace Saul, and who's rising in power. One day, Saul even runs into people singing jubilant songs about how much tougher David is than Saul (18:6–9). So as time goes on, the soothing effect of David's playing is, let's say, mitigated.

The evil spirit continues to torment Saul like a cat with a mouse. The very day after Saul hears the "Anything Saul can do, David can do better" song, the evil spirit again "forcibly enters" Saul, making him so agitated that he raves.[7] Now, if you Google "raving like a," you'll get an autocomplete of "lunatic," but that isn't what's happening here. The Hebrew verb means "raving like a prophet."

This is the word used about prophets possessed by the spirit of the Lord, like the spirit-struck prophets Saul encounters as they prophesy ecstatically outdoors for all to hear. When God's own spirit is the cause, the verb is commonly translated as something like "be in a prophetic frenzy" (e.g., NRSV; 10:5–13; 19:18–24). When the evil spirit enters Saul, he behaves the same way—but in the privacy of his own home, with no prophetic message. He's frenzied, raving like a spirit-struck prophet, but without the prophecy. He's been struck with a spirit alright, just not the right one.

Day after day, Saul raves, and David plays the lyre. But after such daily torment, no relief can be found. One day, Saul hurls a spear at David, trying to pin him to the wall, but David escapes. The scene closes with a recap of the divine setup: Saul is afraid of David "because the Lord was with him, but had departed from Saul" (18:10–12).

The third vignette is a short and not-at-all-sweet reminder that Saul's torment is ongoing. Once again, an evil spirit from the Lord comes upon Saul, David strums the lyre, Saul is driven over the edge and tries to spear David a second time, and David escapes (19:9–10).

After that, David remains on the run for a very long time, with Saul in pursuit.

The first of these three scenes begins with the spirit *of* God leaving Saul and the evil spirit *from* God terrorizing him. One spirit leaves, another comes. When God's own spirit abandons Saul and moves to David, it makes room for the evil spirit to attack Saul. As different as the Saul story is from the Micaiah story, this is what happens there too. The prophet Zedekiah sucker punches Micaiah because he understands the implication of Micaiah's vision, even if he doesn't buy it: that the spirit of God has departed from him and moved to Micaiah. Meanwhile, having just predicted Ahab's victory, Zedekiah himself is under the deluding influence of the spirit of false-hood. In these stories, it seems to be a basic rule of cosmic physics that no two spirits can occupy the same space at the same time.

It makes sense that God's own spirit and the evil spirit can't both be present. They operate in the same spaces and work in similar ways. When the evil spirit arrives, its movements mirror those of God's spirit in these same stories. Each spirit "forcibly enters" people (16:13; 18:10) and "departs" from people (16:14, 23), and each causes some kind of spirit-struck "raving" (18:10; 19:20), with identical Hebrew terminology for each of these.[8]

Entering and departing in the same way is logical enough, if this is how a formless spirit influences a person. The "raving" is where the mirror image goes *Poltergeist III* (1988). God's own spirit can trigger ecstatic prophecy, but the evil spirit from God triggers the outward behavior of spirit-struck prophecy—absent the prophetic part. Saul "raves," but with no divine communication to pass on.

Saul is often said to be delusional in these raving and spear-chucking episodes, but that's not quite accurate. After all, David *is* coming for the throne, and eventually gets it. Attempts at the remote diagnosis of Saul miss the point. If Saul is delusional, it's because he's been deluded.

The "evil spirit" isn't identical to the "spirit of falsehood," who hatches a plan to get a king killed and achieves its goal but apparently isn't evil. The two spirits do share a mode of attack, though. The spirit of falsehood enters the prophets, causing them to deliver false prophecy, to speak something prophetic that isn't true. The evil spirit enters Saul, causing him to speak something prophet-*ic* that isn't prophecy. The spirit of falsehood's infiltration generates a false message, while the evil spirit's triggers empty prophet-miming, prophetic behavior devoid of a prophetic message. Both of God's ethereal emissaries inspire varieties of hollow prophetic speech.

We don't get the video feed from the back room showing God's interaction with the spirit this time, but we can still clearly see God's motives. When God deploys the spirit of falsehood, its assignment is to take down a disobedient king. God also sends the evil spirit to terrorize Saul as reprisal for his disobedience, as minor as it is. Saul's downfall is a slower process, sparked by the effects of the evil spirit dismantling its victim, never ending until Saul is in the ground.

The evil spirit triggers a conflict between Saul and David that simmers for the remainder of Saul's life. After David's second escape from the spear-hurling king, he flees, Saul hot on his trail. Saul pursues him *daily* (1 Samuel 23:14). Once, when David has a chance to kill Saul, he spares him, with this ominous warning: "The Lord will judge between me and you! He will take vengeance against you for me. . . . May he fight my fight and vindicate me against you" (24:12–15). We saw God pick his horse, so as Saul's story tumbles toward its fateful conclusion, we're bracing ourselves for Saul to meet an inglorious end.

Sure enough, the Philistines kill Saul's three sons and leave Saul badly wounded. Saul asks his armor-bearer to finish the job, but when the armor-bearer can't bring himself to do it, Saul kills himself. When the Philistines return the next day, they cut off Saul's head and fasten his mangled body to a wall (31:1–10). The evil spirit from God has driven Saul raving and fighting right over the edge.

"An Evil Spirit" Divides and Conquers

That wasn't the first time God deployed an evil spirit. For that, we need to look back to a time before there was ever a king—at least, a legitimate king. As the Bible tells it, Israel was ruled by a series of military heroes. One of them, Gideon, had seventy sons with his various wives, and an additional son with his concubine in Shechem (Judges 8:30–31). That son is Abimelech, and this is his story.

When Gideon dies, Abimelech is done being the seventy-first wheel. His "legitimate" brothers are ruling, but Abimelech gets the leaders of Shechem to support him in a bloody coup. Abimelech and his hired guns go out and slaughter his brothers, and the leaders of Shechem make Abimelech their king (9:1–6). But Abimelech—like Saul, and like Ahab—isn't God's chosen ruler, so you can probably guess this won't end well. God, not one to sit back and see how things pan out, taps a member of his divine entourage to take care of business. The scene is depicted in Judges: "God sent an evil spirit between Abimelech and the leaders of Shechem, and the leaders of Shechem double-crossed Abimelech" (9:23).[9]

We lucked out with Micaiah's inside scoop about the spirit of falsehood. This time we have no such advantage. As in the vignettes of the evil spirit that terrorized Saul, this fleeting reference is our only glimpse of the spirit, an ephemeral flicker we see out of the corner of our eye—and before we can register what we've seen, it's gone. What lingers in view once again, as in the stories of Ahab and Saul, is the effect of the spirit's activity. It leaves its signature: deception, discord, and death.

This is psychological manipulation at its finest. Remember those campaigns on Facebook "seemingly with no specific intent other than to foment discord"? Here's how that works:

The evil spirit infiltrates, coming between Abimelech and the Shechemites. The Shechemites double-cross Abimelech, backing a challenger to his rule. Then an Abimelech loyalist runs a triple-cross, posing as one of the rebels while plotting an attack against them. He stands by the challenger's side as Abimelech's army advances, reassuring him that no attack is coming: What's wrong, he asks, you think those look like men rushing down the mountain toward you? Silly goose, those are just shadows (9:25–36).

They're not shadows. This ripple effect of duplicity and deceit leads to Abimelech slaughtering untold masses of people in Shechem and then killing another thousand who've fled to a stronghold that he burns down (9:45–49). When he tries to set another tower on fire, a woman at the top drops a grinding stone on his head, crushing his skull. As he lies dying, he asks his armor-bearer to finish him off with a sword so that no one can say a woman killed him (9:53–54). Unlike Saul's armor-bearer, this one doesn't hesitate to get the job done. He runs a sword through him. Abimelech is dead.

The evil spirit's work is finished. It instigates treachery, and shortly thereafter nearly everyone involved is dead. The ruler God rejects is violently eliminated, his conspirators are slaughtered, and (no surprise) the further death toll is enormous. Discord, deception, death.

The three victims of spirit attacks we've seen so far suffer three of the most notoriously ignominious deaths of the Bible. In biblical order: Abimelech, Saul, and Bad King Ahab.

We don't need a witness to a closed-door heavenly meeting to know God's motives. God doesn't just want Abimelech deposed, he wants payback. God sends the evil spirit in revenge for the seventy brothers of Abimelech, so that their blood will be on the heads of Abimelech and his Shechemite conspirators (9:23–24). God "repaid them for the evil they had done" (9:56–57). Done and dusted. In a tour de force, the evil spirit sows discord and deceit between the men until they and countless others are eliminated.

Rumor Has It . . .

Several generations after the disposal of Ahab, the Assyrian king Sennacherib falls victim to a spirit sent by God. When we met Sennacherib before, you'll recall he had Jerusalem in his crosshairs, causing desperate King Hezekiah to invoke God "who dwells among the cherubim," to prove his divine might—which God did, sending his angel to kill 185,000 Assyrian soldiers (2 Kings 19:14–19, 35). But what happens to Sennacherib? It turns out God has a more creative strategy for taking care of him.

The Assyrian king taunts Hezekiah and intimidates the people of Jerusalem: "Don't let Hezekiah deceive you!" yells Sennacherib's messenger, "and don't let Hezekiah make you trust the Lord!" (18:29–30). In what will turn out to be perfect dramatic irony, Sennacherib has just suggested that everyone *else* is going to be deceived. We should be on high alert.

Hezekiah consults the prophet Isaiah, who delivers God's explanation of how he plans to handle Sennacherib: "I will put a spirit in him and he will hear a rumor, and he will return to his land and I will make him fall by the sword in his own land" (19:6–7). This isn't God's first rodeo. It worked with Ahab, and it'll work with Sennacherib. This time, though, God puts the deceiving spirit directly into the king he wants to knock off, not into his advisors. God gathers the divine troops. He sends an angel to slaughter the Assyrian soldiers—and something else comes for Sennacherib.

No juicy details this time, just God's matter-of-fact statement that he'll put a spirit in Sennacherib to deceive him into returning to Assyria to get killed. God explains his plan, and the reader sees the brutal results unfold. Whatever the rumor is, Sennacherib heads home, where his own sons take their swords and slaughter him (19:36–37).

Another king, another spirit, another deception, and another disgraceful, bloody death.

Doesn't it seem like spreading a rumor to hurt someone should be . . . beneath God? Maybe it's hard to resist using the supernatural weaponry at your disposal when you know it's so effective. In *The Umbrella Academy*, the superhero Allison only has to whisper, "I heard a rumor," and whatever she says next will be believed. Even Allison—aka The Rumor—tries to swear off her powers after seeing the damage they cause. But God doesn't seem to mind the dubious morality of psychological manipulation.

Sennacherib made his own meager attempts at psyops. First, he tried to psych out the people of Jerusalem by claiming that Hezekiah was deceiving them, and that God couldn't be trusted. Later, he warned Hezekiah, "Don't let your God, whom you trust, deceive you" (19:10). No match for God when it comes to psychological warfare, Sennacherib fails. God seems to retort through the deployed spirit, "How's *this* for deceit?"

Mass Attack: Spirits of Distortion and Stupor

On two occasions, God sends a spirit to act against an entire population. Both times, the spirit is nearly imperceptible—but our examinations of other spirit attacks have yielded a pattern that surfaces here too.

Both incidents are described by Isaiah. In the first oracle, God lays out a plan of attack against Egypt. First, he plans to incite the Egyptians against one another—like he did with Abimelech and the Shechemites. Next, he'll leave Egypt emptied of spirit—like he did to Zedekiah and Saul. Then he's going to confuse Egypt so that the people will rely on futile divination and false sources—like he did with Ahab (Isaiah 19:2–3). Taken individually, each similarity to a spirit attack might seem coincidental. But these reverberations of multiple incidents of spirit infiltration, all packed into two verses, build to a blunt statement: the leaders of Egypt have been "deceived," because "the Lord mixed within it a spirit of distortion" (19:13–14).

We see only the faintest silhouette of the spirit, but recognize its handiwork. The result: all of Egypt is led astray "like the stumbling of a drunk in his vomit" (19:14).

A nation can't up and die like the individual victims of other spirit attacks, so instead Egypt is threatened and humiliated. The image is as disturbing as any bloody slaughter we've seen: the Egyptians will become like women "trembling with fear before the raised hand that the Lord of Armies swings against them" (19:16). A violent God looms over them. He strikes—fade to black.

The second time God deploys a spirit against an entire region, the target is Jerusalem. In this oracle, Isaiah's back to his frequent focus on the threat of Assyrian attack. Only here, God's on the Assyrian side. Jerusalem has sinned, Isaiah says, and God is threatening a devastating siege against the city, along with a battery of other consequences.

"Ariel, Ariel," God begins his address to Jerusalem (29:1). This is sometimes translated "Lion of God," but at best it's a nasty play on words, since Jerusalem isn't called this anywhere else in the Bible and the word means something totally unrelated in the next verse—and it's not pretty. In Hebrew, *ariel* means the "altar hearth" on which things are slaughtered and burned (as in Ezekiel 43:16). God continues, "I will cause distress to Ariel; there will be mourning and lamentation, and the city will be like an *ariel* to me," like an altar where blood is spilled (Isaiah 29:2). God describes his military invasion of the city, and its fatal consequences. He tells the people they will speak from deep beneath the earth, that their voices will come from underground like a ghost, and that they'll "chirp" from the dust, which is how Isaiah describes the eerie sounds of ghosts elsewhere (29:3–4; see 8:19). You'll be mourned, God says to Jerusalem, after I lead this deadly assault that turns the whole city into an altar for slaughter.

A brief moment of hope follows, but then it all comes crashing back down. The storm after the calm brings the pinnacle of God's threat: a visit from our ephemeral interloper. A few chapters earlier, Isaiah described the terrible effect of the spirit of distortion, when Egypt would be led astray "like the stumbling of a drunk in his vomit." Now he turns and says something similar to Jerusalem: "Stupefy yourselves and be stupefied, blind yourselves and be blind! Be drunk, but not from wine—stagger, but not from a drink" (29:9). Be dazed and confused—but not from any substance. Isaiah explains why the people fall into such a discombobulated state: "Because the Lord has poured upon you a spirit of stupor" (29:10).

Like the spirit that was "mixed into" Egypt, this spirit takes a form that can permeate a population, and it's "poured upon" Jerusalem. Also like the spirit of distortion, the spirit of stupor makes people stagger around stupefied like they're drunk out of their gourds. But that's only one symptom of the spirit's infiltration.

Isaiah details its immediate effect: Stagger around, he tells the people of Jerusalem, "because the Lord has poured upon you a spirit of stupor, and has shut your eyes, the prophets, and covered your heads, the seers." God uses the spirit of stupor to obscure prophecy. Like all of its cohort, this spirit shrouds reality from the eyes of its prey. In Jerusalem's bleakest hour, in the chaos and desperation of war, all radio signal is cut off. God has pulled the plug.

We've seen spirits engage in each major type of psyops—spreading disinformation, fomenting discord—and now we see the final piece of the triad, blocking access to information.

Spirits of falsehood, of rumor, distortion, and stupor bring false prophecy, no prophecy, prophetic speech absent a prophetic message. Evil spirits sow discord and deadly violence. People are deceived, rendered delusional, and dazed. The spirits of God's entourage leave their signature at every crime scene.

The next spirit seems different—at first.

"A Spirit Brushed by Me"

In each previous incident, the spirit has been implicitly formless as it sweeps through the human realm. Even the spirit of falsehood, whom Micaiah sees step forward from among the divine entourage in heaven, is invisible in the mouths of all the prophets. But one man has a bona fide spirit sighting—on earth.

For this story, we return to the book of Job, where God and the Adversary have just conducted the Job experiment. God gave the Adversary the nod to torture Job and crush his children to death, and we left Job sitting in ashes, scratching the inflamed boils that covered his body. But here's what happens next: Job's friends come to visit, they mean well but tensions escalate, and they have an increasingly hostile exchange with Job that lasts for virtually the entire rest of the book. One by one, they accuse him of having brought his troubles on himself, unrelenting in their challenges to Job to think about what sin he may have committed to deserve this awful fate.

The first to speak up is Eliphaz. What he says will lay the groundwork for everything that follows. He asks Job, "Remember now, who that is innocent has perished? Where were any righteous people disappeared?" (Job 4:7). He's just kicked off the conversation by telling Job that his dead children weren't so innocent.

If Eliphaz left it at this, maybe Job could bear it. But he goes further. He tells Job that his insight comes from a divine source:

> A word was brought stealthily to me, my ear caught a whisper
> of it—
>> amid unsettling thoughts from visions at night,
>>> when deep sleep falls upon people,
>> fear came over me, and trembling,
>>> and made me shudder to the bone—
> A spirit brushed by my face;
>> the hair on my flesh bristled.
> It stood still, but I did not recognize its appearance;
>> a form was right before my eyes.
> There was silence—and I heard a voice:
> "Can a human being be more in the right than God? Can a man
> be purer than his maker?" (Job 4:12–17)

Eliphaz remembers his goosebumps as the spirit brushed by his face. He describes hair-raising, bone-shaking fear. After he feels the spirit on his face, it halts right in front of him. He sees a physical form before his very eyes. It's indescribable. As the narrator of H. P. Lovecraft's story "The Outsider" says when he catches a glimpse of what has just sent people fleeing, "I beheld in full, frightful vividness the inconceivable, indescribable, and unmentionable monstrosity. . . . I cannot even hint what it was like."[10]

The spirit stands before Eliphaz, not unlike how the spirit moved in Micaiah's vision, when it "stood before the Lord" in heaven—only this time it's happening on the ground.

Given that in Micaiah's vision the first words out of the spirit's mouth are, "I'll deceive him," we'd do well to enter in with a touch of healthy suspicion when the spirit speaks to Eliphaz. Sure enough, it begins, "Can a human being be more in the right than God?"

The best lies, they say, contain an element of truth.

The spirit's point seems generally right, doesn't it? But this isn't an abstract Grand Theological Truth to be snipped out and pinned to a bulletin board, surrounded by other favorite quotations. It's a line interjected into an ongoing debate, and the subject of that debate matters. The issue in dispute is whether Job brought his troubles on himself. Job argues that because he's innocent, God has unjustly afflicted him and should be held accountable. When the spirit says these words to Eliphaz—"Can a human being be more in the right than God?"—it's taking the other side in that dispute. But the entire premise of the book is that Job *is* blameless, and God *has* afflicted him.

Job's innocence is even given as the reason for the divine experiment in the first place. God and the Adversary agree to find out whether innocent Job can be corrupted. They torture him to find his breaking point. The words of the spirit might not be false per se, but they're sure as hell false in their application to Job.

The spirit knows exactly what it's doing. In its next words, it casually mentions that divine beings aren't trustworthy. The greater point the spirit is making is that *people* are flawed, but the way it expresses this is like a private joke with God. The spirit says of God,

> Look, he doesn't trust his servants,
>> and he charges his angels with error—
> How much more so, those who live in houses of clay,
>> whose foundation is in the dust. (Job 4:18–19)

In the same breath as emphasizing that human beings are flawed—which is certainly the point Eliphaz takes from the spirit's speech, applying it to Job for the rest of the book—the spirit has just said that God's divine messengers can't be trusted either. Choice words from a dissembling spirit.[11]

We don't need a vision of the heavenly council to know where this spirit comes from. Eliphaz explains that "a word" was brought to him, which is Bible shorthand for "a word from God." He specifies that this divine message was brought to him "when deep sleep falls upon people," using a term that almost invariably refers to a "deep sleep" or "stupor" (*tardema*) that God first causes and then utilizes. Elsewhere, God does this, for example, to give messages to people he's put to sleep (Genesis 15:12), and to obscure prophecy (Isaiah 29:10). Where this exact phrase, "when deep sleep falls upon people," is used again later in Job, it's explicitly a "deep sleep" that God causes so that he can give people scary messages (Job 33:15).

This message is chilling too. Not to Eliphaz—he'll be fine. Granted, the spirit gives him the heebie-jeebies and he shudders to the bone, but his fear in that moment of phantasmagorical presence is nothing compared to the long-term effects of the spirit's psychological toying, and that part isn't aimed at him. The spirit appears to Eliphaz, but its misleading question, "Can a human being be more in the right than God?" is aimed at Job.

Eliphaz functions somewhat like a prophet, receiving "a word" from the spirit and delivering it to its intended recipient. But this is no ordinary prophetic message. Eliphaz introduces it: "A word was brought stealthily to me, my ear caught a whisper of it." Stealth, whispering . . . there's something fishy about this divine message. It turns out this is more like the other spirit incidents than it first seemed—and especially like the one other story of an embodied spirit, who uses prophets to pass on its false message.

But God's strategy this time is different in one crucial way. When Ahab's prophets receive their message from the spirit of falsehood,

God's plan is for Ahab to believe it. Not so with Job. This time, the intended recipient knows full well that the spirit's message is false. Job realizes that in his particular situation, he's "more in the right than God," and he spends virtually the rest of the book taking God to task. This is the only time a deceptive spirit's target knows the message is false—and it's perfectly in keeping with the divine manipulation of the target that we've already seen. God is screwing with Job again.

This isn't a momentary mind game. It lays the groundwork for protracted psychological torment. The spirit whispered to Eliphaz that people can't be more in the right than God, prompting Eliphaz to tell Job that he's wrong to question God—that his unspeakable losses must have been his own damned fault. Job's other friends follow suit with a battery of diatribes, pelting Job with the message that it's all his doing, right down to the lost lives of his children. And thanks to the spirit, it's all framed as being rooted in a word from God.

Job didn't get to read the prologue. The reader knows that the catastrophe came from God and the Adversary performing an elaborate experiment on Job, but all Job has is his deepest certainty that he did nothing to deserve this. Job knows it in his bones, but he's subjected to his friends' unremitting affirmations of the divine message that God doesn't cause the innocent to suffer (*but he did!*) and so Job must have brought this on himself (*but he didn't!*).

This is expert psychological manipulation, twisting the knife as Job hears over and over that he has only himself to blame, all rooted in this divine message. God uses the stealthy, whispering spirit to distort the truth, gaslighting his victim.

Apparently, the Job experiment isn't over.

Even the Adversary spoke more truthfully. He asked if Job worshipped God for nothing, suggesting that Job's righteousness was tied to protection from suffering. Job later argues precisely that his righteousness should merit divine protection. So with his original question, "Does Job fear God gratis?" and its implied *no*, the Adversary is right. The spirit, sent next to mess with Job, also poses a question about Job's righteousness: "Can a human being be more in the right than God?" This also has an implied *no*, but we've seen the tapes. Job is innocent, and this is why God has the *satan* torment him. The answer to the spirit's disingenuous question of whether a man can be more in the right than God, then, is *yes*. Emphatically, yes. The dissembling spirit distorts the truth more than the figure eventually called Satan and the "father of lies" (John 8:44).

The Deceiver of the World

By the time of the New Testament, divine deception is seen as so malevolent that it becomes a core part of the job description of Satan, the "father of lies" and "deceiver of the whole world" (Revelation 12:9). That's Satan—go big or go home. He sometimes engages in small-scale ops, deceiving one mark at a time, but mass deception is where he really shines.

God's manipulative spirits had done this job well. Because it's so blatantly wicked, though, the role of deceiver is transferred to Satan's jurisdiction . . . mostly.

And yet, when he sees fit, God still deploys his spirit of deception.

One Final "Operation of Deceit"

The New Testament letter of 2 Thessalonians—where earlier we saw angels doling out vengeance—warns people about what to anticipate as the end times approach. It starts with something predictably Satany. But then the warning veers into unexpected territory— unexpected, that is, unless you've been tracking the activities of God to this point. The writer worries that people have been deceived

MANIPULATIVE AND MIND-ALTERING SPIRITS   193

about the end times, and explains that an antichrist figure called "the man of lawlessness" will come "in accordance with the supernatural operation of Satan, with all power and signs and wonders of falsehood, and with all unrighteous deception" (2 Thessalonians 2:9–10). So far, so good. This is just what we'd expect from Satan—signs and wonders that perpetrate falsehood, and every kind of deception.

But the sentence doesn't end there. The supernatural operation of Satan is characterized by deceit "for those who are perishing because they did not receive the love of truth, that they might be saved—and for this reason, God sends them a supernatural operation of deceit, so that they will believe the falsehood" (2:10–11).

God's at it again.

In the New Testament, even after deceit has decisively come under the purview of Satan, God sends deceit so that people will believe falsehood. The awkwardness of this moment is inescapable. Deceit isn't just Satan's business in the New Testament *in general*. It's identified as his signature pursuit *in this very passage*. God engages in what was described moments earlier as the characteristic activity of Satan. We saw God and Satan like this once before, synchronized in split screen, peas in a pod.

But since when does God deceive people single-handedly? He's got a specialist for that. Lo and behold, 2 Thessalonians doesn't say that God deceives the people himself, but that "God sends them a supernatural operation of deceit, so that they will believe the falsehood." So what's a "supernatural operation of deceit," and what does it mean for God to "send" it?

Bear with me for a moment, because the Greek word here matters: God sends an *energeia* of deceit. This noun means "activity" or "operation," especially denoting "divine or supernatural action."[12] It's used eight times in the New Testament, and refers every time to the operation of a supernatural figure. It's most often the *energeia* of God, and once—two verses earlier in this very text—the *energeia* of Satan.[13] Each time, the phrase specifies whose *energeia* it is. The "*energeia* of deceit" is no exception.

Deceit isn't simply the result of God's own *energeia* (supernatural operation), which it would be hard for him to "send." Let's compare another example of the phrase. In Colossians, where the result of God's *energeia* is the resurrection, God doesn't send an *energeia* of Jesus-raising; you can't send your own supernatural activity of a result. That's as nonsensical in Greek as in English. Rather, it's "the *energeia* of God, who raised [Jesus] from the dead" (Colossians 2:12). That's how the word is used in the New Testament: *energeia* of divine figure, results stated separately. In Colossians, the result is the resurrection; in Thessalonians, the result is "that they will believe falsehood." In Colossians, the *energeia* is God's, so it's not something he can "send." In Thessalonians, God "sends" the *energeia*, because in this case it's not his own: it's the supernatural operation of Deceit.

This doesn't mean Deceit is literally a name. It probably refers to the supernatural figure by its defining trait, just like another writer refers to God by a defining trait with the phrase "the *energeia* of his mighty power" (Ephesians 1:19). Nametag or no, we can recognize the figure whose supernatural operation causes people to believe falsehood. We've seen God send such a figure many times before.

It's nice to know who we're dealing with—but for anyone hoping they'd seen God's violent deployment of monsters ratcheted up in the New Testament for the last time, this is not good news. Not only does God still send out an emissary of deceit, he now does it in perfect parallel with Satan in *his* efforts to deceive.

Some readers will surely want the New Testament to show a nice, sharp distinction between the activities of God and Satan, relegating the monstrous God and God's monsters to the Hebrew Bible. After all, once Satan has morphed into the master of evil and father of lies, you kind of hope God will let that stuff go. You'd want God's goals and Satan's to be different from one another—and their spirits, too. It should be easy as pie to tell them apart.

Another New Testament letter lays out that exact hope. This writer, too, is concerned about deception as the end times draw near. He writes of antichrists and falsehood in the last hour, and he, too, explains that he's writing this out of worry about people being deceived (1 John 2:18–26). He dwells on the issue of discerning between what comes from God and what comes from the devil (3:4–10 and elsewhere). And then he starts talking about spirits.

"Do not believe every spirit," he says, "but test the spirits to determine whether they are from God, because many false prophets have gone out into the world" (4:1). In other words, spirits that are *not* from God spread falsehood through prophets, so you have to test the spirits. If a spirit acknowledges Jesus, he explains, then it's a spirit from God, "and every spirit that does not acknowledge Jesus is not from God; this is the spirit of the antichrist" (4:2–3). In his conclusion on how to discern these spirits, he titles them: "From this we know the spirit of truth and"—wait for it—"the spirit of deceit" (4:6).

In 1 John, then, the spirit of deceit is from the antichrist. It's a Bad Thing, and wielded by Bad. This is also explicit in another New Testament letter, where the writer warns that people in later times will listen to "spirits of deceit" and teachings of demons (1 Timothy 4:1). There, too, the danger is that these spirits will persuade people who hear their false messages. Spirits of deceit are still active in the New Testament. They're just usually part of Satan's entourage—not God's.

So in Thessalonians, no wonder the supernatural operation of deceit that God sends sounds just like the supernatural operation of the antichrist and Satan two verses earlier. The purpose of both supernatural operations is to spread falsehood: the *energeia* of Satan is characterized by deception and "wonders of falsehood," and then God sends people the *energeia* of deceit "so that they will believe the falsehood." Two supernatural operations; two toxic infusions of falsehood. It's not a coincidence that the *energeia* of deceit is just like the *energeia* of Satan. The figure God sends is by this point generally in Satan's employ.

The spirit of deceit operates in 2 Thessalonians as God's deceptive spirits always have, prompting people to believe falsehood that leads to their doom. Its supernatural operation is like Satan's because divine deceit has come to be understood as so wicked that it's now among Satan's principal functions. But God still uses the same means—and to the same end.

If we've learned anything by now, it's that just when you think it can't get worse, it gets worse. God's not even just sending the operation of deceit to hoodwink the people *generally*. He does it "so that they will believe *the* falsehood"—the same falsehood already spread by the operation of Satan.[14] God uses the same method as Satan because he shares the same goal.

A reader of 2 Thessalonians might long for the clear-cut good guys and bad guys of 1 John, which has about the moral ambiguity of a 1950s *Lone Ranger* episode. As different as the two letters are, though, they share a profound concern about people being led astray: "Let no one deceive you," they both warn (2 Thessalonians 2:3; 1 John 3:7). But 1 John says this in the context of distinguishing between what comes from God and what comes from the devil, with "the spirit of deceit" neatly in column two.

The writer of 2 Thessalonians is more like Clint Eastwood in *Unforgiven* (1992), who's seen the ways of the world and has no use for pretense. He flashes this alarm signal just before the references to the twin operations of Satan and God. He tells the people not to be shaken by any false message purporting to be authentic, whether by a *spirit*, word or letter, warning them, "Let no one deceive you." Then, having just warned people not to be deceived by a spirit with a false message, he goes on to explain that God will send the supernatural operation of deceit so that the people will believe falsehood.

Let no one deceive you . . . except God.

The winds shift, and an idea is born in an unsuspecting mind. Doom is on the horizon. What's been set in motion can't be stopped.

The stealthy spirits of God's entourage in the Hebrew Bible and New Testament specialize in mental manipulation. Like others of God's supernatural cohort, spirits have been imagined in a variety of ways since the biblical period—but always as a little too close for comfort. The fear of spirits is much older than the Bible, and has thrived throughout the generations.

Possibly no monster in this book has been wielded in more perverse, destructive ways—by people, that is. In some Christian subcultures, there's a veritable free-for-all around the idea that spirits infiltrate and manipulate people's lives, and it's a pernicious form of social control. Don't approve of someone's convictions, actions, or identity? Attribute it to a "spirit of [thing you dislike]." Feminism? A spirit of rebellion! Queer? Gotta know that's some kinda spirit! The claim of cause and effect can work the other way around, too. The founder of one evangelical ministry attributes stalled goals and short-lived relationships to a "spirit of abortion," providing a handy list of things she says can open you up to "harassment by this spirit," including abortion—or even thinking that someone's abortion might have been the right choice—and having sex outside of marriage.[15] In claims like these, the implication is that the Bad Spirits come from

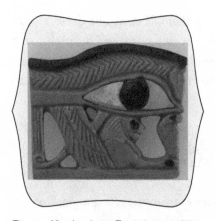

Figure 13. Ancient Egyptian wedjat eye amulet for warding off evil. Two uraeus serpents rear up at the inner eye, and a lion lies beneath, covered by a wing. (Third Intermediate Period, ca. 1070–664 BCE.)

Figure 14. Early Christian amulet for warding off evil. This side shows a winged figure surrounded by magical symbols. The other side shows narrative imagery from several scenes in the New Testament. Both sides bear inscriptions against varieties of evil.

Figure 15. Kabbalistic personal amulet against spirits, demons, and all manner of harm, written for a woman named Esther bat Miriam. The parchment shows fold creases and stains, indicating that it was carried around (18th–19th century).

Figure 16. Kabbalistic amulet to protect a house against evil spirits, along with a litany of other sources of harm (1832). If only King Saul, raving and hurling spears in his own home, had had one of these . . .

Satan. It's like they've got the devil down there going, "We've got a spirit for that." (I can't *wait* to hear what they think I've got.) In some of these degrading accusations, the effects on human lives are probably no better than in the ancient stories.

But for all the fear in some corners of spirits sent by the devil, the picture in the Bible is far more disturbing.

God's psychological warfare artists are virtuosos, adapting as needed to do their work on a single high-priority target, a group, or an entire population. His furtive spirits plant lies, obfuscate reality, and foment discord. They expertly go undetected in most missions. When they're spotted, it's a calculated part of the plan. The uniquely capable divine operatives bring about God's vengeance and his peculiar will as no other member of the entourage can.

Satan may be called the "deceiver of the whole world," but God is the commander of the heavenly army who dispatches his deceiving spirits, taking aim at Israelite kings and foreign kings, towns and cities and nations, the innocent subject of experimentation still locked in the divine laboratory—and finally, all of the people worldwide "who are perishing because they did not receive the love of truth," so he targets them with deceit leading to their eternal condemnation. Maybe God is the real "father of lies."

In the final verses of the New Testament, it is written that no one who practices falsehood will enter the new Jerusalem (Revelation 21:27; 22:15). This could pose a problem for the Almighty.

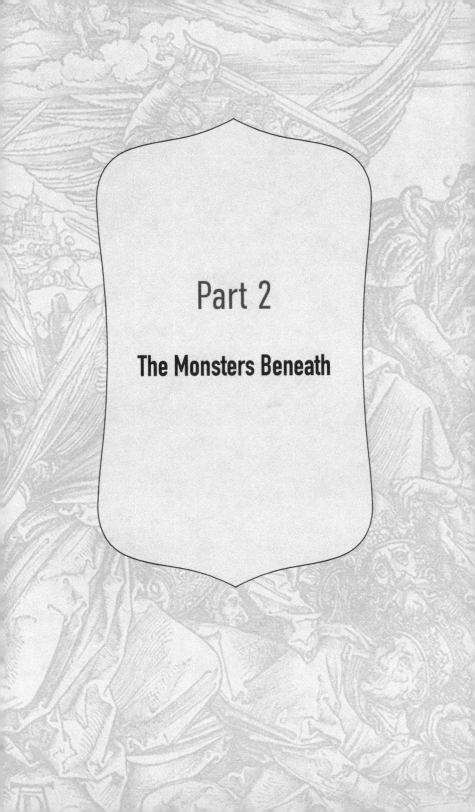

Part 2

The Monsters Beneath

7

The Sea Monster

Beneath the surface, something is moving. The dark water is too alive. The great white locks onto its next target. Water turns to wine. The massive predator devouring swimmers off the coast of Amity Island, forever reminding us that we never really know what lurks beneath, continues to terrify long after Chief Brody has killed the monster and escaped the sea alive (*Jaws*, 1975). "I used to hate the water," he says as he swims for shore with his one surviving shipmate, who responds, "I can't imagine why."

The vast open water stretches beyond what any eye can see, containing things beyond what anyone can know. What gigantic and petrifying creatures must dwell there! Sea monsters emerge and endanger from ancient legend to modern classic. Scylla snatches up sailors with the rows of razor teeth in her six heads atop snaky necks. The kraken brings down ships whole with its many arms, staring down sailors with its giant black eyes. Cthulhu terrorizes, that gelatinous squid-dragon with tentacles dangling from his horrible head.

The great beasts rising from the sea are incomprehensible, dwelling in the furthest reaches of the *elsewhere* and *beyond*. For all humankind from every varied terrain, this is the ultimate uninhabitable realm of the earth.

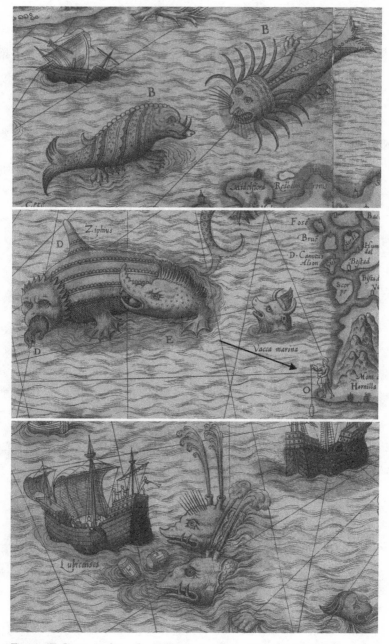

Figure 17. Section of the *Carta Marina* by Olaus Magnus, 1572, followed by details from the map.

Sea monsters loom large in the cultural imagination, as they have since long before there was a Bible.

Some monsters are born to be killed. It's not always permanent—monsters do have a way of resurfacing—but while the role of some monsters is to menace or destroy, others are there as conquests for gods and heroes to prove their strength. The primary role of the sea monster in the Bible is not to kill, but to be killed.

From the reputation Satan has gained over the last two millennia, you might think he was God's original nemesis. But long before there was a Christian devil, God had a first worst enemy: the great mythical sea monster, best known by the name Leviathan.

God has a tumultuous relationship with the sea monster. In a number of texts they fight to the death (God wins), though as we'll see, that's not all there is to their complicated dynamic. This cosmic showdown of god versus sea monster has roots deep beneath the biblical texts. Among the colorful variety of ancient Southwest Asian traditions of gods battling sea monsters is even a Canaanite myth in which the god Baal kills the monstrous sea serpent Litan, whose name and description are echoed in the Bible. The sea monster is God's most ancient foe, and the reader roots for God to kill it.

Between the Devil and the Deep Blue Sea

Most of the time when the Bible mentions the sea monster, it's getting its head bashed in. Psalm 74 offers a dramatic description of God's defeat of the monster. Before that resolution, things aren't looking too good for God's people. The psalm describes how enemies have violated the sanctuary, taken axes to it and set it on fire. The poet has one hope: that God will conquer Israel's enemies like he vanquished his own:

> You split the sea with your strength;
>> you shattered the heads of sea monsters upon the water.
> You smashed down the heads of Leviathan;
>> you gave him as food to the people, to the desert crea-
>> tures. (Psalm 74:13–14)

This monster is so forbidding that the mere memory of God's ancient victory over it is meant to reassure people looking at their hacked-up, burned-down sacred space.

It's hard not to be forbidding when you have a lot of heads. God smashes the heads—yes, plural—of Leviathan.

Not too many for God, though. God can haul up a sea monster and thrash it back down on the surface of the water. God's cracking skulls.

It's not enough just to crush the multiple heads of Leviathan. God desecrates his corpse. Remember Bad King Ahab, whose blood was licked up by dogs? The insult to Leviathan's dead body is worse. God feeds his carcass to the people dwelling in the desert—apparently picking up the corpse and chucking it a few miles inland—with leftovers for the wild animals.[1]

An oracle in Isaiah also calls up the memory of God's ancient victory over the sea monster. Isaiah uses another name for the monster, Rahab (no relation to the biblical woman whose name looks the same in English, but is different in Hebrew):

> Awake, awake, put on strength, Arm of the Lord!
> Awake, as in the days of old, generations of long ago!

> Was it not you who hacked Rahab to pieces, who pierced the sea
> monster? (Isaiah 51:9)

Both here and in Psalm 74, God slaughters his opponent himself, preferring to use divine hitmen only for human targets. Psalm 74 had God in unarmed combat with the sea monster, crushing its many rearing heads. In Isaiah 51, God is armed, chopping up the sea monster and piercing it with some divine weapon we can only imagine. In these two scenes, God's vanquishing of the dread sea monster is securely in the distant past.

But the best monsters never stay dead.

The sea monster is God's forever foe, fought and slain in days already ancient to the biblical writers but promising to resurface for another round, destined to be slain again in the most distant future. God's conclusive victory is still to come, Isaiah declares:

> On that day, God with his fierce and huge and strong sword will
> punish Leviathan the fleeing serpent, Leviathan the twisting ser-
> pent, and he will kill the sea monster that is in the sea. (Isaiah 27:1)

God is once again armed in that promised future, apparently. He slaughters Leviathan with his enormous, terrible sword while the monster twists and flees. But the irony of the forever fight is that through an assurance that God *will* slay the monster in a final showdown, the monster grows even larger. It won't be killed only once—it's like a recurring nightmare. God will always have to battle this monster.

This primordial creature is the Hebrew Bible's poster child for the dangerous looming enemy that must be defeated, so much so that Egypt and other regional enemies are sometimes referred to metaphorically as sea monsters.[2] It's no wonder, then, that in the

New Testament the sea monster develops from the great enemy into *the* Enemy.[3]

The evolution is spectacular. The sea monster becomes a "giant red dragon" with seven heads, "the ancient serpent who is called the devil and Satan, the deceiver of the whole world" (Revelation 12:3, 9; similarly 20:2). The language and imagery for the devil in these apocalyptic scenes are taken from the sea monster texts.

Where the Hebrew Bible refers to the sea monster, or even to Leviathan by name, the ancient Greek Septuagint (the Greek version of the Bible used by New Testament writers) uses the word *dragon*. The descriptions in Revelation of the devil as a giant, ancient "dragon" and "serpent" in particular are lifted from the Isaiah text we just saw, where Leviathan is both serpent and sea monster—or, in the Septuagint, "serpent" and "dragon" (Isaiah 27:1). The sea monster has become the very picture of the devil. You know you're bad to the bone when you make a good template for the Prince of Darkness.

From the first clash to the final epic battle, the sea monster is a foe for all time. This seems like a smooth trajectory if we gaze back into the mythical past: biblical writers repeatedly invoke the memory of God's victory over the monster. And looking unfathomably far into the future, the writer of Revelation identifies the great dragon and ancient serpent as the devil himself. Everything would lead us to expect consistent animosity between God and this enemy. But God's proclivities are never quite what we expect, are they?

The Heart Wants What It Wants

Slaying, smashing, crushing, piercing. From all we've seen, God is dead set on vanquishing his eternal enemy, who does seem in need of a good walloping. By all accounts, we should be cheering and raising victory fists in the air each time we see God conquer the damned thing. But elsewhere, it's a different story: God delights in his sea monster.

A God's Best Friend

Leviathan is praised as a thing of wonder in Psalm 104. The psalm marvels at creation: God stretched out the heavens like a tent, set the earth on its foundations, covered it with the ancient deep like a garment, and made the streams flow. There are branches for birds and grass for cattle. God made moon and sun, darkness and light; wild animals prowl at night, and people work all day until the evening comes.

Does this sound familiar? It should. The first twenty-three verses of the psalm name almost every facet of creation from Genesis 1. But in Genesis 1, the pinnacle of creation is humankind. The poet of Psalm 104 takes a very different view of the culmination of God's creation:

> Lord, how many are your works!
>> In wisdom you have made them all;
>> the earth is full of your creatures.
> There is the sea, great and wide;
>> creeping things without number are there,
>> living creatures small and great.
> There ships go,
>> and Leviathan, whom you formed in order to play with
>> him.[4] (Psalm 104:24–26)

Here the pinnacle of creation is *Leviathan.* And that's not all. In Genesis 1, God finishes with humankind, having finally created something "in his image" (1:26–27). Aren't we the cat's meow. But in the psalm, God finishes with Leviathan—having finally created his companion. He's God's pet.

When Crowley, *Supernatural*'s demon king of hell, keeps a hellhound as a pet, the audience understands that this reflects something hellish about Crowley ("The Devil You Know," *Supernatural* S5 E20). In Psalm 104, when God creates the sea monster as his puppy, we see a reflection of something monstrous in God.

The poet continues, directly following up this praise of Leviathan among all God's creatures:

> All of them look to you to give them their food in due season.
> You give to them and they gather it up;
> You open your hand and they are satisfied with good things.
>   (Psalm 104:27–28)

How recently we saw God slaughtering Leviathan, crushing the multiple heads of the ancient monster and feeding his carcass to the people of the desert! And yet, here is God now, playing with Leviathan and feeding the monster out of his open hand.

For the Love of Leviathan

We've seen the sea monster from two very different angles. A trusting pet looks to God for food and care. Also: heads are smacked down onto the surface of the water, a creature is pierced, a monstrous serpent twists and speeds through the deep. But for all this, we've hardly caught a glimpse of the monster's body.

One biblical book includes an extended, graphic description of Leviathan. The speaker is the one who knows him best: God.

God is addressing Job. We've witnessed what leads up to this scene multiple times, since there are so *many* monsters in the book of Job. A quick recap: God and the Adversary agree to experiment on innocent Job, curious whether he can be corrupted. God instigates it, and the Adversary's game to do his part. After sending the Adversary to kill Job's children and leave Job himself in physical agony, God sends a deceiving spirit with the message that Job is at fault. Job is consumed with grief and angry with God, who doesn't appear to be taking his calls. Only near the end of the book does God *finally* respond—but only to say to the bereaved, tormented subject of his experiment, "Gird up your loins like a man!" (Job 38:3).

With those opening words, God delivers a long speech that pointedly doesn't answer anything Job has been asking throughout his suffering. Instead, God's speech runs through the whole of creation, a lot like Psalm 104. But this time the tone isn't so serene. In a litany of rhetorical questions, God reminds Job who's who: "Where were you when I laid the foundations of the earth?" (38:4). You just know he's angrily gesturing toward the clouds: "Have you seen the storehouses of hail that I've saved for a time of trouble?" (38:22–23). After cataloguing the waters, the stars, and so on, God moves on to the next phase of creation, the animal kingdom (38:1–39:30). God gets oddly aggressive in this part of the survey of creation too, explaining to Job that the reason the ostrich's babies get killed is because it's a Bad Parent. After sending a spirit to blame Job for the death of his own children, this is no innocent zoological observation.[5] It's a slap in the face.

After the sun and moon and clouds and animals, we teeter on the edge of where we'd expect to find human beings as the crown of creation. We meet something very different instead.[6] As his long, glorious finale, God describes Leviathan.

In the praise of creation in Psalm 104, Leviathan found his place of pride even after humankind. God's speech in Job one-ups this, leaving out human beings altogether. Leviathan is the apex of creation—not after people, but *instead* of people. This is God's first hint of what he'll soon reveal, as if to say, "I made the world for this monster, not for you."

Then God starts in with another battery of questions: "Can you pull out Leviathan with a fishhook? . . . Can you put a rope in his nose? . . . Will he speak soft words to you? Will he make a covenant with you? Will you take him as a servant forever? Will you play with him like a bird?" (Job 41:1–5). Will you spear him, harpoon him, and let the traders haggle over him? (41:6–7).

The contrast with God's rhetorical questions about the earth is jarring. Those questions had pointed to God's control over creation: he determined the earth's measurements, made the boundaries of the sea (38:5, 8). This time, God's questions emphasize how Leviathan is beyond all control. Job can't go fishing for Leviathan and sell him to traders. But what isn't said here is, neither can God.

Some interpreters suggest that these questions point to things that Job can't do but God can, which is an idea with a high theological-comfort quotient. It has additional appeal, since the image of God playing with Leviathan "like a bird" would tie in nicely with Psalm 104, where God created Leviathan in order to play with him. But all swirled together within this series of questions, God also asks whether Leviathan speaks softly to Job and makes a covenant with him. If God's rhetorical questions suggest that he himself could harness Leviathan, then they also suggest that Leviathan speaks tenderly to God and that the two have a covenant.

Neither option is particularly comforting. Either God created a monster beyond his control and let him loose, or he plays with Leviathan while the sea monster whispers sweet nothings in his ear.

God has some last words of advice before coming to the climax of his speech. First, he warns of Leviathan's power. Lay a hand on him once, God says, and you'll never try it again; no one's so fierce that he should try to rouse the monster (41:8, 10). But then God veers off into threats and warnings about his own power, like a man puffing up his chest as he heatedly steps in to defend his beloved: "Who then will stand before me?" (41:10). God returns to the "gird up your loins like a man" theme, challenging, "Who will confront me, and I'll repay him? Under the whole of heaven, who?" (41:11). Try me, says God. Come at me!

With this, God turns to his awe-filled description of Leviathan:

> I will not keep silent concerning his limbs,
>> his mighty power, and his incomparable form;
> Who can strip off his outer garment,
>> who can penetrate his double coat of armor?
> Who can open the doors of his face,
>> his teeth of terror all around?
> His back is rows of shields closed up with a tight seal,
>> coming one after another so that not a breath can come between them.
> One is fused to the next;
>> they clasp each other and cannot be separated. (Job 41:12–17)

The details are alarming. Our eyes might be drawn first to his mouth, as with so many classic befanged monsters. Leviathan's giant jaws open wide to reveal terrifying teeth "all around." The Hebrew literally means "encircling." I can tell you that if you ask a roomful of students to draw what they think that mouth looks like, every picture will be different and none will be anything you want to meet in the sea. Those jaws are "the doors of his face"—not just the doors of the mouth, as in other poetry (Micah 7:5), but giant doors that open up the whole face. His enormous jaws are heavy and powerful, impossible to pry open.

His scales are like impenetrable fused shields, and even that's just the outer layer of a "double coat of armor." The terrifying teeth and hard scales give Leviathan a feel that's more crocodilian than serpentine, but with utterly unnatural features that take him far outside the scope of any living creature. His fantastic monstrosity becomes more glaring as God continues:

> His sneezes flash forth light;
>> his eyes are like the eyelids of the dawn.
> Out of his mouth go flaming torches;
>> sparks of fire escape!
> Out of his nostrils comes smoke,
>> like a basket with bulrushes ablaze.
> His breath could kindle coals;
>> flame comes out of his mouth.
> In his neck lodges strength;
>> terror dances before him.
> The folds of his flesh cleave together,
>> hard-cast and immovable.
> His chest is hard as a rock,
>> hard as the bottom grinding stone.
> When he rises up, gods fear!
>> at the crashing, they are beside themselves. (Job 41:18–25)

Leviathan breathes fire. It's like a blowtorch from his fang-ringed mouth, and smoke from his nose. At the best of times, sparks escape his jaws. His eyes glow red like the first glimmer of dawn.

Now, there's not many a sea creature with any neck to speak of, but Leviathan has a neck of brute strength. Even the folds of his flesh—literally "the drooping parts"—are hard-cast, a Hebrew word used to describe metal. His chest is like stone, and not just any old rock, but the hardest bottom grinding stone against which other things are broken to pieces.[7]

This section of the poem ends with a vivid image of the sea monster rising up and then hitting the water again with a thundering splash. Remember the good old days when the image of Leviathan hitting the water was invoked in celebration of his defeat, like the scene of a cosmic action flick where God finally vanquishes the monster? "You shattered the heads of sea monsters upon the water; you smacked down the heads of Leviathan!" (Psalm 74:13–14). This time is different. Leviathan lifts himself out of the water—and gods fear! At his crashing back down, even the gods panic.

And it's no wonder:

A sword reaching him will not endure,
      nor spear, dart, or javelin.
He thinks of iron as straw,
      and bronze as rotten wood.
The arrow cannot make him flee;
      sling-stones become chaff to him.
Clubs are reckoned as chaff;
      he laughs at the shaking of javelins.

His underparts are like the sharpest of potsherds;
      he crawls like a threshing sledge in the mud.
He makes the deep boil like a cauldron;
      he makes the sea like a pot of ointment.

Behind him, he leaves a shining wake;
      one would think the deep to be white-haired.
He has no equal upon the earth,
      a created thing without fear.
He looks upon everything lofty,
      he is king over all the proud. (Job 41:12–34)

As God paints a picture of Leviathan's body, he pauses between describing his neck and chest and his underparts for an interlude about how no weapon forged against him can stand: even if a spear were to reach him, it would break. Iron and bronze are like straw and rotten wood to him, cudgels and sling-stones like wind-blown chaff.

God has one more part of Leviathan to describe. The monster's underside is like razor-sharp potsherds—and if I've learned anything from *Swamp People*, it's that on anything even vaguely crocodilian, this should be the softest part. Not so with Leviathan. His belly is so jagged and sharp that he cuts into the ground as he crawls. That's right, the ground. The sea monster can come out of the ocean straight toward you like that girl in *The Ring* (2002) crawling out of the TV. He crawls up onto the land, scraping as he goes.

If there is any lingering question about how impossibly monstrous Leviathan is, here's another clue: he boils the deep as he swims through it. He does breathe fire, after all. His body also leaves the sea "like a pot of ointment," whatever that means—maybe he oozes slime. He shoots through the water, leaving a shining wake. Does this white trail come from his speed alone, or from the high boil the beslimed water reaches the instant he moves through it?

Leviathan has no equal, God concludes: he is the only created thing with no fear. He is unparalleled, reigning over all.

THE SEA MONSTER   219

There's no one else God talks about the way he talks about Leviathan. In all of God's speeches in the Bible, nothing compares to this twenty-three-verse description of Leviathan's incredible body, part by part. In the speeches of human beings, though . . .

Ever read Song of Songs? The lover describes his beloved's form in intimate detail, savoring each part, poetically exploring her whole body with amazement:

> How beautiful you are, my darling,
> > how beautiful!
> Your eyes are doves
> > behind your veil.
> Your hair is like a flock of goats
> > moving down Mount Gilead.
> Your teeth are like a flock of shorn ewes
> > that have come up from the washing,
> > each of which has a twin,
> > and not one of them is left without.
> Your lips are like a scarlet thread,
> > and your mouth is lovely.
> Your temples are like halves of a pomegranate
> > behind your veil.
> Your neck is like the tower of David,
> > built in courses;
> > upon it hang a thousand shields,
> > all of them shields of warriors.
> Your two breasts are like two fawns,
> > twins of a gazelle
> > that feed among the lilies. . . .
> You are altogether beautiful, my darling;
> > there is no flaw in you. (Song of Songs 4:1–5, 7)

He begins with her eyes, then describes her hair, her teeth, her lips and mouth, her temples, and moves down to her neck, and then her breasts. When the young woman in turn describes her beloved, she doesn't address him directly, but boasts of him to other women. She begins with his skin, then his head and hair, his eyes, cheeks, and lips, then moves to his arms, his belly, and down to his thighs:

> My beloved is radiant and ruddy,
>> standing out among ten thousand.
> His head is fine gold;
>> his locks are wavy,
>> black as a raven.
> His eyes are like doves
>> beside springs of water,
>> bathed in milk, sitting well in their place.
> His cheeks are like beds of spices,
>> silos of fragrance.
> His lips are lilies,
>> dripping with myrrh.
> His arms are rods of gold,
>> set with topaz.
> His belly is a panel of ivory,
>> inlaid with lapis lazuli.
> His thighs are alabaster pillars,
>> set upon foundations of gold.
> His appearance is like Lebanon,
>> distinguished as the cedars.
> His mouth is sweetness itself,
>> and he is altogether lovely.
> This is my beloved and this is my friend,
>> daughters of Jerusalem. (Song of Songs 5:10–16)

To most readers of the Bible, this form of poetry must seem unique to the Song of Songs. It isn't. The slow gaze down the loved one's body, pausing to praise each place the eye falls—the Song of Songs includes some memorable examples of this, but it's actually a well-known genre of poetry outside of the Bible, called a *wasf* (Arabic for "description").[8] Here's a snippet of an ancient Egyptian *wasf*:

Long of neck, white of breast,
her hair true lapis lazuli.
Her arms surpass gold,
her fingers are like lotuses.[9]

Even from this brief excerpt, the style of the Egyptian poetry has a familiar feel after reading the Song of Songs. The poetic form would have been even more familiar to an ancient reader. Think about how we recognize the tone of a limerick by its familiar contours: when you hear, "There once was a girl from Nantucket," you know generally what sort of poetry you're dealing with. We know the genre, and know to expect something light-hearted and likely (ahem) discourteous. In a similar way, an ancient reader or listener would recognize the tone of a *wasf*, understanding the sentiments it conveys. And also like a limerick, the composition of a *wasf* would not happen by accident in the hands of a poet.

God describes Leviathan's body as if gazing slowly over each part. This is not a biology lesson. It's a *wasf*. Don't worry, that doesn't mean it's sexual, like in the come-hither Song of Songs (the hubba-hubba *wasf* is just one type)—but it is positively an expression of intimate knowledge and passionate love.

God begins, "I will not keep silent concerning his limbs, his mighty power, and his incomparable form," and then describes Leviathan's skin, face, and teeth, his back, his eyes, mouth, and nose, then moves down to his neck, the flesh of his body, his chest, and finally his underparts. The Leviathan *wasf* ends with overall praise, as *wasfs* often do. In the Song of Songs, the beloved man is summed up as the altogether desirable lover and friend, and the beloved woman as altogether beautiful, having no flaw. God finishes his *wasf* the same way: Leviathan surpasses all others, having no fear. God's poem is an expression of love, and he lingers over every detail.

Contrast this with how God relates to Job. The first part of God's speech was already dismissive, jettisoning humankind from the survey of creation. The Leviathan *wasf* twists the knife. Job has cried out, pleading for God to respond to him in his suffering, devastated at God's utter silence. There is, it turns out, something God "will not keep silent" about. When he finally answers, he says, "My heart belongs to another."

Mortal enemy, eternal beloved—if we needed more evidence of God's ambiguous stance toward the monstrous, we're looking it right in the glowing red eyes.

We see God killing the sea monster over and over. It's satisfying every time, because the way the Bible almost always presents it, the gigantic terror of the sea *must* be destroyed. We don't want Chief Brody to decide that on second thought he loves the shark and prefers to play with it off the coast of Amity Island, pausing occasionally to recite love poetry in its name.

But God has already demonstrated that his loyalty isn't to human beings. He's shown this clearly—though he's never quite admitted it before. It turns out his true loyalty is something he can shout from the rooftops. In God's definitive picture of creation, by far the longest and most elaborate description of creation out of his mouth in the entire Bible, he omits human beings. Leaving the poet of Psalm 104 in the dust, the psalmist who recognized Leviathan as the pinnacle of creation, God swaps out any description of humankind for a classic descriptive love poem about the infamous sea monster.

To be fair, Leviathan is a better match for God. People can be so . . . *moral*. God identifies with the monster, and with the monstrous.[10] Leviathan can never be tamed, and neither can God.

The sea monster is wholly separate from God's entourage. God never deploys Leviathan on a mission or commands him to strike. His relationship with the sea monster is different. In that relationship, and in his own effusive words, God's allegiance comes into painfully sharp focus. We finally know where we stand.

8

Shades, Ghosts, and Other
Living Dead

"He's in a better place."
Hit with grief, I found few attempts at reassurance as cutting as this. It's an understandable hope, the desire for a final, definitive okay-ness: to say see, in the end, *that* is where we stand.

For some, it's a desire that also stems from a belief that this is what the Bible says about death. But the erasure of death as cruel—not only to the bereaved, but to the dead—is not a comfort. It makes a mockery of the grief that will not bear a sunshiny spin. Sometimes it's more comforting to know that even the Bible speaks of the hollow nothingness that meets the dead.

The Bible, so often both profoundly relatable and kind of bizarre, expresses this through monsters.

We see people die all over the Bible, in manners dramatic, tragic, or matter-of-fact. Those people are not in this chapter. But a few times, we also see people after their deaths. And I'm not talking about images of heaven, or even hell. I'm talking about the living dead.

The dead we encounter in the Hebrew Bible take one of two main forms: the shades who dwell in the underworld and interact at most with other dead people, and the ghosts who communicate with the living. Shades and ghosts aren't different supernatural species, the way ghosts and angels are (remember, the dead never become angels in the Bible). They reflect different modes of existence, with different relationships to the world above. It's similar to the way *ghost* in English is mostly reserved for imagining the dead who intrude upon the world of the living, while other terms are used for the dead who stay cooperatively where they belong.

In the Bible, where the dead belong isn't always where you'd hope. In the Hebrew Bible, the dead all dwell in the underworld, often called Sheol or just "the pit." The idea of heaven as people today might think of it is nowhere to be found—God lives there with his monstrous underlings, but it's not an afterlife destination. Hell hasn't been invented yet. Eternal fiery torture is just a twinkle in its Daddy's eye. In the end, the underworld is home to all, righteous and wicked alike. It's not torment, but it sure isn't bliss. As classic monster geography goes, it's hard to beat. It's the ultimate *elsewhere* and *beyond*, removed from human society but with an easy way in and a teeny-bit-too-accessible way out. It's creepy and lifeless— except for what ought to be either more or less alive than it is. The underworld is bleak, dark, and silent.

It's not all bad, though. The dead are gone, but not forgotten. That's the goal for the afterlife, at least. Remembering the dead was pivotal for their wellbeing, as we see from biblical texts to tomb inscriptions.[1] The hope wasn't to go to a Good Place instead of a Bad Place, but to be remembered rather than to be forgotten. Remembrance was how the dead lived on.

Some of this looks different by the time of the New Testament, where heaven becomes a destination for the select dead. This sounds like a nice development until you recall the other innovation, the one where lots of people get to burn in hell forever. (As with many theological developments, you win some, you lose some.) But neither part of that begins in the New Testament. The distinction between everlasting blessing and shame shows up already in the book of Daniel, and the contrast between an afterlife of peace and one of fiery punishment is featured in other pre-Christian Jewish writing (e.g., 1 Enoch 21–22, 54). The shift from Sheol to heaven and hell is a gradual process. And it's still underway in the New Testament, which reflects a variety of ideas about afterlife locations and conditions. There are still images of the underworld within the New Testament, as we'll see, and even images of Sheol in post–New Testament early Christian writing.[2] If you're looking for the comfort of a secure idea of heaven, it will have to come from something later than the New Testament.

He's Created a Monster!

Ghosts and shades aren't part of God's entourage, but they do reveal a God-monster dynamic that shows some of God's more troubling interpersonal tendencies. After considering biblical reflections on what it's like to be dead, we'll see some good old-fashioned spookiness. This journey into another dimension isn't about ghost stories, but ghosts' stories. We're taking a monster's-eye view now. And we have a lot at stake—because this time, the monster is us.

The inconvenient dead lurk in biblical texts cherished through the ages. There's nothing reassuring about the dead who "go down into silence" and "sit in darkness" (Psalm 115:17; 143:3; Lamentations 3:6). Their not-living conditions aren't the stuff of hymns.

Imagine yourself in the role of the semi-animate shades floating through the underworld, or of the ghosts that chirp and mutter from beneath the earth.

What's it like to be the monster?

Into the Darkness

Psalm 88 addresses precisely this question. The poet is sure that death is near, but that's not the worst of it. Feeling on the verge of death, the poet confronts the true horror: the afterlife.

> I am counted among those descending to the pit;
>> I have become like those who have no help,
> Cast off among the dead,
>> like the slain who lie in the grave, whom you remember
>>> no more, and they are cut off from your hand.
> You have laid me in the lowest pit,
>> in darkness, in the depths. (Psalm 88:4–6)

Death is, first, a descent. There's no highway to heaven, no shining light through pearly gates. (There are also no angels—so we can be grateful for that, at least.) The dead settle into the pit, into the lowest depths beneath the earth, into darkness.

This isn't a punishment. It's the last trip *everybody* takes. The poet looking toward this dismal future is among the faithful (88:1–2). But this earnest prayer turns to frank acknowledgment of the fate that awaits the dying.

The dead are "those who have no help." They're "cut off" from God. This isn't a punishment either, it's simply the way of the underworld. God no longer remembers them. Can't place the face, name doesn't ring a bell. This is God we're talking about, *God*-God, creator of humankind . . . who lays the dead out in a dark pit and never thinks of them again.

God's immediate loss of interest in the recently departed would be troubling under any circumstances. Imagine, though, that your entire hope for the afterlife depends on being remembered. This is what bestows the sole form of immortality, and without it you vanish. But God forgets about the dead in the underworld—hey, out of sight, out of mind—which is why the dead need the living to provide them with everlasting life. God's not good for it. Like the prophet Isaiah says, "Those who go down to the pit cannot hope for your faithfulness" (Isaiah 38:18). God ghosts the dead.

The desperate poet takes a new tack. If God isn't swayed by the pleas of the dying, maybe the prospect of missing out on praise will do the trick:

> Do you work wonders for the dead?
>> Do shades get up and praise you?
> Is your steadfast love recounted in the grave,
>> your faithfulness in Abaddon?
> Are your wonders known in the darkness,
>> or your righteousness in the land of forgetting?
>> (Psalm 88:10–12)

The "I can't praise you if I'm dead" strategy is a bit of a Hail Mary pass, but anything's worth a shot, given the dismal facts of the life for the dead we've just heard about. The dead don't praise God—because they have no reason to. God doesn't do anything for the dead, the poet writes; God's love and faithfulness aren't visible from the grave. This is pretty much as far from the image of the dead joining angels praising God in heaven as we can get.

The poet calls the underworld by one of its more foreboding names: Abaddon, place of destruction and ruin. It's not terribly surprising that the dead wouldn't declare the love and faithfulness of the God dropping bodies there.

But that's not the only reason the dead don't praise God. The underworld is also "the land of forgetting." Once the shades have been consigned to the "land of forgetting," even God's former faithfulness fades like a dream.

It's mutual, and it's hard to say which is worse: that God doesn't even remember the dead once they're gone, or that the forgotten dead in the depths of the underworld are like zombies, having lost even their own memories. They're still vaguely sentient, these semi-animate shades who are cut off and "have no help"—but they don't get up, they don't praise, and they don't remember.

Let's hope the dead forget, though. At least this would bring relief from the sense of being drowned by God, as the poet goes on to describe. Drowning your victims doesn't seem godlike—not so much for its violence as for its particular m.o. That might be because this imagery usually shows up where poets are pleading for God to save them from drowning, not where God's the one drowning them.

The poet of Psalm 88 tells a different story:

> You have afflicted me with all your breaking waves. . . .
> Your fury has swept over me,
>   your terrors have ravaged me.
> They surround me like water all day long,
>   they have engulfed me altogether. (Psalm 88:7, 16–17)

Compare that with a passage from a poem within the story of David:

> For the breaking waves of Death encompassed me,
>   the torrents of doom terrified me;
> The cords of Sheol surrounded me,
>   the snares of Death confronted me. (2 Samuel 22:5–6)

The two passages share similar imagery, structure, and even specific vocabulary. But the rest of the poem in 2 Samuel is about God rescuing David, drawing him out of mighty waters. And isn't that how it should be? How we *want* it to be? That God will sweep in and pluck the drowning sufferer from the waves? Hell, even in the book of Jonah, where God's the one who chucks Jonah into the deep blue sea in the first place, God *still* hears Jonah's plea for rescue from drowning and saves him. In Psalm 88, not only does God decline to save, God's the one holding the poet's head underwater.

God has another split-screen moment here. The poet of 2 Samuel 22 ascribes the breaking waves to Death (or death, which is still not great); Psalm 88 ascribes the waves, the fury, the terrors, all unequivocally to God. The first poet cries out, *The cords of Sheol surround me!* Our poet cries out, *The terrors of God surround me!* It's not the pain of death itself now, but of God's actions, which the poet introduces as intentional and born of anger: "Your rage leans hard on me" (Psalm 88:7). Death and Sheol are secondary. The writer knows God as the true source of suffocating terror.

For the poet of Psalm 88, this is about literal death and dying, not a metaphor for danger or despair, as in some texts. It's about descent to the pit, at the hands of God, to become one of the forgotten shades.

The shades abide their muted existence in the underworld, a place of no light, no help, no praise—neither any new reason to praise in the afterlife, nor any memory of things praiseworthy. The blasé deity is done with them. God deposits the dead in the darkness and never looks back. The dead are only returning the favor.

In the Midst of the Darkness

It's an ancient version of a modern classic: "You're going down, sucker." The prophet Isaiah taunts the king of Babylon, congratulating him on the warm welcome that awaits him—by the dead, as he joins them in the underworld. "Sheol below shakes for you, to greet your arrival; it rouses the shades for you" (Isaiah 14:9).

Figure 18. Miniature of "The Three Living and the Three Dead" from the *De Lisle Psalter* (ca. 1308–1340). In the story, three decaying corpses appear and give warnings about the inescapability of death. Worms crawl around the belly of the dead figure on the left.

If you were hoping that Psalm 88 was the gloomy view of one depressed poet, that Isaiah might envision a brighter afterlife—sorry, no. Isaiah describes how Sheol rouses the shades to greet the newcomer. Even in Sheol, the shades need to be awakened in order to interact. Their default state is a sort of suspended animation.

Then the shades speak. In creepy unison, they say to the king, "You, too, have become as weak as we are!" (14:10). This is what awaits the dying. Not glory, but weakness.

Lord knows, the hope for an eternal distinction between Us and Them (whoever the We and They are) is widespread and relished. But don't look for it in Isaiah. What sets the king's wretched fate apart from everyone else's is just the degree of gloating it warrants.

Isaiah describes the undifferentiated dead in Sheol again in another oracle, and this time he brings it on home. We land back in that horror montage leading up to the demon Haby's invasion of Israelite homes. Isaiah writes, "The dead do not live, shades do not rise—you have punished and destroyed them, and wiped out all memory of them" (Isaiah 26:14).

Isaiah could have read the bleakest parts of Psalm 88 and said, "Yep, that checks out." At least in the psalm, God only forgets the dead himself, leaving their afterlife in the hands of the living, who can memorialize them and keep them alive. In Isaiah, God punishes the people by wiping out any memory of them, extinguishing not only their life, but their afterlife.

When Isaiah comes to the more upbeat part of his oracle, check out what changes: "Your dead will live! Their corpses will rise! Awake and sing, you who dwell in the dust! . . . The earth will push out the shades of the dead" (26:19). We've gone from "The dead do not live, shades do not rise," to "Your dead will live! Their *corpses* will rise!" If you read that really fast you can pretend it's a good thing. But the dead don't suddenly have a better quality of afterlife. When people are dead and buried, they stay in their semi-animate state. It's just that now the earth is vomiting out their corpses. The final line might be the most disconcerting: it's only corpses that rise, and they're still shades when the earth pushes them out. What is walking around out there?

Up from the Darkness

The dead aren't always content to remain silent and listless in Sheol. Sometimes, ghosts down in the depths of the underworld make eerily inhuman sounds that can be heard topside. That chilling tidbit comes from Isaiah, too. In an oracle about necromancy, he describes people suggesting to one another, "Consult the ghosts and familiar spirits that chirp and mutter!" (Isaiah 8:19). In another of Isaiah's oracles, God warns people that when he's through with them, they'll speak from beneath the earth and "chirp" like ghosts (29:3–4).

And then there's the time we witness a ghost rise to have a chat with the living.

In this scene the prophet Samuel is dead, and his ghost has been not-living in the underworld. This isn't because the prophet broke bad. He's in the underworld because that's where everyone goes. Live Sam was always faithfully on the side of God, and God on the side of Live Sam. Once he dies, though, hey, relationships change—just like the poet of Psalm 88 expects. Samuel has been let go.

King Saul, the story unfolds, goes to visit a necromancer in Endor. In later interpretation this woman is called "the witch of Endor," but she's not a witch in the Bible. There's a Hebrew word for that, and it's not used here. Frankly, a "witch" would be tame in comparison. This woman is a specialist in raising the dead for the purposes of communication. In Hebrew, she's called a "ghost-diviner."[3]

The story begins with a reminder that God was refusing to talk to Saul. You see, ever since God switched his affections to David, removing his spirit from Saul and sending an evil spirit to rile him up, God no longer gives Saul the time of day. Saul keeps seeking God's help, but God won't answer (1 Samuel 28:6). So, frightened and in desperate need of guidance before heading into battle, King Saul decides to try to contact the ghost of Samuel. Samuel once had his back—until the time Saul failed to execute God's hit order against the Amalekite king, at which point Samuel washed his hands of Saul and refused to ever speak to him again (15:1–35). But right now, Saul is hoping the dead prophet can let bygones be bygones.

To complicate matters, all necromancers have been exiled—by Saul. This doesn't reflect poorly on the necromancer, though. After all, Saul also slaughters eighty-five priests (22:17–18). It's just that

King Saul is always shooting himself in the foot, so naturally as soon as he gets rid of the necromancers, he finds that he needs one. And, in a charming moment right out of an upstairs-downstairs comedy, the king's servants know just where to go to find one. The group heads out in the dark of night so that Saul, in disguise, can seek the services of the woman who can summon ghosts from the earth.

Saul arrives in Endor and makes his request to the necromancer: "Divine for me by a ghost, and raise for me the person I tell you to" (28:8). She does. Necromancy is presented here as authentic and effective, as it is in several other biblical texts. The necromancer does her work without a hitch, raising the ghost for Saul, and characters and narrator alike all find this perfectly reasonable.

For anyone with miraculous resurrection on the brain: the necromancer raises a ghost, not a body. The writer provides a careful reminder that Samuel had died and been buried in the city of Ramah—not Endor. What the necromancer raises from beneath the ground is the ghost of Samuel.

The ghost has to rise up through the earth in order to appear at ground level. The necromancer describes it as it's happening: "I see a supernatural being coming up out of the ground" (28:13). She sees an old man rising up, wearing a robe. He's a little like the "Subway Ghost" who shows Patrick Swayze how to save the day (*Ghost*, 1990)—still recognizable, deeply cranky, eventually helpful, and still wearing his old clothes.

Saul can hear the ghost clear as day, and there's no question about its identity. It's Samuel, through and through. The ghost of Samuel asks Saul a question, and the two have a conversation, just like old times.

And this is the question the irritable ghost of Samuel asks: "Why did you shake me to bring me up?"

Up. Not down.

This line is consistently translated, "Why have you disturbed me by bringing me up?" (e.g., NRSV, NASB, NKJV, NIV), but that misses Samuel's state in the underworld. The first verb literally means to "shake" something, like when God shakes the earth (Job 9:6). The second means "*in order to* bring me up." It's not that being summoned disturbed Samuel, but that his ghost had to be shaken awake in the underworld in order for it to be raised.

This is pretty grim, even on its own. But we've seen the dead shaken awake in Sheol before. It's the same image we saw in Isaiah's oracle to the Babylonian king: "Sheol below shakes," the prophet says; "it rouses the shades for you" (Isaiah 14:9). Sheol shakes, like a supernatural underworld earthquake, to wake its residents—at least into a more animate state of deadness. Same idea, same Hebrew verb (in intransitive and transitive forms), as in our ghost story. Samuel asks, "Why did you shake me to bring me up?" because just like the shades in Isaiah who need to be shaken awake to greet one king, the ghost of Samuel in the underworld has to be shaken awake for another. The state of those shades in Isaiah seemed pretty dismal— and Samuel has met the same fate.

If already the ghost of a prophet needs to be shaken out of its semi-animate state in Sheol, you might hope that at least God would be the one to do it. But God's no more in control of what happens than Samuel is. He'd refused to get involved with King Saul's tiresome pleas for help. The raising of Samuel's ghost happens by the necromancer's power alone. God has no say in the matter.

When the conversation between Samuel's ghost and Saul begins, the writer repeats that God had cut Saul off from all divine communication, as if to stress that the power enabling this act of supernatural communication was Definitely Not God. Saul complains to the ghost that God has "departed" from him, and the ghost confirms, you got that right, "the Lord has departed from you," both using the same language from the story of how this all began, when the spirit of God departed from Saul, vacating the premises for the evil spirit (1 Samuel 16:14; 18:12; 28:15–16). God is still emphatically not with Saul, and the ghost itself confirms that it sure isn't there on God's behalf.

Abandoning Saul in favor of David was one thing. We find out now that God has abandoned the ever-faithful Samuel, too. Raised for a moment, he'll descend again when the necromancer's work is done, returning to the semi-animate state of the shades—cast off, in the darkness, forgotten.

Then again, hell is not a huge improvement. Forgetting the shades is more merciful than what develops later. As Jesus explains from the boat to all those gathered on the shore, his angels will chuck people "into the furnace of fire, where there will be weeping and gnashing of teeth" (Matthew 13:41–42; and once more for those in the back, 13:49–50). People will be tortured with fire and sulfur, and the smoke of their torment will rise forever and ever (Revelation 14:10–11; 20:15; 21:8).

This is a god you *want* to forget you.

More comforting concepts of the afterlife develop too, of course—at least, if you're betting you're on God's good side. Though be advised, the New Testament is inconsistent about how to avoid burning in hell, which is really not cool for something so high-stakes. In one of the final visions of the New Testament, the voice from heaven announces, "I am the Alpha and the Omega," and then gives a handy breakdown of the hellbound, including big baddies like murderers—but also liars, and for god's sake "the fearful" (Revelation 21:6–8).

Ideas about the afterlife are still in flux in the New Testament. The criteria for how to avoid hell are a moving target. Hell itself shifts shapes, too.

The word *hell* in English Bibles reflects an attempt to harmonize a range of New Testament terms—Hades, Gehenna, Tartarus, the abyss—each with its own nuances. Among those is the Greek word for Sheol. *Hades* was the word for Sheol in the Septuagint, the Greek translation of the Hebrew Bible used by New Testament writers. So when New Testament writers use *Hades*, it reflects a continuity with Sheol that you wouldn't catch in translation.

Jesus tells one parable in which we get to zoom in on an individual afterlife, and it turns out to capture a moment in the transition from Sheol to two separate afterlife locales. There's a rich man in Hades, and somewhere that's visible to him, a poor man in the company of Abraham. The rich man wants help because, as he calls over to Abraham, he's "in agony in these flames" (Luke 16:24). This is "Hades"—the writer's using the Greek word for Sheol—and everyone's within earshot. The two distinct areas, an unpassable chasm apart, might even be two "compartments of the underworld."[4] More to the point, the underworld's gotten spicier, now featuring fiery torture for the dead—and also, in the worst possible tandem development, complete consciousness.

The New Testament hasn't settled on one image of hell (or how to steer clear of it), but even this snapshot of a transitional stage is worse than anything we saw in the Hebrew Bible. The last time we zoomed in on someone in the afterlife, he was only aware of having been shaken awake. The worst Samuel got was cranky cosmic jetlag—the worst he was conscious of, at least.

In retrospect, God's utter lack of concern for the shades in Sheol may be our best hope. Of course, "on the brighter side, it's better than hell" is a low bar. There's a *Choose Your Own Adventure* in here somewhere.

It's clear how disturbing people found the idea of being forsaken and forgotten in Sheol. The later theological need to change that narrative, still in process throughout the New Testament, reveals deep discomfort with the notion of a hollow nothingness awaiting us all. Is the desire to see differentiation and justice in the afterlife only a matter of hope for ourselves, or is it also a hope to redeem the character of God?

Then again: eternal fire-torture. It's not *entirely* clear that this development is redemptive for God's character. Sheol was desolate, but it's no match for being cognizant of one's eternal agony in flames.

At least the semi-animate dead aren't cognizant of their loss of humanity. For that, you need to be just on this edge of descent into the pit—like the poet of Psalm 88, who faces that nightmarish metamorphosis and grieves the betrayal by the God who created human beings, only to drown them beneath the waves of his divine fury and cut them off forever, never tossing a glance back.

And yet, here in this bleakest of biblical moments, an ultimate reality of the human experience is given voice, recognized as it is nowhere in the pictures of a happy afterlife. Rage, rage against the dying of the light.

Do any of the other monsters we've met stop to wonder how they became monsters? This must be the unique purview, and curse, of the human being. The poet contemplates the dematerialization from full-color human life into the remote existence of a shade, becoming a monster at the hands of a monster.

Doomed to repeat the sins of the Father, the people go forth and create monsters of their own. This time, the monster was us—next time, it's Them.

9

Giants

Every type of monster we've met so far shows some internal variety—cherubim statues and the living cherubim-chariot, or the formless lying spirit in the mouths of Ahab's prophets and the gaslighting spirit who brushes by Eliphaz, looks him in the eye, and starts posing questions. When we meet biblical giants, we need to pull back and notice a broader type of variation. The giant tales comprise two different kinds of myths. One reflects the writers' ideas about certain divine beings in heaven. The other reveals views of certain people on earth. Content warning: both are horrible.

The first kind shows up once in the Bible, spanning just a few verses, but its imprint may well be familiar thanks to its massive pop culture afterlife. In a fleeting picture of a distant mythical past, like a fragment of a dream, it imagines the world before the flood, when the nephilim walked the earth.

The second kind of myth imagines specific people as giants. These stories are written as if they're historical. (They're not.) This phenomenon isn't unique to the Bible, it's wildly problematic, and we need to snap to attention.

Monsterization is nothing new—and it's not just talk. Describing people as monstrous, as aberrations and somehow not perfectly human, serves to rationalize persecution, oppression, racism, and murder. From the medieval Christian monsterization of Jews and Muslims to the present-day monsterization of gender-nonconforming people, people with disabilities, Black people, and more, people have characterized those who differ from them as monstrous, sometimes to horrific ends.[1] If certain people are "monsters," it becomes seemingly heroic to defeat them.

Every Body Has a Backstory

The fleeting tale of the birth of half-divine, half-human nephilim is scarcely more than a snapshot in the Bible. A rich modern mythology has grown up around the nephilim (*Supernatural*, *The Mortal Instruments*, *Fallen*, *Magic: The Gathering*), but in the Bible itself they're not even the main characters of their own story. The biblical tale is one of how they came into being—of monsters created through monstrous acts.

Rosemary's Babies

The beginning of Genesis tells tales of the early generations of humankind and the Very Bad Things they do. Adam and Eve defy God, Cain murders Abel. Things aren't going according to plan with these people. Then it turns out God's got his own family scandals. Tucked between the stories of Cain and Abel and the flood, there's a vignette involving the divine family. Like other early Genesis stories, where people are eyeing fruit in Eden and building a tower in Babel, this one too is about a threat to the boundary between the human and divine realms. But this time, the breach comes from the divine side.

The women on earth are minding their own business when the "sons of God" (generic lower-level divine beings, not the specific species called angels) notice them, think they're attractive, and impregnate whomever they want. The offspring are called the nephilim, and are described as famous ancient mighty men:

> When humankind began to multiply on the face of the earth and daughters were born to them, the sons of God saw the daughters of men, that they were attractive, and they took women for themselves, whomever they chose. . . . The nephilim were in the land in those days (and also afterward), when the sons of God had sex with the daughters of men, and they bore them children. They were the mighty men of old, men of renown. (Genesis 6:1–4)

In the grand tradition of cleaning up the Bible, a lot of translations say the sons of God took "wives" (NRSV, NASB, NKJV). But the Hebrew word means "women," and though the phrase elsewhere can refer to marriage, the point in this story is explicitly that the divine beings liked what they saw and "took women for themselves, *whomever they chose.*" Two verses later, this is summed up bluntly as the time "when the sons of God had sex with the daughters of men." As in so many stories of gods having their way with women (a dime a dozen for Zeus alone), it's not marriage, it's rape.

Centuries later, the noncanonical book of Enoch will develop these ideas into a complex saga about angels (or "watchers") going bad, raping women and being punished by God. But in Genesis, the predatory divine beings aren't the focus. The godlets rape women and vanish from the story. The focus is on the nephilim, and how they came to exist—not the violation of the women, but the violation of the boundary between realms, between natural and supernatural species. The Genesis text doesn't emphasize that it's rape, but that it's interspecies sex. Even the terminology, repeatedly juxtaposing "the sons of God" and "the daughters of men," highlights the difference in species. It's like a divine being's version of bestiality, and it results in monstrous, hybrid offspring. This is the semidivine island of Dr. Moreau.

The word *nephilim* may even mean something like "monstrous births." It's plural (like *seraphim, cherubim*), so if you've learned a day of Hebrew in your life, the insistent pop culture use of "a nephilim" will be like nails on a chalkboard. The word has something to do with falling, but the nephilim aren't "fallen" in a theological sense. That concept develops later. They also didn't "fall" from heaven, since they were never in heaven to begin with. Elsewhere, the noun refers to fetuses that are "fallen"—that is, miscarried (Job 3:16; Psalm 58:8; Ecclesiastes 6:3). While nobody really knows its meaning in Genesis 6, a strong possibility is that the word for miscarried fetuses is used here in the broader sense of "anomalous" or so-called "monstrous births," which people were remarkably fixated on in other writing from the region.[2]

As classic monster traits go, it's hard to get more explicitly hybrid than being introduced through the story of your parents' cross-species sexual encounter. The partly human, partly divine nephilim are the ultimate category violation, who are the product of the ultimate boundary violation.

The writer of Genesis says nothing more about the nephilim, who are assumed to be familiar: they're the famous ancient mighty men. The Hebrew doesn't even specify that they're giants, though the Greek Septuagint renders both "nephilim" and "mighty men" in verse 4 as "giants." This is a logical assumption, since it was common in regional mythology for semidivine offspring to be giant.

Whatever the original intention, the Genesis 6 tale becomes the origin story for giants. The Septuagint already reflects that understanding, and it's explicit in some Jewish apocalyptic literature like

1 Enoch and the Book of Giants, where divine beings rape women and the hybrid offspring are giants.

The nephilim are giants the next time they show up in the Bible, too. When members of Moses' band of wandering Israelites first encounter the inhabitants of Canaan, they describe them as giants—and as Nephilim, now used as the name of an ethnic group. In one go, this turns the Genesis 6 tale into an origin story for giants, and into an origin story for some of the people of Canaan.

As we move ahead in the Bible to the episode when the nephilim resurface, it's no longer monsters we see. Now, it's monsterization.

Who's Creating Monsters Now?

In ancient literature, one common type of monsterization goes beyond describing people in monstrous terms. Writers depict tribes of monstrous people living in lands that are themselves portrayed as unfamiliar. (This is where your ears might prick up if you already know the biblical stories of the giants of Canaan.) Sometimes these monstrous groups are the indigenous inhabitants of a desired land, as in the writing of Megasthenes following Alexander the Great's invasion of India.[3] There are all sorts of wild physical anomalies: dog-headed people, the umbrella-footed (what better to shade yourself with than your single giant foot?), those whose feet face backward, and the classic: giants.[4]

Some tales of monstrous tribes living in unfamiliar lands were written by people who had actually traveled and encountered unfamiliar people, and some weren't. But even tales that had roots in encounters with real people obviously don't portray . . . well, real people. In ancient discourse, not unlike today, observers see individuals whose cultural norms differ from their own—customs, clothing, diet, speech, values—and a "monstrous people" is born.[5] As monster theorist Jeffrey Jerome Cohen puts it, "The monster is difference made flesh, come to dwell among us."[6] Monstrosity is in the eye of the beholder.

I'll Eat You Alive

Egypt is in the rearview mirror. God is leading the Israelites through the wilderness, pausing occasionally to attack them along the way when he gets mad, shooting fire and plague at them (Numbers 11:1–3, 33–34). Moses sends some men to scout out the land of Canaan and report back. He adds a minor assignment that turns out to set up a major revelation: to bring back some fruit (13:17–20).

The scouts set out. They find fruit, alright. They cut down a branch with a cluster of grapes so large that two men need to carry it on a pole between them. It's said repeatedly to be a single cluster, meaning that it has one stem so enormous it can bear up the whole load. The beloved image of Israelites carrying giant grapes isn't just conveying how bountiful the land is; it's ominous foreshadowing, like Jack climbing the beanstalk and finding a suspiciously giant copper pot. This is the giant fruit of giant *giants*.[7] Gives a whole new meaning to "You will know them by their fruits" (Matthew 7:16).

The scouts come back. They've got some good news and some bad news. The land is flowing with milk and honey—good news—"and *this* is its fruit," which brings us to the bad news. They finally say who they saw there, using a name the characters recognize: it was the Anakim. The scouts drop this bombshell in front of all the Israelites, so even before they describe the giants, a hullabaloo ensues.

An aggressive outlier among the scouts, Caleb, silences the people. He wants to go back and take possession of the land right then and there, sure the Israelites can take them. The rest of the scouts beg to differ.

Figure 19. Scouts carrying giant grapes. Detail from the façade of the Duomo, Milan.

The scouts make their case: "It's a land that eats up its inhabitants, and all the people we saw in it were of great size. There we saw the Nephilim (the Anakim are among the Nephilim), and we were like grasshoppers in our own eyes—and also in theirs!" (Numbers 13:32–33).[8]

There it is. The inhabitants of the land have been identified first as giants—let's call that Level One monsterizing—and then as a specific breed of giants descended from the hybrid offspring of natural and supernatural species. Level Two goes all in, assigning them an abhorrent origin and making them a violation of the natural order.

As disturbing as all the monsters we've seen so far have been, at least they were *monster*-monsters. Suddenly we're up against something quite different—and not better.

Despair runs through the crowd. The people weep and wail and want to go back to Egypt. Caleb and his one ally, Joshua, insist that "the land is very, very good," and add, "If the Lord is pleased with us, he will bring us into this land and give it to us, a land that flows with milk and honey" (14:7–8).

They could have stopped there: land good, God good. But they continue. They warn their fellow Israelites, "Do not fear the people of the land, for they are our food; their protection is removed from them, but the Lord is with us. Do not fear them!" (14:9).

Hold everything, the people are our *what*? Our food? Keep in mind that the rest of the scouts just warned everyone that the land "eats up its inhabitants." Caleb and Joshua's remark isn't a throwaway line, it's a rebuttal: the land doesn't eat its inhabitants, *we* do! Those people are our food, and we'll eat them alive.

God's got an opening here. This is his chance to take the moral high ground. Instead, he sides emphatically with Caleb and Joshua, who've just described people as nothing more than food to be devoured. And those who don't want to fight the giants, God promises to kill off. "Your dead bodies will fall in this wilderness!" he repeatedly vows (14:22–35).

God makes good on his promise. First, he strikes the scouts with a fatal plague (14:36–37), and then wipes out countless others in various ways over the course of the Israelites' continued wanderings. One time, fire shoots out of God and consumes 250 men (16:35). Later, God kills another 14,700 Israelites with plague (16:45–49).

This all culminates in the incident of the seraphim-snakes in chapter 21, bringing us full circle back to the first horror story in this book.

One vignette in this death-by-divine-hand series seems like the kind of perfect retort God would only look back and *wish* he'd thought of in the moment. Some men challenge Moses's authority, saying he hasn't brought them into a land of milk and honey. (To be fair, he hasn't.) God makes the ground open its mouth and swallow them whole (16:30–33). God's gone from straightforward divine vengeance to mocking people to death: You're scared that the land of Canaan eats up its inhabitants? I can make the land of this here desert eat up its inhabitants—who at present, my friends, are you.

Chomp, chomp. Delicious.

Caleb's retort as he tried to rally the Israelites was essentially, "The land doesn't eat up its inhabitants, we do." God one-ups him: "*Any* land will eat up whomever *I make* it eat up, Israelites included." No reason left not to head into the land of the giants, then.

Monsterization takes a bow. It has served its purpose well. The inhabitants of the land are giants! Not only that, they're even Nephilim! We'll eat them for breakfast. Rather than disavowing that hot take, God doubles down, eliminating the opposition one group of Israelites at a time. Go forth and slay the giants.

Deja Vu

Later, Moses retells the story of the scouts to the surviving cohort as they prepare to finally enter the land of Canaan. This version zooms out, and we get to see what's been going on throughout the region. First, Moses recalls how terrified the people had been when the scouts reported: "The people are bigger and taller than we are—the cities are big, and walled up to the sky!" (Deuteronomy 1:28). In Numbers, we saw the giant produce; here, we have the giant city, walls built alarmingly high. Moses assures the people that God will fight for them. Then, the backdrop: God will help them defeat giants so they can settle in the land he's giving them. Just like he's helped other people conquer other giants and settle in other lands.

Yeah, that part of the story doesn't get as much press.

The tidbits come out piecemeal. Moses continues his story: God told the Israelites wandering in the wilderness not to go up against Moab because he'd already given that land to other people, namely the Moabites. But it turns out the land wasn't empty when he gave it to them. The narrator interjects some backstory we haven't heard before: a tribe of giants called the Emim used to live in Moab, and they were every bit as tall as the Anakim, but God gave their land to the Moabites instead (2:9–10). The narrator reveals that several of the neighboring lands were also once inhabited by giants—but God conquered each group of giants and gave the land to the people he chose. The Zamzummim used to live in Ammon, and they too were every inch as tall as the Anakim, but God vanquished those giants as well: "The Lord wiped them out from before the Ammonites, so they could dispossess them and settle there in their place" (2:19–21).

Then come two more groups, the Horim and Avvim, who aren't explicitly described as giants, the way the Emim and Zamzummim are, but the narrator includes them as examples of the same phenomenon, explaining that God wiped out giants for the Ammonites "just as he did for the descendants of Esau who live in Seir, when he wiped out the Horim from before them, so they dispossessed them and settled there in their place to this day. And the Avvim, who were living in villages as far as Gaza, the Caphtorites who came from Caphtor wiped them out and settled in their place" (2:22–23). God moves people around like chess pieces, knocking off indigenous giants and placing whomever he chooses in their land.

If this seems to you like a lot of names to take in, you're not alone. The narrator mentions a couple of times that the Israelites just call all giants "Rephaim"—even though the giants of each land had distinct names. Take a moment to appreciate the layers here. The Israelite narrator, aware of a convention of blurring the groups, takes pains to clarify that all giants aren't the same, explaining that while they've all been considered Rephaim, the Moabites call the giants of Moab "Emim" and the Ammonites call the giants of Ammon "Zamzummim" (2:11, 20).[9] This careful explanation distinguishing the various populations of giants is all still within a mythology where every land has an indigenous population of giants warranting slaughter. But they're *different* giants.

One of the slaughtered giants gets a name: Og, king of Bashan. Moses is further along in his story now, reminding the people how they defeated Og and conquered his region, leaving no survivors. Our narrator, ever interested in giant lore, explains that the whole region used to be called the "land of the Rephaim," and that Og was the last of the Rephaim. We get a bit of juicy detail here: giant King Og's bed was made of iron and measured thirteen and a half feet long by six feet wide (3:11, 13).

But not even the narrator's preoccupation with explicating giant mythology can overshadow the priorities of the characters them-selves. Moses uses the Og story to take aim at the next targets, asserting that just like God conquered Og, God will conquer the next kingdoms for the Israelites too. Don't fear them, Moses says, because God himself is fighting for you (3:21–22).

That promise is where Moses had begun, when he retold the story of the scouts. Later, he returns to this theme again: once the Israelites are all up to speed, he looks ahead, assuring them that God will go before them as a "consuming fire" and wipe out the mighty Anakim so the Israelites can dispossess them (9:1–3). And you can be sure God's good for it—since this is precisely what the narrator says God already did for the Ammonites and others, with the giants of *their* lands (2:21–23).

One difference in wording stands out. This time God is a "consuming fire," as traditionally translated. "Consuming" has the poetic advantage, but the word is an everyday one we've seen before: "eating." The objects here, let's recall, are people. Good to know he's still eating people alive.

You Animal

Our first close-up of a giant, King Og of Bashan, was hardly more than a tantalizing glimmer. For our next giant sighting, we skip ahead to a time when Israel is already established in the land. Saul is king, though mediocre and insecure (especially since the attacks by an evil spirit from God have already begun). As the scene opens, the Philistine and Israelite armies are facing each other on mountain-tops, with a valley between them. A Philistine giant comes out to challenge any Israelite who will face him: Goliath of Gath, coming in at over nine and a half feet.

Goliath is wearing a bronze helmet and full armor. The coat alone weighs over 125 pounds, and he's also wearing bronze shin guards, with a bronze scimitar slung between his shoulders. He's carrying a spear, the shaft of which is like a weaver's beam. The spearhead alone weighs more than fifteen pounds (1 Samuel 17:4–7).[10] From helmet to shin guards and everything in between, he's loaded up with the weight of a good-sized refrigerator.

Goliath dares anyone to come on down: "I defy the ranks of Israel today! Give me a man, so we can fight each other!" (17:10). Saul's shaking in his boots, but here comes young David, who's been off feeding his father's sheep. He shows up just in time to hear Goliath's challenge, which he accepts. This plan is met with some skepticism. David claims that he's had to kill lions and bears that attacked his family's flocks. At first, it seems he's just proving his heroic experience—but then he explicitly compares Goliath to one of the animals he's killed. He tells Saul, "Your servant has killed both lion and bear, and this uncircumcised Philistine will be like one of them" (17:36).

They give David armor, but he can't walk in it (highlighting Goliath's comfort sauntering around in his refrigerator). Instead, David opts for a stick, a sling, and a few stones, and heads out to face Goliath. The two trash-talk a bit. *Goliath*: "Am I a dog, that you come at me with sticks? . . . Come at me! I'll feed your body to the birds of the air and the wild animals of the field" (17:43). *David*: "I'll strike you down and cut off your head, and give the corpses of the Philistine army to the birds of the air and the animals of the earth" (17:46). Goliath gets up—which implies that he's been sitting down, maybe in casual mockery of David—and approaches. David runs at him and reaches into his pocket for a stone. The rest is (not) history.

David's sure of his victory from the start, because God is on his side. Even his description of Goliath as an animal that needs to be put down presents God as the one to do it. Right after comparing Goliath to one of the animals he's killed, he adds that the God who saved him from those animals will save him from "this Philistine" too (17:37).

David's trash talk is also all wrapped up in the idea that God will fight the giant for him. David tells Goliath that God's about to deliver him up so that David can cut off his head (which he does, after his more famous first move). Goliath is going down, and the whole Philistine army with him, because "the battle is the Lord's" (17:46–47).

"Am I a dog?" asks Goliath in his final moments—right before he's put down like the other animals David killed, with God on his side.

Along with a few other individual giants whose slayings merit one-liners, Goliath is the last of the biblical giants. But wait . . . weren't the giants defeated in the conquest of Canaan, and wasn't King Og said to be the last of the giants when he was killed? For that matter, shouldn't the original nephilim have all drowned in the flood?

Ancient Jewish writers noticing these biblical inconsistencies suggested ideas about what might have happened. One rabbinic text, for example, spins a tale about how giants survived the flood, simultaneously playing on the notion that King Og was the last surviving giant (Deuteronomy 3:11). In this charming vignette, Og is among the original giants, and when the flood comes, he hunkers down on a rung of the ladder on the outside of the ark. Noah, having cut some sort of deal with him, bores a hole in the ark and feeds the giant through it.[11]

Staying within the biblical tradition, though, there's no way to explain away the discrepancies. Like so many classic monsters from Leviathan to Michael Myers (of the *Halloween* franchise), biblical giants are survivors: each time it seems they've been eradicated, they resurface in some slightly varied form, ready to go after the next storyline's heroes with renewed vigor.[12]

After a good thrashing at a few key points, this long-surviving foe, simultaneously superhuman and subhuman, is eventually wiped out for good.[13] At each stage, the giants are God's to vanquish. "The Lord your God is the one fighting for you," says Moses. "The battle is the Lord's," says David. God finally uses that almighty power to help his people fight the monsters that surround them. Unlike with the array of monstrous creatures he uses to threaten and kill people from Genesis through Revelation, this time God is super gung-ho about slaying the monsters. This time. When they're people.

These giants aren't monsters—they're human beings who have been monsterized. And specifically, they're foreigners. The Israelites

Figure 20. "Og, riding gaily on the unicorn behind the Ark, was quite happy." Illustration and caption from *Jewish Fairy Tales and Legends*, Gertrude Landa, 1919.

encounter group after group and individual after individual who are primarily identified as foreigners, and secondarily as giants.

First, this is the premise of the story of the scouts, who are sent to find out what the people of Canaan are like. Then, we move to the story of the Israelites wiping out the population of Bashan and defeating their king, Og. The narrator slips in the parenthetical comment that Og was the last of the Rephaim, and one can still gawk at his giant iron bed. Later, we meet Goliath, who isn't even purportedly from a distinct ethnic group of giants—he's a Philistine through and through, their warrior, their pride, introduced as "Goliath of Gath" (a Philistine city) and repeatedly called "this Philistine." The other scattered references to giants are also all about foreigners, including several Philistines and one Egyptian, and each reference includes a focus on killing them.[14]

It's only certain people who are identified as giants: a group of Anakim in Canaan, a single giant among the Philistines. But the presence of the monsterized foreigners in the spotlight colors the whole group, valorizing the violent defeat of them all. A few giants here and there, and all of Canaan is ripe for conquest. Goliath is an aberration among the men of Gath, but as the public face of the Philistines in the Bible, his anomalous form as a giant in need of a good slaying casts a monstrous shadow on the whole Philistine army—and they become monstrous by association. Monstrosity is a color that bleeds.

Biblical giants are born to be conquered. Their form intimates a kind of ancientness: they are the Before people. Even the giants who have nothing to do with the Israelites—the indigenous populations conquered by the Ammonites, Moabites, and so on—are the Before people of those lands.

It would have been enough to cast these various people as giants, and some even as nephilim, those scandalous aberrations of almighty proportions—but it doesn't end there. The monsterized foreigners are giants to be slain, food to be eaten, and animals to be killed.

The horror here isn't historical, it's theological. First of all, the archaeological evidence demonstrates that there was no "conquest" of Canaan. What's more, even archaeologists who disagree about many other things agree about this: a lot of the population that would become ancient Israel were in fact indigenous to Canaan, and developed a separate identity over time.[15] The Israelites didn't come into the land and bash a bunch of people on the head because they saw them as monsters. It was later ancient Israelite writers who looked back and imagined themselves heroic in the face of a mighty and even monstrous opponent.

The story of the scouts is doing some heavy lifting. It introduces the entire myth of conquest—which extends through several biblical books and is internally wildly inconsistent—and kicks it off with a picture of going up against giants. The Goliath story, written long after the time of David, reinforces the image of the monstrous enemy. These giant stories aren't reports of monsterization in the moment, but retrojections imagining Israelites as heroic monster-slayers.

This doesn't make it better. The monsterizing fiction has a violence all its own. Real-time monsterization does one kind of damage. The fantasy of having long ago vanquished a monstrous enemy—with God's help—does another.

As the inhabitants of Canaan are reinterpreted as monstrous, we witness the biblical writers' creation of monsters, and of their own identity in contrast: They are giants, We are altogether distinct, and what's more, we're heroic and God is demonstrably on our side. (This was presumably not a spontaneous invention, but a belief that developed over time.)

Then, it turns out this isn't just about Israel or the land of Canaan. God conquered the giant inhabitants of other lands, too. This pattern in the biblical writers' views of the distant past, times already ancient to them, doesn't only reinterpret the Israelites as heroic—it reinscribes God as reliably on the side of the conquerors of indigenous populations.

I'm writing this as I live on Lenape tribal lands where European colonists, seeing what is now the United States as their promised land, their Canaan to conquer, monsterized diverse Native peoples in many ways. One stands out: Captain John Smith wrote of meeting the Susquehanna that "they seemed like Giants to the English." He describes one man, "the calfe of whose leg was 3 quarters of a yard about, and all the rest of his limbes so answerable to that proportion." Echoing the depiction of Goliath, he adds, "His arrows were five quarters long," in a wolfskin quiver slung over his back.[16]

Far more often, the colonists described diverse Native peoples as "animals" and "wild beasts"—directly related to the intention of displacing and killing countless people.[17] Hugh Henry Brackenridge, a Pennsylvania Supreme Court justice, wrote of "the animals, vulgarly called Indians": "I am so far from thinking the Indians have a right to the soil" that they "ought to be driven from it."[18]

The monsterization was biblically infused and religiously continued. One early seventeenth century Virginia poem referred to Native Americans as "men-monsters."[19]

Let's not gape in amazement that such things were said and done, as if they're a thing of the past. We still do this. Those monstrous descriptions of Jews and Muslims haven't gone anywhere, and continue to serve as justification for violence. Rates of lethal violence against people who are trans or gender nonconforming have increased over the last decade.[20]

In his grand jury testimony, the white six-foot-four police officer who killed Michael Brown described his perception of the Black eighteen-year-old: "I felt like a five-year-old holding on to Hulk Hogan. . . . Hulk Hogan, that's just how big he felt and how small I felt just from grasping his arm."[21] The two were within an inch of the same height.

The biblical battles of conquest of a giant-filled land weren't historical events, but the consequences of the types of beliefs the stories reflect are devastatingly real. Interpreting the Other as somehow less than human—then and throughout the centuries—has obviously disastrous results, for individuals and for entire populations.

Moving from this modern reality back to the ancient fiction with an acute sense of the horrors both of monsterization and of religiously justified acts of violence, the question is sharper than ever. How can slaughtering and displacing monsterized indigenous populations be something God would get behind? But, as the Bible tells it, he's been game for a very long time. He comes down hard on the side of the giant-slayers time after time.

We've now seen many a monster in the company of God, supernatural creatures and divine hitmen he keeps in his entourage and deploys at will against his human victims. But the monsterized foreigners? *That's* company he won't keep.

Part 3

The God-Monster

10

The Monster of Monsters, the Wonder of Wonders

"You're quoting me out of context," objects the president. Richard Nixon sits accused of criminal activities, growing defensive in a tough interview (*Frost/Nixon*, 2008). British journalist David Frost presses on. Nixon explains that when you're in charge, you have to do things "that are not always in the strictest sense of the law legal, but you do them because they're in the greater interests of the nation." With a look of astonishment at the admission, Frost then asks, "Are you really saying that in certain situations the president can decide whether it's in the best interests of the nation, and then do something illegal?" Nixon answers, "I'm saying that when the president does it, that means it's not illegal."

In my imagination, I have this clip at the ready for every time someone responds to the horrific actions of the biblical God with the claim that no matter how vengeful or barbaric it may look to us, he's God and therefore his actions are right and good—in other words, that when *God* does it, that means it's not horrific.

There's a robust religious impulse to polish God's image, to defend and excuse God's acts in the Bible. But what if we don't let the biblical God-character off the hook just for being God?

We've seen this God do bad, bad things. He rarely does his own dirty work, instead deploying an array of monstrous creatures to get the job done, and always just the right monster for the moment: seraphim to threaten and intimidate people into submission, cherubim to guard the gateways and periodically to burn down portions of the earth and usher in divine destroyers, the Adversary to condemn and torture the innocent, spirits to gaslight, demons to destroy, and for a good old-fashioned slaying, perhaps an angel (if the angels aren't too busy dragging people to hell or murdering masses of the earth's population). This God dispatches members of his monstrous entourage left and right against his human targets. What's more, *this* is the "heavenly host"—that is, the army of God. Every single type of divine being shown acting in God's service in the Bible injures, threatens, tortures, or kills on his command.

The way in which I am *most* like Augustine (okay, possibly the only way) is that I think the monsters of the Bible demonstrate something about the biblical God. [*Peeved side-eye from Augie.*]

Is there room for wonder, I asked, many monsters ago? Are there marvels to behold? If monsters reveal something about their world, what do the monsters of God's entourage reveal?

As problematic as your regular old divine violence is, what's worse is this: God's use of the monster militia shows a certain cold premeditation. If the violent flare-ups of God's blazing wrath are the crimes of passion of the divine world, then his deployment of monstrous underlings, each kind with its own specialty, are the systemic violence. It's a chillingly organized way to kill people.

The monsters don't only play out their individual scenes: they show us their god. Every biblical monster torturing, gaslighting, bloodying, and slaughtering people on God's orders is a neon sign pointing to its commander, the God-monster.

The God-Monster

God's monstrosity isn't metaphorical. He doesn't just act monstrous— he also has his own array of classic monster traits.[1] Even sticking just to texts already explored in detail earlier in this book, we can see God exhibiting one monster trait after another. It's like going down a diagnostic checklist, and things are not looking good.

God's giant size is on display—if we're not too distracted by the seraphim flying around him—when the prophet Isaiah describes him sitting on his throne, with just the bottom of his robe alone being huge enough to fill the entire temple (Isaiah 6:1).

He has lethal superpowers, like shooting rays out of his hand (Habakkuk 3:4). We've also seen him consume people with fire that blasts out of him when his anger is kindled (Numbers 11:1–2; 16:35), and we've watched as he zaps people with plague (Numbers 11:33; 14:36–37; 16:45–49).

God is sometimes amorphous, like the looming threat of John Carpenter's The Fog (1980). When the "cloud of the Lord" settles upon the tabernacle, even Moses can't safely enter, now that the dangerous "glory of the Lord" is there (Exodus 40:34–38). The cloud isn't just the horse he rode in on. The Hebrew word trans-lated "tabernacle" (mishkan) comes from the verb "dwell" or "settle" (shakan), referring to the dwelling place of God—and what "settles" or comes to "dwell" (shakan) there is the cloud (40:35). Even within amorphous appearances, God's got range. When he descends onto the top of Mount Sinai, the people see thick smoke "because the Lord had descended upon it in fire" (19:18).

Elsewhere, God appears in a more defined physical form. Defined as what, exactly, is harder to say. When the prophet Ezekiel has a vision of "the appearance of the likeness of the glory of God," he describes seeing "something like a human form," but the top half of the something-like-a-body is like glowing mineral or metal, and the bottom half is like fire (Ezekiel 1:26–28). Even God's physical hybridity one-ups every other monster.

God is also a shapeshifter. In addition to the different forms in which he appears to prophets in visions, he changes forms on earth. We've just recalled seeing him manifested both in cloud and in fire. If anyone's keeping the heebie-jeebies at bay by figuring that at least those happen on discrete occasions, sorry: while leading the Israelites through the wilderness, God switches it up for optimum visibility, going before the people in a pillar of cloud by day and a pillar of fire by night (Exodus 13:21–22).

A lot of instances of divine form-changing also entail realm-crossing, like when God descends from heaven and covers the tabernacle. Later, just as the spirit of falsehood stands before God in heaven and shifts shape to become formless in the mouths of the prophets, God, too, is pictured as physically upon the heavenly throne, but can enter someone as a spirit on earth, like when the spirit of the Lord enters David (1 Samuel 16:13). We've also witnessed a cosmic battle in which the God of heaven comes to attack the earth and sea. When he lands on the earth, it shakes. He shatters the mountains, tramples the sea on horseback, and brandishes a bow and arrow (Habakkuk 3:3–15).

The God-monster commands people to fear him (Deuteronomy 6:1–2, 13, 24). Readers frequently soften this "fear" of God to "awe," making it palatable as some reverent human response to the numinous. But no: "Your terrors have ravaged me," says the poet (Psalm 88:16). When Jesus sends out the apostles, he encourages them not to fear those who can only kill your body, but not your soul—instead, says he, "fear him who can destroy both soul and body in hell" (Matthew 10:28). That terrifying figure Jesus has destroying you in hell isn't Satan, it's God. When God says "fear me," he means FEAR ME.

In the Bible's ancient context, it makes sense that God is a monster. The divine and the monstrous are all intertwined in mythology from this region, like the god-monsters we met in the introduction, the giant, fire-breathing Marduk and the divine sea monster Tiamat. Monstrous behavior's not a deal breaker, either. Throughout the region, the defining trait of gods isn't goodness—it's power. The "goodness" of gods runs the gamut, just as with people. Sure enough, while there are biblical texts that describe God's goodness, there are many more that are focused on his power, and that describe God as being primarily concerned with the perception of his power. For instance, we saw God harden Pharaoh's heart to prevent him from letting the Israelites go, explicitly in order to have a chance to prove his divine power (Exodus 7:3–5). God then proves that power through the plagues, which he caps off with a flourish, sending the Destroyer to slaughter children. If that's not a vivid enough example, elsewhere God conveys in so many words that his power isn't limited to goodness: "I am the Lord, and there is no other: I form light and create darkness; I make peace and create evil. I, the Lord, do all these things" (Isaiah 45:6–7). When God says "I create evil," he means I CREATE EVIL.

For biblical writers, the portrayals of God's monstrosity and his monstrous demonstrations of power weren't in conflict with his divinity—they were part of it. Modern assumptions that God must be all good aren't based on the Bible. The "great and terrible" God, as

Moses calls him, really is both great and terrible (e.g., Deuteronomy 7:21). With an understandable urge to tame the God-monster, we often render this "awesome" instead of "terrible"—though when Moses uses the same phrase again right afterward to describe the "great and terrible wilderness" filled with seraphim-snakes and scorpions (8:15), we take it at face value. It means the same thing both times. God is as terrible, as dangerous and deadly, as the desert. He has revealed himself through the monsters under his command, and he has revealed his own monstrosity. He has warned people to fear him and explained that he creates evil. If we should take him at his word anywhere, it's here.

"You're quoting me out of context," objects the God-monster.

Yes and no. Yes, God in the Bible is far more complex and multifaceted than just being the monster king. He's not plain old bad. He's incredible, ineffable, glorious . . . and *also* very, very bad.

The Bible is full of wonderful passages portraying the goodness of God, describing God's love, mercy, and everlasting faithfulness; passages that uplift the weary and sustain the desolate, that bring a sense of hope and peace to the devastated.

And—threaded tightly throughout, inextricable in the fabric of the Bible—are the great many passages depicting God doing violent and twisted things, the passages that pull back the curtain and reveal the God-monster.

If we want to understand the Bible, we can't take just the merciful portrayals and gloss over the monstrous ones. These disconcerting descriptions of God doing one terrible thing after another are in the Bible for a reason, and it's not enough to pull a Nixon, claiming that when God does it, that means it's *not* horrific.

The Bible is better for going on the record with God's monstrosity. The Bible is a wonder.

Book of Wonder

The Bible is a compilation of countless people's diverse perspectives from different places and times. Some of these perspectives complement each other, and some conflict—and the Bible is all the richer for it.

In particular, the Bible has a complicated relationship with God and God's monstrosity. Different texts reflect vastly different views of God's violence. Some biblical writers describe God doing horrible things but attempt to justify it, placing blame squarely on the human actors for their disobedience. (This doesn't quite solve the problem, since the divine "you drove me to it" tenor of that remains, in theological terms, icky.)

Other passages don't blame the victims. Among those, some biblical writers simply don't offer explanations for God's deadly deployment of monsters against an innocent population. We saw that approach in the story about the seventy thousand victims of God's giant plague-shooting angel when King David sinned. Other parts of the Bible wrestle with God's monstrosity head-on, like the book of Job, devoted to the innocent protagonist's struggle with his suffering at the hands of an unjust God.

This complexity is part of what gives the Bible its depth and dimension. To pick and choose from its collection of voices and highlight only the more theologically palatable, the more confident that God is a safe space (while cherubim beg to differ), flattens the Bible, turning it into the Wonder Bread of world literature, rather than the genuine wonder that this multifaceted ancient anthology really is.

Instead of discounting these difficult texts and settling for a simplistic, party-line Bible, we can embrace the rich diversity of perspectives within its pages. We can appreciate the array of ancient ruminations on God and the world, these many disparate voices with all of their complex and diverging viewpoints. Yes, even on God's monstrosity. Especially on God's monstrosity.

A few years after the end of the Holocaust, the American philosopher of religion and rabbi Abraham Joshua Heschel wrestled with the question of God's place in horrors so grave it felt "sinful for the sun to shine." After observing that it certainly seemed like God must be either guiding events or at best indifferent, Heschel went on to offer rational arguments to explain why God wasn't at fault, pointing to various biblical texts along the way. Yet then, after all this, he concluded by simply quoting one of the psalms of protest in its entirety.[2] The psalm accuses God of the abuse of his people despite their steadfastness: you have rejected us and degraded us, you've set us up to be slaughtered; we've been faithful to you, but you have crushed us (Psalm 44). With his logical explanations for God's behavior complete, Heschel gave this poet the last word.

Like the psalms that accuse God of abandonment and abuse, the biblical texts that depict God's deployment of monsters and exhibit God's own monstrosity give room for our grief, anger, and protest.

We can hold God accountable. The writer of Psalm 44 would be baffled by the modern rhetoric that God is all good, all the time. The validity of calling God out is part of biblical tradition. Mixed in and among other perspectives in the Bible, we're confronted with a persistent thread of texts that depict a monstrous God acting with cold premeditation, dispatching his entourage of monsters to commit horrific acts. Rather than discreetly setting those texts aside, we can value them for how they validate the reality of the human experience, as we live our lives in a world that is unpredictable, unjust, and at times monstrous.

Grappling with the monstrous divine is in some ways at the heart of the Bible's sense of what it means to be the people of God. The very name *Israel* is explained in Genesis as meaning something like "one who wrestles with God," a name bestowed on the early patriarch, Jacob, after he wrestles with the divine being who attacks him one night. Jacob then names the place in commemoration of having lived through an encounter with God. The writer, reflecting on what makes Israel Israel, tells this story set even in ancient Israel's distant past, as if to say, We've survived many things, even God.

It's a far cry from "thoughts and prayers."

How poignant it is that many of the Bible's ancient writers didn't pretend that everything would be fine if people would just trust in God. Sometimes, they said, God is why things aren't fine at all. Some of the writers lamented, protested, and struggled with God's monstrosity. Others bluntly described holy terrors at his hand without overt question or quandary. Even as we reel at the horrors they pin on God—and they don't shy away—there's something powerful in their refusal to look at the world around them and conclude that God is only ever trustworthy and good.

Confronting God's monsters—and the God-monster—shows us a multifaceted picture that's less rosy than we might wish, but more realistic. This is part of the Bible's sense of what it means to live in our chaotic and violent world. This is part of God's profile in both the Hebrew Bible and the New Testament, inextricable from the rest.

If we tame the monsters, and the Bible itself, we'll miss the complex beauty and poignancy of the Bible's collection of voices— how these ancient thinkers reflected on the nature of God and the world, how they wrestled and pondered. The Bible isn't a solution to the struggles of life, but a reflection of them.

The troubling depictions of God and his entourage add a vital dimension to the diverse anthology we call the Bible, as these writers grappled with the messiness of the world and God's place in it. Rather than writing magically intuited God-facts, they felt the realities of the world around them and gave them expression. They ruminated, they contemplated, they struggled and they speculated, much as we do now.

Acknowledgments

E ven as someone always fond of a good monster story, this has been a disconcerting book to write. While I was writing about plagues of flies, lice, and locusts, my home was invaded by ants that turned out to be feeding on termites. "They'll swarm when those chemicals hit," our exterminator said. "It'll be like a horror movie in here."

More seriously, as I wrote about plague demons, locking out Haby, and the multitudes descending into darkness, we tried to lock the doors against a frightening pandemic while people died in the hallways of hospitals filled to capacity. As I wrote about injustice in the heavenly court and the targeting of the innocent, the Supreme Court of the United States decided that an earlier ruling against a Christian baker who refused to bake a cake for a gay couple had involved hostility against religion, yet decided that Trump's explicit "Muslim ban" had not.

Monsters are fun, but monstrosity is real, and takes as many forms as monsters do. It can be a lot to sit with—so first, thank you to my readers and to all of the people who've been game for thinking seriously about these unsettling texts with me.

I'm grateful to my agent, Giles Anderson, for his support and essential guidance. Among other things, it was Giles who convinced me that I needed to open up in the introduction and include something about my personal experience, to let readers know why I find these grim parts of the Bible compelling. Although I resisted, the book is more meaningful to me this way, and I hope to others as well.

Many, many thanks to Lil Copan, my brilliant editor at Broadleaf Books, who offered invaluable feedback along with constant enthusiasm for the project. I'm deeply grateful for her suggestions about how to sharpen the manuscript. This book wouldn't be what it is without her. A heartfelt thank you to the design team for the amazing cover and very cool interior, and thank you to everyone at Broadleaf.

I'm fortunate to have worked with another brilliant editor earlier in the process as well. Jana Riess's insightful suggestions, questions, and guidance were crucial in this book's development. She helped me to follow my best ideas, reminding me often to pare down the lengthy technical treatments I was accustomed to from my work for specialists. Where my citations ranged from the academic style of noting everything in existence to the absurdly (I prefer to think "charmingly") discursive, Jana asked repeatedly: Do you really need this footnote?[1]

I'm indebted to Thea Portier-Young, who read the entire manuscript and provided generous and perceptive comments. At a writing retreat in Alexandria a few years earlier, as I dug into this book and she began work on *The Prophetic Body*, her early feedback on a section of the cherubim chapter was very helpful. I'm grateful to Mark Leuchter for his comments on the final manuscript, and to Robyn Whitaker, who lent her expertise in the book of Revelation.

Until March 2020, I enjoyed regular shared writing days with Stephen Russell, as I worked on this book and he worked on *The King*

---

1. No, I do not.

and the Land and on *Space, Land, Territory, and the Study of the Bible.* Writing is mostly a solitary endeavor, and these communal work days were precious. It was a loss not to be able to continue this during the pandemic, while I completed this project and Stephen began his on the Bible and the Morant Bay Rebellion in Jamaica.

I'm thankful to my colleagues at Union Theological Seminary, and owe particular thanks to Sarah Azaransky, David Carr, Jeremy Hultin, Jerusha Rhodes, and Andrea White for their support. I first taught a course based on my ideas about biblical monsters in 2013, and my work benefited from the lively, rigorous engagement of many students in that seminar and each iteration thereafter. I thank my colleagues at Jewish Theological Seminary, who invited me to teach Monster Heaven there as well. Among so many thoughtful students in Monster Heaven over the years from both UTS and JTS, a special thanks to those with whom I had inspiring and thought-provoking conversations in the months or years afterward: Roni Tabick, Jeremy Tabick, Carolyn Klaasen, Miya Lee, Jessica Christy, and Eva Suarez.

I had the distinct privilege of presenting parts of this work in a range of contexts—universities, seminaries of very different orientations, synagogues, and churches—where I benefited from the opportunity to engage with people coming from a great variety of perspectives. I especially want to thank Ted Lewis of Johns Hopkins University for inviting me to give the Thirty-Third Annual Samuel Iwry Lecture in November 2019, Joel Kaminsky of Smith College for inviting me to give the Annual Lecture in Ancient Studies in April 2019, and Chris Hays and Carly Crouch for inviting me to speak at Fuller Seminary in May 2019. I first publicly presented this work at the American Academy of Religion in 2017 in a session organized by Kelly Murphy, Joseph Laycock, and Steve Wiggins, featuring a terrific line-up of presenters with Timothy Beal as respondent. I offer my deepest thanks to all of the people who participated in each of these events. I thank my gracious hosts at various churches and synagogues, and am grateful to those who asked interesting and surprising questions after these talks. Having you all as conversation partners, for moments or for years, has enriched my work and been a delight.

I've benefited from rich conversations in less formal contexts as well. I'm particularly grateful to Jill Hicks-Keaton and Lauren Winner for key moments. Thank you to Sarah Shectman for eleventh-hour transliteration advice, to Simcha Gross for help with incantation bowls, and to Damien Kempf for help with a medieval French manuscript.

A decade ago, editor Susan Reed and I had a long conversation full of laughter and the whispered exchange of mischievous ideas. She began encouraging me to write for nonspecialists, and I'm thankful to her for it.

Going a bit further back: thank you to my fifth-grade teacher, Mr. Merle-Smith, who one day handed each kid a few stapled pages from a cuneiform dictionary, some clay, and a stylus, letting us each compose whatever we wanted. I made a cuneiform tablet that said, "Monster eat male cow." And so it began.

But further still: I pause to remember my grandfather, Rezső Sajó, who planned to work in the family's antiquarian bookshop but was killed in a Jewish forced-labor battalion in January 1943; my grandmother, Jolán Szántó Hámori, who survived through astounding courage, strategy, and luck, and then ate off cheery yellow plates, of which I've broken only a few, and who made a Hungarian chocolate cake I'll forever strive to imitate; my grandfather, Ferenc Hámori, who survived unspeakable losses and sat in the backyard painting landscapes that hang on our walls. I remember my grandfather, Charles Enselberg, who fixed up hearts and did silly dances in the living room; and my grandmother, Minna Stitch Enselberg, who played a mean game of bridge and still bought her candy on the Lower East Side well into her nineties. My dear parents, Andras Hamori and Ruth Enselberg Hamori, are now the most wonderful grandparents a kid (or his mama) could ever want.

I am sorely aware of the insufficiency of this statement, but have nowhere more public to make it: I thank Maria, whose last name and identity my family has not been able to uncover; Maria, who sheltered my father for a time during the Holocaust in Budapest. We don't know your full name or who your descendants might be, but we remember you.

On a happier note: this book is dedicated to my husband, Jack, who knows more about ancient monsters than he would have ever anticipated, and to our son, Jonah, who spent his toddlerhood listening to my private explanations of why he wasn't *really* cherubic (after whoever gave the intended compliment was safely out of earshot). To you, with all my love and appreciation.

Notes

Monster Heaven

1 Stephanie Dalley, "The Epic of Creation," in *Myths from Mesopotamia: Creation, the Flood, Gilgamesh, and Others*, rev. ed. (Oxford: Oxford University Press, 2000), 236, 253–57.

2 Or, as two monster theorists have put it, "Sometimes all that separates a god from a monster is a dedicated PR team." Natasha L. Mikles and Joseph P. Laycock, "Five Further Theses on Monster Theory and Religious Studies," in *Religion, Culture, and the Monstrous: Of Gods and Monsters*, ed. Natasha L. Mikles and Joseph P. Laycock (Lanham, MD: Lexington Books, 2021), 4.

3 On these and other types of hybridity, see Noël Carroll, *The Philosophy of Horror: Or, Paradoxes of the Heart* (New York: Routledge, 1990), 32–34.

4 The *rudis indigestaque moles* in 1.7 is part of a longer description of amorphous chaos: Ovid, *Metamorphoses* 1.1–20.

5 While the Hitchcock film is better known, credit for this classic horror story belongs to Daphne du Maurier, author of "The Birds," 1952. On the phenomenon he calls "massification," see Carroll, *The Philosophy of Horror*, 50.

6 The "monsters among us" trope (like the vampires of *True Blood* "coming out of the coffin" and assimilating into non-monster society) has punch precisely because it plays against the expected idea.

7 "Report: Leading Cause of Death Still Venturing beyond the Pines," *The Onion*, March 23, 2016; https://tinyurl.com/45mt8pep.

8 Carroll, *The Philosophy of Horror*, 34–35.

9 Framing this concept in Freudian terms, see Timothy K. Beal, *Religion and Its Monsters* (New York: Routledge, 2002), 4–5.

10 Augustine, *The City of God* 21.8. Many monster scholars present Augustine's etymology as being factual, but the prevalent view among modern scholars of Indo-European linguistics is that *monstrum* is derived from *moneo*, "remind, advise, warn." Michiel de Vaan, *Etymological Dictionary of Latin and the Other Italic Languages* (Leiden and Boston: Brill, 2008), 367.

Seraphim

1 Kristine Phillips, "'We Knew the Ship Was Doomed': USS *Indianapolis* Survivor Recalls Four Days in Shark-filled Sea," *Washington Post*, August 20, 2017, https://tinyurl.com/2rkhr2vj. For updated count: Scott Neuman, "Navy Admits to 70-Year Crew List Error in USS Indianapolis Disaster," *The Two-Way*, National Public Radio, March 23, 2018, https://tinyurl.com/3xmpm9kr.

2 See, e.g., Friedhelm Hartenstein, "Cherubim and Seraphim in the Bible and in the Light of Ancient Near Eastern Sources," in *Angels: The Concept of Celestial Beings: Origins, Development, and Reception*, ed. Friedrich Vinzenz Reiterer, Tobias Nicklas, and Karin Schöpflin (Berlin: de Gruyter, 2007), 163–64; T. N. D. Mettinger, "Seraphim," in *Dictionary of Deities and Demons in the Bible*, rev. 2nd ed., ed. Karel van der Toorn, Bob Becking, and Pieter W. van der Horst (Grand Rapids: Eerdmans, 1999), 742–43.

3 Carroll, *The Philosophy of Horror*, 50.

4 For examples, see Karen Randolph Joines, "Winged Serpents in Isaiah's Inaugural Vision," *Journal of Biblical Literature* 86 (1967): 411–13, and J. J. M. Roberts, "The Visual Elements in Isaiah's Vision in Light of Judaean and Near Eastern Sources," in *From Babel to Babylon: Essays on Biblical History and Literature in Honour of Brian Peckham*, ed. Joyce

Rilett Wood, John E. Harvey, and Mark Leuchter (New York: T & T Clark, 2006), 206–7.

5 Hartenstein, "Cherubim and Seraphim," 166; Othmar Keel and Christoph Uehlinger, Gods, Goddesses, and Images of God in Ancient Israel, trans. Thomas H. Trapp (Minneapolis: Fortress Press, 1998), 273.

6 See examples in R. S. Hendel, "Serpent," in van der Toorn, Becking, and van der Horst, Dictionary of Deities and Demons, 744–45.

7 Nahman Avigad, revised and completed by Benjamin Sass, Corpus of West Semitic Stamp Seals (Jerusalem: Israel Academy of Sciences and Humanities; Israel Exploration Society; Institute of Archaeology, The Hebrew University of Jerusalem, 1997) includes many examples; Keel and Uehlinger, Gods, Goddesses, and Images of God, 29–30, 251– 53, 272–75; Joines, "Winged Serpents in Isaiah's Inaugural Vision," 413–14.

8 Translation of Karen Radner, "The Winged Snakes of Arabia and the Fossil Site of Makhtesh Ramon in the Negev," in Wiener Zeitschrift für die Kunde des Morgenlandes, Vol. 97, Festschrift für Hermann Hunger zum 65. Geburtstag gewidmet von seinen Freunden, Kollegen und Schülern (Department of Oriental Studies, University of Vienna, 2007), 355.

9 I don't say this lightly. It's critical to bear in mind the effects of this biblical metaphor on women who have experienced such abuse, as notes Renita J. Weems, Battered Love: Marriage, Sex, and Violence in the Hebrew Prophets (Minneapolis: Fortress Press, 1995), 8.

10 On supersized gods, see Mark S. Smith, Where the Gods Are: Spatial Dimensions of Anthropomorphism in the Biblical World (New Haven: Yale University Press, 2016), esp. 13–30, 41. On the Ain Dara temple, the closest parallel to Solomon's (contemporaneous) temple in Jerusalem, see Francesca Stavrakopoulou, God: An Anatomy (New York: Knopf, 2022), 29–30, plate 1.

11 Joines, "Winged Serpents in Isaiah's Inaugural Vision," 414–15; Keel and Uehlinger, Gods, Goddesses, and Images of God, 273.

12 Tallay Ornan, "Member in the Entourage of Yahweh: A Uraeus Seal from the Western Wall Plaza Excavations, Jerusalem," 'Atiqot 72 (2012): 15–20; Avigad and Sass, Corpus of West Semitic Stamp Seals, 253–54; Keel and Uehlinger, Gods, Goddesses, and Images of God, 272–75.

13 Joines, "Winged Serpents in Isaiah's Inaugural Vision," 410–15; Keel and Uehlinger, Gods, Goddesses, and Images of God, 273; Hartenstein, "Cherubim and Seraphim," 164; Roberts, "The Visual Elements in Isaiah's Vision," 204–10.

14 Pliny, Natural History 8.30.

15 Related observation by Hartenstein, "Cherubim and Seraphim," 165, 172.

16 Jeffrey Jerome Cohen, "Monster Culture (Seven Theses)," in Monster Theory: Reading Culture, ed. Jeffrey Jerome Cohen (Minneapolis: University of Minnesota, 1996), 12–13.

Cherubim

1 F. A. M. Wiggermann, "Mischwesen A.," and Anthony Green, "Mischwesen B.," Reallexikon der Assyriologie 8 (1994): 222–46 and 246–64.

2 Green, "Mischwesen A.," 255.

3 Dalley, "Gilgamesh," Myths from Mesopotamia, 96–98.

4 Dalley, "The Epic of Creation," Myths from Mesopotamia, 236–40, 251.

5 HALOT, s.v. כרוב I 497 (Ludwig Koehler, Walter Baumgartner, and Johann J. Stamm, The Hebrew and Aramaic Lexicon of the Old Testament, trans. and ed. under the supervision of Mervyn E. J. Richardson. 4 vols. [Leiden: Brill, 1994–1999]. Experts on Mesopotamian monsters disagree about the precise identification. See Wiggermann, "Mischwesen A.," 243, and Green, "Mischwesen B.," 255.

6 On cherubim as Israel's version of the sphinx, see, e.g., Hartenstein, "Cherubim and Seraphim," 159–60; Mettinger, "Cherubim,"

in van der Toorn, Becking, and van der Horst, *Dictionary of Deities and Demons*, 189–190. Against the common conflation of this with a throne, see Alice Wood, *Of Wings and Wheels: A Synthetic Study of the Biblical Cherubim*, BZAW 385 (Berlin: de Gruyter, 2008), 9–33; and Cornelis Houtman, *Exodus*, vol. 3 (Kampen: Kok Publishing House, 2000), 383–85.

7 Story in y. Sheq. 6:1, 49c, and discussion follows; with thanks to Rebecca Scharbach Wollenberg for prepublication access to *The Closed Book: How the Rabbis Taught the Jews (Not) to Read the Bible* (Princeton: Princeton University Press, 2023).

8 See discussion in Mark S. Smith, "Like Deities, Like Temples (Like People)," in *Temple and Worship in Biblical Israel*, ed. John Day, LHB/OTS 422 (New York: T & T Clark, 2005), 3–27.

9 On various difficulties of Ezek 1:13, see Moshe Greenberg, *Ezekiel 1–20: A New Translation with Introduction and Commentary*, Anchor Bible 22 (Garden City, NY: Doubleday, 1983), 46.

10 Jo Ann Hackett, *The Baalam Text from Deir ʿAllā*, HSM 31 (Chico, CA: Scholars Press, 1984), 87.

11 Moving beyond that, see Raanan Eichler, "The Meaning of ישב הכרבים," *ZAW* 126, no. 3 (2014): 369; and Houtman, *Exodus*, 385.

The Adversary

1 Carol L. Meyers and Eric M. Meyers, *Haggai, Zechariah 1–8: A New Translation with Introduction and Commentary*, Anchor Bible 25 (Garden City, NY: Doubleday, 1987), 115; Jason M. Silverman, "Vetting the Priest in Zechariah 3: The Satan between Divine and Achaemenid Administrations," *Journal of Hebrew Scriptures* 14 (2014): 4–7.

2 For a treatment of this dynamic in Job engaging psychological analysis of intimate-partner violence, see Marlene Underwood, "'Battered Love': Exposing Abuse in the Book of Job," in *Womanist Interpretations of the Bible: Expanding the Discourse*, ed. Gay L. Byron and Vanessa Lovelace (Atlanta: SBL Press, 2016), 165–84.

3 On "pure garments," see Meyers and Meyers, *Haggai, Zechariah 1–8*, 190.

4 Meyers and Meyers, *Haggai, Zechariah 1–8*, 187–88; James C. VanderKam, "Joshua the High Priest and the Interpretation of Zechariah 3," *Catholic Biblical Quarterly* 53 (1991): 555–58, 569–70; Silverman, "Vetting the Priest in Zechariah 3," 22.

5 Meyers and Meyers, *Haggai, Zechariah 1–8*, 182.

6 As Meyers and Meyers observe, "The Accuser appears in a bad light in this passage because he is unaware of the change in policy. . . . He is using irrelevant and dated evidence; he has not rebelled against Yahweh's authority." Meyers and Meyers, *Haggai, Zechariah 1–8*, 186–87.

7 See *HALOT*, s.v. רעה 1262–64.

8 E.g., Exod 32:12, 14; Deut 32:23; Jer 26:3, 13, 19; Joel 2:13; Jonah 3:8–10 and 4:2.

9 Satan also develops in complex ways in postbiblical Jewish writing, but never achieves the prominence he has in Christian theology. I address only the latter here because popular notions about Satan come largely from Christian ideas.

10 On God's agency, see Ralph P. Martin, *2 Corinthians*, 2nd ed., Word Biblical Commentary (Grand Rapids: Zondervan, 2014), 606, 611, and Murray J. Harris, *The Second Epistle to the Corinthians: A Commentary on the Greek Text*, The New International Greek Testament Commentary (Grand Rapids: Eerdmans, 2005), 855–56.

11 Satan still requires God's go-ahead; see, e.g., Harris, *The Second Epistle to the Corinthians*, 856; Colin G. Kruse, *2 Corinthians*, rev. ed., Tyndale New Testament Commentaries (Downers Grove, IL: InterVarsity Press, 2015), 265.

12 Raymond F. Collins, *1 & 2 Timothy and Titus: A Commentary*, The New Testament Library (Louisville: Westminster John Knox, 2002), 50; Gordon D. Fee, *The First Epistle to the Corinthians*, rev. ed., NICNT (Grand Rapids: Eerdmans, 2014), 228–34.

13 Monster theorist Jeffrey Jerome Cohen dedicates one of his central theses to the ways in which monsters resist categorization, thus

challenging the categories themselves. As he concludes, monsters are "full of rebuke to traditional methods of organizing knowledge and human experience." Cohen, "Monster Culture (Seven Theses)," 6–7.

The Destroyer and Other Angels

1 Precious Moments, https://tinyurl.com/yc53dss3, accessed March 7, 2021.

2 Not even in Dan 9:21; John J. Collins, *Daniel: A Commentary on the Book of Daniel*, Hermeneia (Minneapolis: Fortress Press, 1993), 351–52.

3 With thanks to my former Monster Heaven student, Rev. Eva Suarez, for this image.

4 Josephus, *Antiquities of the Jews* 19.8.2.

5 Jesus gives a long description of the end of the age that takes two chapters in Matthew's Gospel. (You have to wonder at what point the disciples sighed and made a mental note not to ask again.) The suggested division of labor between Jesus and the angels seems to vary through Matt 24 and 25.

6 Quoted with permission of the student, Danielle Williams.

7 I make the comparison with apologies to Tchaikovsky. As he considered composing this celebration of military triumph, he wrote, "It is impossible to tackle without repugnance this sort of music which is destined for the glorification of something that, in essence, delights me not at all." Geoffrey Norris describes the *Overture* as having a "famously over-the-top coda," which would also make a good subtitle for Revelation. "Tchaikovsky's 1812 Overture: The Complete Guide," *Gramophone*, May 1, 2018: https://tinyurl.com/3h5cnzvp.

8 On rebellious angels, see Kelley Coblentz Bautch, "The Fall and Fate of Renegade Angels: The Intersection of Watchers Traditions and the Book of Revelation," in *The Fallen Angels Traditions: Second Temple Developments and Reception History*, ed. Angela Kim Harkins, Kelley Coblentz Bautch, and John C. Endres, SJ, The Catholic Biblical

Quarterly Monograph Series 53 (Washington, DC: The Catholic Biblical Quarterly Association of America, 2014), 69–93.

9 On bound angels, see Kelley Coblentz Bautch, "Heavenly Beings Brought Low: A Study of Angels and the Netherworld," in *Angels: The Concept of Celestial Beings: Origins, Development, and Reception*, ed. Friedrich Vinzenz Reiterer, Tobias Nicklas, and Karin Schöpflin (Berlin: de Gruyter, 2007), 459–75.

10 Once again, the New Testament writer has picked up an image from the Hebrew Bible and gone completely off the rails with it. Here, he takes a poetic metaphor (Joel 3:13) and turns it into a horrifying vision of something angels will do to human beings.

11 Gabriel is named in Dan 8:16, 9:21, and Luke 1:26; Michael in Dan 10:13, 21; 12:1, Rev 12:7, and Jude 9. Note that Satan's name is only his job title, while angels are given names like people.

Demons in God's Ranks

1 Fox News footage: Caleb Parke, "Trump's Spiritual Adviser, Paula White, Prays to Stop 'Every Demonic Network' against Him," June 21, 2019, https://tinyurl.com/mwmdy9hf.

2 Kyle Mantyla, "Trump Faith Adviser Paula White Dedicates White House as 'Holy Ground' Sanctified by 'The Superior Blood of Jesus,'" Right Wing Watch, Sept. 11, 2019, https://tinyurl.com/mvuznjz5.

3 Even in Ps 91, where angels and demons are mentioned in closest proximity, the angels guard people from lions, snakes, and toe-stubbing, not from the demons (91:11–13).

4 See, e.g., Karen Sonik, "Mesopotamian Conceptions of the Supernatural: A Taxonomy of *Zwischenwesen*," *Archiv für Religionsgeschichte* 14 (2013): 114–15.

5 The word in Isa 34:14 refers to an animal, and is surrounded in the text by all sorts of other animals.

6 N. Wyatt, "Qeteb," in van der Toorn, Becking, and van der Horst, *Dictionary of Deities and Demons*, 673–74; Johannes C. de Moor, "O

Death, Where Is Thy Sting," in *Ascribe to the Lord: Biblical and Other Studies in Memory of Peter C. Craigie*, ed. Lyle Eslinger and Glen Taylor, JSOT Supp 67 (Sheffield, UK: JSOT Press, 1988), 99–107.

7 As in a talmudic line taking Ps 91:7 as referring to demons (b. Ber. 6a).

8 Matthias Henze, "Psalm 91 in Premodern Interpretation and at Qumran," in *Biblical Interpretation at Qumran*, ed. Matthias Henze, Studies in the Dead Sea Scrolls and Related Literature (Grand Rapids: Eerdmans, 2005), 185.

9 Michael D. Coogan and Mark S. Smith, "Baal," in *Stories from Ancient Canaan*, 2nd ed. (Louisville: Westminster John Knox, 2012), 141, 147.

10 Sheol is sometimes personified in poetry, usually alongside Mavet or Abaddon (e.g., Hos 13:14; Hab 2:5; Isa 5:14; 28:15–18; Ps 49:14; Prov 27:20), but is never depicted with the agency ascribed to Mavet and Abaddon.

11 Maciej M. Münnich, *The God Resheph in the Ancient Near East*, ORA 11 (Tübingen: Mohr Siebeck, 2013), 129–30, 148–50; Edward Lipiński, *Resheph: A Syro-Canaanite Deity*, OLA 181, Studia Phoenicia 19 (Leuven: Peeters, 2009), 104–8.

12 Elsewhere I render this "the Lord," but it's a name, like Resheph. Münnich, *The God Resheph in the Ancient Near East*, 131, 150–51; Lipiński, *Resheph*, 96–98.

13 Münnich, *The God Resheph in the Ancient Near East*, 132, 150; Lipiński, *Resheph*, 111.

14 Münnich, *The God Resheph in the Ancient Near East*, 217.

15 Münnich, *The God Resheph in the Ancient Near East*, 225, 264.

16 Münnich, *The God Resheph in the Ancient Near East*, 8–9.

17 Münnich, *The God Resheph in the Ancient Near East*, 218.

18 Coogan and Smith, "El's Drinking Party," in *Stories from Ancient Canaan*, 172.

19 Cyrus H. Gordon, "ḤBY, Possessor of Horns and Tail," *Ugarit-Forschungen* 18 (1986): 129–32.

20 So too Gordon, "ḤBY, Possessor of Horns and Tail," 130, and P. Xella, "Haby," in van der Toorn, Becking, and van der Horst, *Dictionary of Deities and Demons*, 377.

21 These include inconsistencies of spelling and grammatical gender.

22 Mark S. Smith and Wayne T. Pitard, *The Ugaritic Baal Cycle*, vol. 2, *Introduction with Text, Translation, and Commentary of KTU/CAT 1.3–1.4*, Supplements to Vetus Testamentum 114 (Leiden: Brill, 2009), 249, 252.

23 One cool talmudic text (b. Pes. 111b) refers to Qetev of Deut 32:24 and Qetev of Ps 91:6 as two types of Qetev demons, differentiated by the time of day they appear.

24 Münnich, *The God Resheph in the Ancient Near East*, 220.

25 Paolo Xella, "'Le Grand Froid': Le dieu *Baradu madu* à Ebla," *Ugarit-Forschungen* 18 (1986): 437–44. P. Xella, "Barad," in van der Toorn, Becking, and van der Horst, *Dictionary of Deities and Demons*, 160–61.

26 The plural is used here, as at times for the god too. Lipiński, *Resheph*, 236, 246.

27 The phrase is a particular verb form (the hiphil of *sgr*), accompanied by one of three prepositions meaning "to" or "into the hand of" (*le*, *'el*, or *beyad*). See *HALOT*, s.v. סגר I 743.

28 Deut 23:16; Josh 20:5; 1 Sam 30:15; Amos 1:6, 9; Lam 2:7; Ps 30:8; Job 16:11. Even in Ps 78:62, where God "handed his people over to the sword," the sword is a synecdoche for the swords brandished by people.

Manipulative and Mind-Altering Spirits

1 "Careers and Jobs," U.S. Army. https://tinyurl.com/bdfb5w8t. Accessed April 5, 2020.

2 Mike Isaac, "Facebook Finds New Disinformation Campaigns and Braces for 2020 Torrent," *New York Times*, October 21, 2019, https://tinyurl.com/52xwnnbw.

3 "Careers and Jobs," U.S. Army.

4 For my more technical analysis of many of these texts, see Esther J. Hamori, "The Spirit of Falsehood," *Catholic Biblical Quarterly* 72 (2010): 15–30.

5 Isaac, "Facebook Finds New Disinformation Campaigns," October 21, 2019.

6 Throughout these vignettes, the phrases "evil spirit *from* the Lord" and "evil spirit *of* the Lord" (or God) are synonymous, as is clear in their back-to-back uses in 1 Sam 16:14–16. The sense of the latter is the same as in "an angel *of* the Lord."

7 This verb, meaning to "force entry into" (*HALOT*, s.v. צלח), sometimes describes the movements of God's own spirit too, as when it enters David in 1 Sam 16:13.

8 For detailed discussion, see Hamori, "The Spirit of Falsehood," 19–20.

9 Here too, there's a hint of God swapping out his own spirit for the evil spirit. Other leaders during this period receive God's spirit (Judg 3:10; 6:34; 14:19; 15:14), but God rejects Abimelech and sends the evil spirit instead.

10 On the indescribable monster in horror, see Carroll, *The Philosophy of Horror*, 20, 33.

11 Side-eye from Epimenides of Crete, murmuring, "All Cretans are liars."

12 This is the sense beyond the Bible, too, as in the Letter of Aristeas 266, in which persuasion is achieved by "the *energeia* of God"; H. G. Liddell, R. Scott, and H. S. Jones, *A Greek-English Lexicon*, 9th ed. with revised supplement (Oxford, 1996), s.v. ἐνέργεια.

13 Eph 1:19; 3:7; 4:16; Phil 3:21; Col 1:29; 2:12; 2 Thess 2:9, 11. One text refers to the *energeia* of the superhuman body of Christ (Eph 4:16). All other references are to the *energeia* of a divine being.

14 As Gordon D. Fee explains, "God thus sends them a powerful delusion so that they will believe the lie. . . . And this is not about just any falsehood, but *the* lie, the ultimate falsehood generated by the Evil One." Fee, *The First and Second Letters to the Thessalonians*, The New

International Commentary on the New Testament (Grand Rapids: Eerdmans, 2009), 295.

15 Marilyn Conrad, "Spirit of Abortion," Covenant Keepers, July 10, 2019; https://tinyurl.com/yruz8tv9.

The Sea Monster

1 Many translations skip over the people dining on Leviathan, leaving only the animals. It's conceivable that there are no *animals*—the word for "desert creatures" might refer to desert-dwelling people (*HALOT*, s.v. צי II 1020)—but the previous noun unquestionably means "people." Best case scenario, the people aren't eating Leviathan *alone*.

2 Safwat Marzouk, *Egypt as a Monster in the Book of Ezekiel*, FAT 2: Reihe, 76 (Tübingen: Mohr Siebeck, 2015).

3 For discussion of this development, see Beal, *Religion and Its Monsters*, 71–82.

4 While many translations prefer the more theologically comfortable interpretation that Leviathan plays alone, there's significant scholarly recognition of God playing with him, e.g., John Day, *God's Conflict with the Dragon and the Sea: Echoes of a Canaanite Myth in the Old Testament* (Cambridge: Cambridge University Press, 1985), 72–73; Jon D. Levenson, *Creation and the Persistence of Evil: The Jewish Drama of Divine Omnipotence* (San Francisco: Harper and Row, 1988), 53–54. Based on this verse, in the Talmud God plays with Leviathan for three hours a day (b. Abod. Zar. 3b).

5 Pointing out the cruelty of this line, Brian R. Doak, *Consider Leviathan: Narratives of Nature and the Self in Job* (Minneapolis: Fortress Press, 2014), 1–2.

6 Behemoth, the last creature described before Leviathan, is just a hippopotamus; e.g., Michael V. Fox, "Behemoth and Leviathan," *Biblica* 93, no. 2 (2012): 261–63.

7 I am indebted to my former student at Jewish Theological Seminary, Jessica Belasco, for this description.

8 For background, see Michael V. Fox, *The Song of Songs and the Ancient Egyptian Love Songs* (Madison: University of Wisconsin Press, 1985), 228–32.

9 Translation of Egyptian love song no. 31 in Fox, *The Song of Songs and the Ancient Egyptian Love Songs*, 269.

10 Beal, *Religion and Its Monsters*, 47–55; Carol A. Newsom, *The Book of Job: A Contest of Moral Imaginations* (New York: Oxford University Press, 2003), 245, 251–52.

Shades, Ghosts, and Other Living Dead

1 On ritual care for the dead, funerary inscriptions, and more, see Matthew J. Suriano, *A History of Death in the Hebrew Bible* (New York: Oxford University Press, 2018).

2 Alan E. Bernstein, *The Formation of Hell: Death and Retribution in the Ancient and Early Christian Worlds* (Ithaca, NY: Cornell University Press, 1993); N. Wyatt, "The Concept and Purpose of Hell: Its Nature and Development in West Semitic Thought," *Numen* 56 (2009): 161–84.

3 See detailed discussion of the terminology and full text, Esther J. Hamori, *Women's Divination in Biblical Literature: Prophecy, Necromancy, and Other Arts of Knowledge*, Anchor Yale Bible Reference Library (New Haven: Yale University Press, 2015), 105–30.

4 William Bales, "The Descent of Christ in Ephesians 4:9," *Catholic Biblical Quarterly* 72 (2010): 88–89.

Giants

1 See, e.g., Sophia Rose Arjana, *Muslims in the Western Imagination* (New York: Oxford University Press, 2015); Debra Higgs Strickland, *Saracens, Demons, and Jews: Making Monsters in Medieval Art* (Princeton: Princeton University Press, 2003); and Jeffrey Andrew Weinstock, ed., *The Monster Theory Reader* (Minneapolis: University of Minnesota Press, 2020), 173–286.

2 Anne Draffkorn Kilmer, "The Mesopotamian Counterparts of the Biblical Nĕpīlîm," in *Perspectives on Language and Text: Essays and Poems in Honor of Francis I. Andersen's Sixtieth Birthday, July 28, 1985*, ed. Edgar W. Conrad and Edward G. Newing (Winona Lake, IN: Eisenbrauns, 1987), 43.

3 Alexa Wright, "Monstrous Strangers at the Edge of the World: The Monstrous Races," in Weinstock, *The Monster Theory Reader*, 176; Rudolf Wittkower, *Allegory and the Migration of Symbols* (Boulder, CO: Westview Press, 1977), 46–47.

4 John Block Friedman, *The Monstrous Races in Medieval Art and Thought* (Cambridge, MA: Harvard University Press, 1981), 5–22. These examples and more come from Megasthenes, Ctesias, writing traditionally attributed to Alexander the Great, and Pliny.

5 Friedman, *The Monstrous Races in Medieval Art and Thought*, 26–36; Wright, "Monstrous Strangers at the Edge of the World," 176–80.

6 Cohen, "Monster Culture (Seven Theses)," 7; on monsterization, see 7–12.

7 As in some ancient stories of Pygmies having proportionally small cattle; Friedman, *The Monstrous Races in Medieval Art and Thought*, 18.

8 The scouts' "unfavorable report" is sometimes assumed to be false, but this Hebrew word also refers to true reports, as in Gen 37:2.

9 I use the Hebrew plural for each group of giants (Emim, Zamzummim) alongside the English plural for the Moabites, Ammonites, and other human populations. While the forms aren't distinct in Hebrew, leaving the Hebrew untranslated is a traditional way to signal mythological nature, as with "seraphim," "cherubim," and "nephilim."

10 P. Kyle McCarter, *I Samuel*, Anchor Bible 8 (New York: Doubleday, 1980), 292–93.

11 Pirkei DeRabbi Eliezer 23; https://tinyurl.com/38zun2we.

12 Brian R. Doak, *The Last of the Rephaim: Conquest and Cataclysm in the Heroic Ages of Ancient Israel* (Boston: Ilex Foundation, and Washington, DC: Center for Hellenic Studies, 2012), 99. On this common monster trait, see Cohen, "Monster Culture (Seven Theses)," 4–6.

13 They're permanently wiped out within the Hebrew Bible. The New Testament monsterizes differently, demonizing people with mental illness or physical disabilities (Mark 5:1–20; Matt 9:32–33; 12:22; 17:14–18).

14 2 Sam 21:15–22; 1 Chron 20:4–8; 11:22–23.

15 William G. Dever, *Who Were the Early Israelites and Where Did They Come From?* (Grand Rapids: Eerdmans, 2003); Israel Finkelstein and Neil Asher Silberman, *The Bible Unearthed: Archaeology's New Vision of Ancient Israel and the Origin of Its Sacred Texts* (New York: Free Press, 2001), 97–122.

16 Karen Ordahl Kupperman, ed., *Captain John Smith: A Select Edition of His Writings* (Chapel Hill: University of North Carolina Press, 1988), 160–61.

17 Claire Jean Kim, *Dangerous Crossings: Race, Species, and Nature in a Multicultural Age* (Cambridge: Cambridge University Press, 2015), 43–52.

18 Kim, *Dangerous Crossings*, 47–48.

19 Christopher Brooke, "A Poem on the Late Massacre in Virginia," *The Virginia Magazine of History and Biography* 72, no. 3 (1964): 259–92. https://tinyurl.com/4asz3v8v.

20 "Fatal Violence against the Transgender and Gender Non-conforming Community in 2021." Human Rights Campaign, https://tinyurl.com/428z2r39.

21 *State of Missouri v. Darren Wilson*, Grand Jury Volume V, September 16, 2014, p. 212.

The Monster of Monsters, the Wonder of Wonders

1 On the value of recognizing God's monstrosity, see also Brandon R. Grafius, *Lurking under the Surface: Horror, Religion, and the Questions That Haunt Us* (Minneapolis: Broadleaf Books, 2022), 145–62; and Kelly J. Murphy, "Leviathan to Lucifer: What Biblical Monsters (Still) Reveal," *Interpretation: A Journal of Bible and Theology* 74, no. 2

(2020): 146–58. For a different perspective on God's monstrosity, see Amy Kalmanofsky, *Terror All Around: The Rhetoric of Horror in the Book of Jeremiah*, LHB/OTS 390 (New York: T&T Clark, 2008), 51–67.

2 Abraham Joshua Heschel, *Man Is Not Alone: A Philosophy of Religion* (New York: Harper & Row, 1966), "The Hiding God," 151–59. I am indebted to my former student, Jeremy Tabick, for drawing my attention to this chapter in a conversation about God's monstrosity.

List of Images

Fig. 1. Levantine stamp-seal featuring a four-winged uraeus serpent. The British Museum, London. © The Trustees of the British Museum.

Fig. 2. Lachish jar-handle impression of a four-winged uraeus serpent. The British Museum, London. © The Trustees of the British Museum.

Fig. 3. Human-headed winged lion (lamassu) from the palace of Ashurnasirpal II in Nimrud. The Metropolitan Museum of Art, New York.

Fig. 4. The pair of lamassu from the palace of Ashurnasirpal II in Nimrud. The Metropolitan Museum of Art, New York.

Fig. 5. Ram-headed winged lion, Phoenician ivory plaque. The Metropolitan Museum of Art, New York.

Fig. 6. The "Prince of Hell," from Les Mérancolies de Jehan Dupin sur les condicions de ce monde (15th century). Bibliothèque nationale de France. Bibliothèque de l'Arsenal. Ms-5099 réserve.

Fig. 7. "Angel," Christian Jorhan the Elder (mid-18th century). The Metropolitan Museum of Art, New York.

Fig. 8. Amulet featuring three angels, from Sefer Raziel (Amsterdam, 1701). Image provided by The Library of The Jewish Theological Seminary.

Fig. 9. Portion of The Four Avenging Angels, from "The Apocalypse," Albrecht Dürer, ca. 1498. The Metropolitan Museum of Art, New York.

Fig. 10. Aramaic incantation bowl. University of Pennsylvania Museum of Archaeology & Anthropology, Philadelphia. Courtesy of the Penn Museum, object no. B2945.